LUBOV BAZAN

A HISTORY OF
BELARUS

A NON-LITERARY ESSAY THAT EXPLAINS
THE ETHNOGENESIS OF THE BELARUSIANS

GLAGOSLAV PUBLICATIONS

A HISTORY OF BELARUS

A NON-LITERARY ESSAY THAT EXPLAINS
THE ETHNOGENESIS OF THE BELARUSIANS

by Lubov Bazan

Translated from the Russian by Callum Walker

© 2014, Glagoslav Publications, United Kingdom

Glagoslav Publications Ltd
88-90 Hatton Garden
EC1N 8PN London
United Kingdom

www.glagoslav.com

ISBN: 978-1-909156-60-9

A catalogue record for this book is available
from the British Library.

CONTENTS

PART 7. THE ESTABLISHMENT OF COMMUNISM (1920-1991)

PART 8. RECENT HISTORY (1991-2012)

FOREWORD

ON 8 DECEMBER 1991 THE PRESIDENT OF THE RUSSIAN
Federation Boris Yeltsin, the Chairman of the Supreme Soviet
of the Belarusian Soviet Socialist Republic Stanislav Shushkevich and
the Chairman of the Supreme Soviet of Ukraine Leonid Kravchuk
signed a treaty in Belovezhskaya Pushcha National Park in Belarus on
the withdrawal of their countries from the USSR and formed a new
political union of three independent states with its capital in Minsk.
Thus, at the stroke of a pen, the Soviet Union as a geopolitical entity
and a subject of international law ceased to exist, making way for new
post-communist states. The Republic of Belarus became a sovereign
nation in the heart of Europe with its territory covering 207,000 square
kilometres and a population of 9.5 million people.

But clearly this does not mean that the history of Belarus only
began after this treaty had been signed in 1991. As a fixed historical
territory, populated by a largely ethnically homogenous people, Belarus
in fact has its origins in the 9th century, with the Principality of Polotsk,
one of the first state entities in Europe.

Due to its geopolitical position, in its early history Belarus found
itself on the juncture of two worlds, two great cultures and ideologies,
becoming a region of mutual interaction between Byzantine Orthodox
and Roman Catholic civilisations. This contributed to the peculiar
political and cultural development that defined the country's historic
role in Europe. In spite of some dramatic historical periods caused by
opposition and conflicts between these two powers, the Belarusian
people preserved their distinctive ethnic and cultural traits that
stayed with them for centuries to come. During periods of active

Polonisation of Belarus, Orthodoxy was an important resistant force that maintained Belarusian language and culture, and in the 19th and 20th centuries, during Russian assimilation, Belarusians managed to preserve their own language and culture as a result of their particular past and resplendence accumulated from centuries old traditions.

Over the course of its history Belarus has been part of various state entities:
- Kievan Rus (9th-13th centuries),
- The Grand Principality of Lithuania (13th-16th centuries),
- The Polish-Lithuanian Commonwealth (16th-18th centuries),
- The Russian Empire (1795-1917),
- The Soviet Union (1917-1991).

A History of Belarus covers major periods of Belarusian history and attempts to reconstruct some peculiarities in detail. Moreover, readers can expect to encounter prominent historical figures throughout the book – princes, generals, politicians and luminaries – to serve as an introduction to the political history, military victories and defeats, and cultural achievements of the Belarusians, starting with material on the existence of Balts and Slavs on Belarusian lands, and ending with the formation of the independent Republic of Belarus in 1991. The factual material in this book is presented systematically and in chronological order. In case of disputable theoretical issues such as the ethnogenesis of the Belarusians, the emergence of the Belarusian language, the Belarusian identity and national consciousness, the problems of the Union between the Orthodox and Catholic churches, the author has chosen to outline all of the prevailing ideas in the field without giving preference to any particular slant.

PART I

HOW IT ALL BEGUN: PREHISTORY AND THE ETHNOGENESIS OF THE BELARUSIANS

ARCHAEOLOGICAL INVESTIGATIONS REVEALED THAT STARTING with very depths of antiquity, Belarus had been a popular site with the first settlement dating approximately 40,000 years ago, during the Palaeolithic Era (Stone Age). Characteristic of this period tools were found at archaeological excavations in the southern provinces of Belarus. It was during this period that people – still Palaeoanthropi with Neanderthals among them – mastered fire-making and produced their first stone tools – arrowheads, knives, scrapers – the most primitive implements known to man. The arctic climate at the time – as Belarus was in the preglacial zone – sustained rather poor vegetation and animal life.

Two of the oldest Palaeolithic human sites are located in Belarus and thought to be 25,000 to 30,000 years old: one on the banks of the Pripyat River near the village of Yurovichi and the other near the village of Berdyzh (1). Only 50 to 60 prehistoric humans would have lived on these sites. Archaeological findings have shown that a tribal community structure existed at the time, and consumption of hunting and fishing produce was collective, with complete equality among members of the community. Several communities would come to be united in a clan, consisting of all of the relatives on the maternal side. Such a clan would occupy a specific territory, operate a common economy and share common property. The total population on Belarusian soil in the late Palaeolithic was no more than several hundred (2).

During the Mesolithic, which for all of Eastern Europe lasted from 9,000 to 5,000 BC, settlements were spreading actively in the territory of Belarus, especially in the Neman, Western Dvina and Dnieper river basins w extensive and rich supplies of fish and waterfowl. After the retreat of the glacier towards the north and the significant temperature increase that occurred in 9,000 to 8,000 BC, Belarus became quite attractive for the rapid settlement of the land. Vast forestation and diverse fauna were more conducive to life. Belarus' settlement during this period primarily came from three directions –from the Russian Plains to the north-east, from the Balkans and the Black Sea to the south along the Dnieper, and from Western Europe through Poland. The people arriving from these areas belonged to different ethnic groups, and so in ethnic terms there has never been a homogenous Belarus.

On the shores of the Dnieper, Neman, Pripyat and Western Dvina archaeologists have found more than 100 Mesolithic sites, each inhabited by 20 to 30 people. The population of Belarus at the time was approximately between 5,000 and 6,000 people whose life style was characterized by the primitive communal system. Based on the obtained data, it'd be safe to conclude that specimens from the same clan used identical methods to process materials, manufacture tools, hunt and fish, and built identical housing structures.

The Neolithic era of human civilisation (the last period of the Stone Age) began at the end of the 5th millennium BC and lasted for more than two thousand years. Society demonstrated a certain ability to adapt to the surrounding environment and put to good use various resources available to humans of that era. The main methods used previously to obtain food, for example, were hunting, fishing and gathering, but in the Neolithic those same methods received what we would call today 'an upgrade'. For example, they learnt to fish using nets, and trained dogs for hunting purposes. Improved means of securing provisions ensured rapid growth of the population. Roughly 600 Neolithic settlements were found in what is now Belarus, accounting for a total population of about 27,000 to 30,000 people. These settlements were still mainly spread in river basins, with the majority in the Pripyat basin and along the Dnieper, but settlements were also found around the many Belarusian lakes formed after the retreat of the glacier.

The most interesting evidence of the late Neolithic era are settlements in the Syanno and Beshankovichy regions of the Vitebsk Province as archaeologists have found not only tools and household utensils there, but also the first small works of art: depictions of birds and animals, and even a small wooden figure of a man. At the same time, archaeological findings have revealed fortified settlements suggesting possible clashes between tribes. These settlements were reinforced by defensive earthen ramparts around them.

So far scientists have been unable to determine the exact ethnicity of Belarus' ancient population during the Palaeolithic, Mesolithic and Neolithic periods. However, archaeological data and studies in historical linguistics, in particular hydronymy (the study of ancient names for rivers and lakes), make it possible to devise an ethnic lineage for some communities living in the Late Stone Age. It's being hypothesized that already in the Bronze Age, at around 2,000 BC, there were Finno-Ugric tribes living along the Western Dvina and Dnieper, and Indo-European tribes along the Pripyat.

Major demographic changes were taking place in Europe at the dawn of the Bronze Age between 3,000 and 2,000 BC: tribes of nomadic herders from the Indo-European ethno-linguistic group were quickly occupying new lands from the Rhine in the west to the Volga in the east, and from the Black Sea in the south to the Scandinavian islands in the north. Slavs as a distinct indigenous ethnic group were part of this Indo-European migration which included Germanic, Baltic, Romanic, Celtic, Iranian and Indian groups.

With Indo-Europeans settling in Eastern Europe, a new era was marked in the development of the region and inevitably changes to the ethnic make-up of Belarus followed. New people brought with them new practices and ideas, and influenced the pre-existing social fabric. More effective bronze tools replaced less effective stone tools, the development of plough farming and animal husbandry created conditions conducive to the amassing of wealth by individual families, which caused envy among others. Such social vices (by today's standards) as robbery and burglary came to be a form of enrichment. As a result, a fortified settlement enclosed by walls behind a deep ditch or earthen ramparts becomes the new, smarter way of protection. More than 1,000 of these settlements have so far been found in Belarus. Archaeologists maintain that between 50 and 75 people would have lived in one of these types of villages, meaning that the total population of Belarus in the Bronze Age may have been between 75,000-100,000 people.

The situation remained relatively stable for a relatively long period of time until the Great Migration between the 3rd and 7th centuries AD following the fall of the Roman Empire. Migration and mobility of Slavs was largely determined by migration of other tribes in the region. The Slavs' homeland was between the Oder and the Dnieper and was named the Prague Archaeological Culture, which by now has been extensively studied by Czech, Polish and Belarusian scientists. During the Great Migration Slavic tribes moved away from their homeland to lands which later became the starting points of their recorded history, and where they still live to this day.

In the 6th and 7th centuries AD some Slavs settled in the south, populating the Balkans in what is modern-day Bulgaria and parts of Greece, and some groups went as far as Spain, Sicily and North Africa. Southern Slavs were formed during the process of assimilating the Thracian population and today these include Bulgarians, Serbs, Croats and Macedonians.

Another stream of Slavs moved during the 6th and 7th centuries from their homeland in the east and settled in the basin of the Dnieper and the Pripyat, having driven away or assimilated the Baltic and Finno-Ugric tribes. Here a new branch of the Slavs was formed and became known as the Eastern Slavs. They stayed in this area until the 8th and 9th centuries, and then moved further afield to settle vast expanses up to the Don, Oka, and Upper Volga. These groups are the modern-day Belarusians, Russians and Ukrainians.

As for the Western Slavs (Poles, Czechs, Slovaks), they stayed in their homelands and there was no migration or mixing. For centuries they lived on their ancestral lands, and their ethnic history does not offer historians as much in the way of disputable material for discussion as the ethnic history of the Belarusians.

Slavs came to Belarusian territory, inhabited by Baltic tribes, in the 6-7th centuries AD. The Slavs moved along the rivers abundant in this area and built fortified settlements as they went, later expanding them into fully-fledged cities. Armed groups always led the way, followed by the agricultural population. The Slavs settled densely in single villages, and the type of housing used at the time was the mud hut. In numerous tombs from this period along the Dnieper, Pripyat and Berezina rivers archaeologists have found items such as typically Slavic pottery and tools, which indicates that the Slavs had already fully settled in this area by the 7-8th century.

In terms of their development, the Slavs were significantly more advanced than the Baltic tribes; they were superior in their social and military organisation and had more advanced forms of economy, in particular agriculture, which the Balts did not know. We do not know how peaceful the coexistence of the two ethnic groups was initially in the Belarusian lands inhabited by the Slavs. Traces of fires have been found at some Baltic settlements from the 7th and 8th centuries AD, which is suggestive of military conflicts.

By colonising the land along the Western Dvina, the Slavs absorbed the cultural and ethnographic features of aboriginal Balts and assimilated them. A portion of the Baltic tribes retreated to the north-west, where they laid the foundations for the formation of the Lithuanian, Yotvingian, Prussian and Lettish ethnic groups. But most of the Balts continued to live where they had lived on what is now Belarus, and their assimilation into the Slavs continued for several centuries until the 12th and 13th centuries, and possibly even later. Thus, the region along the Neman and Western Dvina rivers remained a mixed Baltic-Slavic area. As a result of this blending, a new ethnic group came into being – the direct ancestors of the Belarusians who spoke in Slavic dialects (3). These Slavic tribes – Krivichs and Dregovichs – are often mentioned in medieval historical sources: the writings of the Bavarian Geographer (9th century), the historian Constantine Porphyrogenitus (10th century) and the first Russian chronicle *The Tales of Bygone Years* (12th century). In their culture and language the Slavic and Baltic elements became intertwined, with Slavic features dominating, including language. Information from archaeology and written sources indicate that by the 8th century the Dregovichs and Krivichs had already moved away from a primitive tribal system towards a class-based society. Division of labour had already taken place and political governance - in the form of elected princes - had been established.

Thus, indigenous Baltic tribes became a substrate in the formation of the Belarusian ethnic group. As a result of the Slavicisation of the Baltic population and its merging with the Slavic population a portion of the Slavic people split off into a separate group of Dregovichs and Krivichs, and through their historical and cultural development this led to the emergence of the Belarusian language and the Belarusian people.

This theory on the ethnogenesis of Belarusians appeared in historical academic circles in the 1960s, and was based on extensive material accumulated from archaeological and linguistic research (4). It was called the *Baltic Theory*, but was entirely suppressed by the official Soviet scientific authorities. Until this time, another theory had prevailed as the only existing hypothesis, both when Belarus became part of the Russian Empire and during the Soviet era. It was called the *Belarusian Theory* and was based on the following principles.

The Eastern Slavs came to modern-day Belarus, Ukraine and Western Russia in the 6th and 7th centuries. The appearance of the Slavs in these lands gradually came to be of great importance to the subsequence historical development of the region as it led to a rapid overruling of many primitive societal institutions and facilitated the emergence of cities and the development of feudal relations. It is almost as if the region witnessed, on a small scale, what had happened several centuries before on the borders of the Roman Empire and Byzantium where the arrival of barbarians contributed to the abolition of former societal relations and supported the adoption of new systems. The pace of economic and social development among the Slavs was far more intensive than that of the native tribes, and so the Slavs assimilated them.

In the late 9th and early 10th centuries the processes eradicating the ethnocultural differences between Eastern Slavic tribes intensified. This was due to economic (the development of feudal and trade relations), political (the need to protect themselves from common enemies in the form of nomadic tribes) and cultural (especially after the adoption of Christianity in the 10th century) integration. As a result of the mixing of different tribes – the Krivichs, Dregovichs, Polans, Radimichs, Drevlyans and others – in the 9th and 10th centuries a united Russian people formed in the Middle Overdnieper, with its centre consolidated in the city of Kiev. Its geographical position had many advantages: the city was at the very centre of the Eastern Slavic lands, and was therefore inaccessible to external enemies – the aggressive nomadic tribes. Situated on the banks of the deep Dnieper river, which connected the northern lands with the wealth of Byzantium, Kiev flourished as an important trading centre. The new Russian people started to unite around Kiev, and by the end of the 10th century in the lands surrounding Kiev it was consolidated and assumed its common name – Rus.

According to this theory Ancient Rus, with its centre at Kiev, served to unify the Eastern Slavic tribes in a single community and protect its borders from external enemies – the many thousands of Varangian tribes to the north, and Khazars and Cumans to the south. This state had a common Slavic language and common cultural trends. Then, in the 12th century, as a result of the fall of this first Russian state, the first unified Russian people separated and splintered. On its foundations, during the further course of history, three related peoples came into being: Russians, Belarusians and Ukrainians.

Soviet history officially recognised this version of events, the *Great Russian* theory, in spite of the fact that since the 19th century it had faced considerable opposition. The term "a united ancient Russian people" only appeared in the 1950s, after the publication of Stalin's "scientific" work *Marxism and Problems of Linguistics*, and it soon came to be widely accepted (5). This theory was clearly politically motivated, as it supported the idea of an "elder Russian brother" from which young Belarusians and Ukrainians had descended, and since they were younger then, consequently, their historical choices should always be guided by this principle.

Opponents of the *Great Russian* theory argue that Ancient Rus was not a state made up of Russian people because such a people did not yet exist in the 10-12th centuries; there were various Eastern Slavic tribes each with their own ethnic and cultural characteristics. These characteristics were defined, developed and intensified according to which autochthonous populations these tribes assimilated. Accordingly, the Russian ethnic group was formed on the basis of the Finno-Ugric substrate, the Ukrainian on the Turkic, and the Belarusian through assimilation of the Balts. The Kievan Rus state only united these peoples for a time, but it was not by chance that when this state collapsed in the 13th century it ruptured along the same lines as the initial tribal territories with all of their ethnographic and cultural features. These features were the basis for the ethnogenesis of these three future peoples – Russians, Belarusians and Ukrainians.

There is also a *Great Polish* theory on the descent of the Belarusian people. It denies the existence of an independent Belarusian ethnic group and argues that Belarusians are a Polish people who speak a dialect of Polish formed under the influence and dissemination of Russian. This theory arose in the 18th century in the Polish-Lithuanian Commonwealth and was, of course, politically motivated in order to more successfully implement Poland's hegemonic policy towards Belarus. No scientific evidence stands in support of this theory. Modern linguistic research has convincingly shown that the Belarusian language, in terms of its lexicon, syntax, phonetics and morphology, is an independent Eastern Slavic language.

As for modern Belarusian history, both the *Belarusian* and the *Great Russian* theories continue to exist, but the debate, unlike during the Soviet period, is free and makes use of the very latest historical, archaeological and ethnographic material.

The settlement of the Eastern Slavs on Belarusian lands in the 6-9th centuries coincided with the disintegration of primitive social systems. In the economic life of the agricultural community more and more elements characteristic of individual farms started to appear (6). During this period the socio-political structure was beginning to change and Slavs moved over to a class-based society with the start of an era of military democracies. Class demarcation contributed to the emergence of the first and earliest feudal Slavic states. The first of such states in central Europe were the Bulgarian Empire, the Great Moravian Empire (7), the Serbian Empire and, in what is now Belarus, the Principality of Polotsk.

PART 2

BELARUSIAN LANDS IN THE EARLY MIDDLE AGES

(9-13th centuries)

CHAPTER 1.
The Principality of Polotsk and Kievan Rus

THERE ARE VARIOUS WAYS TO DIVIDE HISTORY INTO DIFFERENT periods; some researchers are guided by socio-economic criteria, whereas others look to politics, statehood or culture. As Belarus has repeatedly changed its allegiance over the course of its history we will elect for the principle of statehood. Based on the political, social and cultural life of the Belarusian people, chronologically the history of Belarus can be divided into 5 periods: Polotsk, Belarusian-Lithuanian, Polish, Russian and its entry into the USSR.

———————◆———————

The first early feudal principalities on Eastern Slavic territory started to form in the 9th century, the foundations for which were created by the former tribal communities. The Slavs' need to defend themselves from hostile nomadic Pecheneg, Cuman and Khazar tribes which regularly carried out devastating attacks on the Slavic settlements contributed to the establishment of military detachments and the appearance of well-fortified cities, the first of which were Novgorod, Kiev and Polotsk.

In the 9th century the northern principalities of the Eastern Slavs headed by Novgorod united with the southern principalities and created a single major power with its capital in Kiev, which historians have named Ancient or Kievan Rus. Based on its social and political system this state was a military monarchy ruled over by the Grand Prince of Kiev. Under the Grand Prince was the state council, the Duma (from the Russian verb *dumat*, 'to think'), which included noblemen – for the most part relatives of the prince and military leaders – called Boyars. The Grand Prince governed the numerous executive bodies, the officials responsible for collecting *dani*, or tributes (from the verb *davat*, 'to give'), court affairs, and the recruitment of soldiers to the prince's detachment. In the lands under the Grand Prince's control the state was run by appointed governors – *posadniki* – (from the verb *posadit*, 'to seat' or 'to implant') and their assistants *tysyachniki* (from *tysyacha*, 'thousand'), which was the name given to the militia during military action.

The lands of the Dregovichs, Krivichs and Radimichs – now Belarus – were incorporated into this Slavic state.

The issue surrounding the origin of the word *Rus*, from which the notion *Rusyn* was also descended, and later *Russian*, as well as the future name of the state *Rusiya* and Russia (*Rossiya*), has caused and continues to spark lively academic debate, with numerous different hypotheses being put forward. In Western European historical sources from the 10-12th centuries, such as the *Annals of Magdeburg*, the term *Rusyn* is used only to refer to the Northern and North-Western groups of Ancient Rus. But with the growth of Rus' territory and population and its increasingly active role in the historical arena of Eastern and Northern Europe, the name gradually spread to cover all Eastern Slavic lands. Thus, the word *Rusyn* was used by neighbouring Western nations to denote all foreigners living to the east, and it existed together with the cognates *Rusy*, *Ruskiya*, *Russkie*, and *Rusichi* which were widely used in Rus itself.

The most popular theory of the origins of the first Russian state and the name Rus is the *Norman Theory*. Normanists trace the emergence of Ancient Rus to the intervention of the Normans and argue that the word *Rus* was initially the name for one of the Varangian tribal unions which subsequently gave its name to the Slavic lands that they came to rule and control.

One of the grounds for this theory is *The Tale of Bygone Years*, a Russian chronicle written in the 12th century. A record exists from roughly 862 AD which reads: "… and in the lands there was war, and they fought amongst themselves. And they decided: let us look for a prince to rule over us and to govern by the rule of law. And they went overseas to the Varangians, to the Rus… and said: our land is vast and abundant, but there is no order in it. Come, reign as princes and rule over us…". Later in the chronicles we read that as a result of this invitation a Varangian detachment led by Rurik and his brothers arrived on the Slavic lands and brought together the many Slavic tribes in the Middle Dnieper basin under their rule (8). The further integration of the Varangians, who were allegedly called Rus, with the Slavic population led to the ethnonym Rus extending to the entire population of the first Ancient Russian state, and the Rurik Dynasty was the first of the dynasties of Russian princes.

The second leading influential hypothesis on the origin of the term *Rus* is geographical. We know that the ancient Slavs always settled along rivers. According to their pagan beliefs the Slavs worshiped rivers, and in the Proto-Slavic language the word for a river was *rusa*. To this day there are many toponyms derived from the root *rus* in Slavic lands. The Neman river, which has been the site of Eastern Slavic settlements since time immemorial, was also called *Ros* in ancient times. There are therefore reasonable grounds for considering this explanation for the origins of the name of the first Eastern Slavic state.

Wherever this name came from, by the 10-11th centuries it had become widespread. The *Hypatian Codex* documents how Slavs, Varangians and many other people from diverse backgrounds served in Prince Oleg's army, and they were all referred to as Rus.

As for the word Russia (*Rossiya*), it came from the Greeks. The Greeks called the inhabitants of Kievan Rus not *Rus*, but rather *Ros*, and hence the word *Rossiya* was formed. By the late 17th century after the church reforms of Patriarch Nikon when thousands of Greek monks came to Russian monasteries to correct their theological books, they propagated the written name Russia (*Rossiya*). Under the reign of

Peter the Great (1672-1725) Russia came to be the widespread official name for the state.

———————◆———————

In view of the constant military strikes, both within the state, and along its frontiers against nomadic tribes, the Grand Prince of Kiev needed a strong army. It consisted of a Grand Prince unit and detachments of his vassals. In certain instances a militia was assembled. He even had his own fleet on the Dnieper, Western Dvina and Berezina rivers and on the Black Sea.

Ancient Rus was made up of various apanage principalities. These apanage principalities were held in vassalage from the Grand Prince. They had to supply him with soldiers, make their detachments available at his request and carry out all orders, in addition to collecting the *dan'* (tribute) from their people and paying it to the Grand Prince's treasury. But in their own lands the apanaged princes enjoyed unlimited power.

Peasant families united by their common economic life created a territorial rural community. The cultivated land, forests and bodies of water were the property of the community. A specific family would make use of its own plot of communal land – its *nadel*, or allotment (from the verb *delit*, 'to share' or 'to divide'). All peasants paid tributes to the state in the form of rye, oats, flax, sheep, chickens, and honey. Money was also paid to the prince. In addition, from the 12th century all rural populations had to pay a tax to the church, called *desyatina* – a form of tithe – which was one tenth of their harvest. There were few slaves – only captive foreigners forced into slavery called *kholopy*, or serfs, who were openly bought and sold. Russians could not be forced into slavery on their own land.

So what sort of position did the Belarusian lands have in Kievan Rus?

The most significant in political terms in the 9-12th centuries was the Principality of Polotsk.

The first mention of Polotsk in chronicles is from the year 862 AD, in which we read that Prince Rurik of Kiev "... distributed the cities among his vassals – one part to the Polotsk vassal, another to the Rostov vassal, and the other to the Beloozero vassal..." (9). Thus, by this time Polotsk must already have been in existence. The very earliest written sources, such as *The Tale of Bygone Years*, and the *Laurentian, Hypatian* and *Novgorod* codices, and the *Livonian Chronicles* write about Polotsk in the 9-10ᵗʰ centuries as the well-fortified cultural and political centre of a rich principality. Polotsk was formed at the confluence of the river Polat and the Western Dvina, giving rise to its name.

Polotsk owed its active trading and wealth to its geographical location and the convenience of its waterways. It was situated on the banks midway down the key trading route of the Western Dvina. This route tracing the Dvina and Dnieper rivers connected the Scandinavian and Baltic states in the north to the Byzantine Empire and the Arabic Caliphate in the South. It was an important waterway for international trading and was called the "waterway from the Varangians to the Greeks".

Polotsk was the social, economic and political centre of a large region in the north-east of what is now Belarus. The Principality of Polotsk bordered with the Novgorod lands to the north, Smolensk to the east, Pinsk to the south, and Lithuanian and Lettish tribes to the west. These tribes were forever dependent on Polotsk, paying it tributes and supplying soldiers to the Polotsk army. Based on current administrative demarcations, the Principality of Polotsk covered the entirety of the Vitebsk Province, the northern part of the Minsk Province and the northern part of the Mogilev Province, accounting for roughly one third of the territory of modern-day Belarus.

The Principality of Polotsk was one of the largest feudal states, comparable with the Bavarian Principality and the Portuguese kingdom in Western Europe, but was not threatened by the raids by nomadic tribes that constantly ravaged the more southern Eastern Slavic lands. The trading route "from the Varangians to the Greeks" on which it was situated contributed to its growing wealth and, as a result, individuality; by the 10th century the population was notable for its ethnic identity, linguistic unity and common culture.

All of this gives us reason to believe that the Principality of Polotsk was the first Belarusian state to have real sovereignty and control over its own destiny. Throughout the 9-12th centuries it had all of the most important attributes of statehood: a legislative authority in the form of a *Veche* (popular assembly), an executive authority governed by an elected prince, its own dynasty, a stable territory and its own army. The Principality of Polotsk pursued its own independent foreign and domestic policy and was remarkable for its political and military activity.

The Principality's economy was based on agriculture and animal husbandry. Primitive methods of economic management – hunting, fishing and gathering – played a subsidiary role. Peasants produced everything that was needed for the sustenance of their families, and only a small number of items such as special tools and aids, pottery, jewellery and adornments were bought from craftsmen or merchants from the cities.

The peasants lived in small villages inhabited by several dozen families and formed a community on a territorial basis. A larger settlement, or *pogost*, would serve as the administrative and religious centre. Small homes were built from wood and had a clay oven to prepare food and provide heating in the winter months.

At the opposite end of the feudal society were the nobles and princes, for whom land ownership served as the economic basis for their power. In the early-feudal period there were different forms of land ownership: patrimonial, where land or a farmstead was owned with the right to sell it or pass it on by inheritance, and landed, where nobles or other influential individuals obtained the land for temporary use in return for their services, in which case they did not have the right to sell it or pass it on to their successors. From the 11th century the main owner of the land was the Orthodox Church and monasteries.

The city of Polotsk comprised a city centre fortified with defensive ramparts and wooden walls, which in ancient cities was called the *citadel* (the Russian word for which, *detinets*, was derived from the word for baby, *ditë*, drawing a parallel between the inner fortress and a child within its mother's womb), surrounding streets and outlying settlements. The city was built entirely out of wood: wood was used for the prince's mansions, homes, farm buildings, city walls, fortifications, and bridges. Trees even lined the streets and pavements.

The prince and his retinue – the standing army of the prince, and the main support for his rule – lived in the city. In military campaigns, militia, called *tysyachi*, would accompany the retinue. The best craftsmen from the surrounding areas came to settle in the city, and Polotsk came to be renowned for its pottery, blacksmiths, leather goods and jewellers. The prince himself always supported arms tradesmen, and often his observers would watch how a combat sword was tempered and how armourers made spears and battle-axes. The price of a good steel sword was equal to the cost of a horse. A feature of a warrior's clothing was iron chain mail made up of tens of thousands (sometimes up to 60,000) metal rings. Polotsk's master archers were famous even in other principalities. From close range even chain mail or shields were unable to defend against steel-tipped arrows. An arrow fired from the best bow could hit a target at three hundred metres.

Between the 10th and 11th centuries the level of independence of the Polotsk princes from the Grand Prince of Kiev first increased and then decreased. It was all determined by military events. In the last quarter of the 10th century Prince Rogvolod ruled over Polotsk and he, having a strong retinue, decided not to obey the Prince of Kiev and chose to rule independently. This prince was the first protagonist in Belarusian history documented in written sources.

After the death of the Grand Prince Svyatoslav of Kiev, when a struggle for the throne had started between his two sons Yaropolk and Vladimir, Rogvolod sided with Yaropolk and refused to hand over his daughter Rogneda to marry Vladimir. During Rogneda's courtship with Vladimir she declared: "I do not want to be enslaved, I want Yaropolk". She was referring to the fact that Vladimir was the son of Prince Svyatoslav and a slave. It was not just a refusal, but an insult.

But in the feud with Yaropolk for the Kiev throne, Vladimir was victorious and gathered an army to wage war against Polotsk to avenge this insult. Of course, it was not so much Rogneda's refusal that was the cause of this campaign, but rather Kiev's constant desire to subjugate Polotsk. Vladimir destroyed and burned the city to the ground for its disobedience, and Rogneda was forced into marriage. Prince Rogvolod, his wife and all of his sons were brutally murdered.

Prince Vladimir (who ruled from 980 to 1015) by this time had not yet turned to Christianity; he was a pagan. His faith meant that he was able to practice polygamy. Alongside the Princess of Polotsk he had a further six wives and many harems of slaves. Chronicles document how Rogneda could not forget and forgive Vladimir for the harm he had caused her, and the violence and destruction of her home city, and at one point attempted to kill him: "One day, when Vladimir came to her and fell asleep, she decided to kill him. But it happened that at that very moment he woke up and grabbed her by the arm. And she said sadly: 'You killed my father and took away my land…' Vladimir snatched the sword from her and wanted to kill his disobedient wife, but their young son Izyaslav also grabbed the sword and protected his mother". This young yet courageous protector surprised Prince Vladimir so much that he spared Rogneda and then ordered the construction of a new city and named it after his son: Izyaslavl (now Zaslavl in Minsk Province). Rogneda and her son were eternally banished to this city and the Prince never saw her again.

In 985, the Polotsk *Veche* invited the young Izyaslav to take the throne as prince, where he ruled until 1001. Written records offer no details of his rule, but later church publications refer to Izyaslav as an active exponent of Christianity and a *knizhnik*, or 'book lover' (from the Russian word for book, *kniga*), the name given to all highly educated people at the time.

The *Veche* was a key feature of political life in the Western and North-Western Principalities of Ancient Rus, including Polotsk. This people's "parliament" performed a legislative function, and the prince and his retinue served as the executive. The *Veche* – the people's assembly

– was formed in Polotsk after other communities in the principality had held their own preliminary *Veche* meetings and representatives of the people had been chosen. The *Veche* invited the Prince to the government, agreed with him the conditions of his reign, and expressed its wishes and demands. If the Prince broke the agreement, the *Veche* could remove him. The *Veche* adopted resolutions that were binding on people of various backgrounds and appointed senior officials. The *Veche* in the Principality of Polotsk lasted until the late 15th century, when the city had become part of the Grand Principality of Lithuania and Magdeburg Law had been adopted.

The *Veche* had the power to declare war and make peace. Its powers extended not only to the capital, but also to the territory and cities around the capital. The Principality of Polotsk incorporated cities such as Minsk, Borisov, Usvyaty and Vitebsk.

A chronicler wrote the following about the *Veche*'s powers: "... and all of the power is taken from the citizens of Novgorod, and Smolensk, and Kiev, and Polotsk, is amassed in the Duma, in the *Veche*, wherein the elders reflect, and enact..." (10). People gathered for *Veche* assemblies when a special *Veche* bell was sounded. All free men, regardless of their wealth, had the right to vote.

The Prince's executive power defended the territory, managed the land, administered "justice", and kept an eye on the trading routes. The Prince of Polotsk "knew his place" and legally had very little influence. When taking the throne, the Prince had to make a strict ritual-like oath to the people. Initially it was an oath to the land, to water, to bread and to arms in front of a pagan wooden idol, and after the adoption of Christianity, in front of a cross. Among the oaths made by the new Prince were promises to protect and defend the territory of the state, not to overturn the decisions of the courts, not to interfere in church affairs, not to deprive free inhabitants of their property, and not to set up restrictions on travel outside the principality.

There is every reason to believe that the process of adopting Christianity in the Principality of Polotsk was very much different to that which took place in Kiev and other lands in Ancient Rus.

All of the chronicles describe the violence and bloody crimes which accompanied the coming of Christianity in many cities, but there are no similar reports for Polotsk. This is due to the fact that Christianity was already widespread in these lands long before Prince Vladimir's ruling on the adoption of Christianity in Ancient Rus; it came peacefully and in a civilised manner. The Princes of Polotsk did not want to see their land as a pagan island in the middle of a Christian Europe; they understood the advantages that the new faith offered the state and the people and so promoted the spread of Christianity by peaceful means (11).

The first source documenting Christianity in the Principality of Polotsk comes in the form of the 9th century Scandinavian work of literature, *The Book of Christianity*. The hero of the saga Thorvald the Traveller, who was sainted following his death, brought Christianity to Iceland, and then went to Jerusalem in the Holy Land. The pilgrim returned through Russian and Belarusian lands, and on the way stopped in Polotsk, where he founded the monastery of John the Baptist, where he was buried.

By 992 the Polotsk eparchy had been created. Compared with Kiev, the church in Polotsk was highly important and its bishops played an active role in the political life of the Principality. In a number of cases social contracts and resolutions on city life were signed in the name of the bishop and stamped with his seal, the most important of which was the seal of the Grand Prince.

In the first few decades of the 11th century the Principality of Polotsk was one of the strongest in military and economic terms in Ancient Rus. This formed the basis for it starting a battle with Kiev for supremacy in the Eastern Slavic world. In 1021 the son of Izyaslav, Bryacheslav, took his powerful retinue to Novgorod, capturing it and plundering rich spoils from the city. Angered, Prince Yaroslav of Kiev caught up with the Polotsk retinue when it was returning from Novgorod and attacked it at the Sudoma river. The Prince of Polotsk lost the ensuing battle between the uncle and nephew. But Yaroslav continued to fear the strength of Polotsk, and in order to appease Bryacheslav allowed him to keep possession of the principality on the condition that the nephew would not take any further action against him. Soon these two princes would walk side-by-side in military campaigns against Lithuania and the Yotvingians to expand and strengthen their north-western borders.

The greatest power and the largest degree of independence came to the Principality of Polotsk in the second half of the 11th century under Prince Vseslav (1044-1101). At the start of his reign construction was started on the St. Sophia Cathedral in Polotsk (one of the oldest churches in Belarus, which still stands in Polotsk to this day, albeit having been heavily restored). Needless to say, the fact that cathedrals to St. Sophia had already been built in Kiev and in Novgorod – two of the most influential cities in Ancient Rus with which Polotsk had been in constant competition – had a considerable impact on the decision to build the large monumental cathedral. In doing so, Vseslav was emphasising the equal standing of Polotsk with Kiev and Novgorod.

St. Sophia in Polotsk was a highly grandiose building for the time. The architecture and the interior of the cathedral was more plain than the cathedrals in Kiev and Novgorod, but this was the essence of its special grandeur and beauty. The restraint of the walls emphasised the narrow, high windows, and under the dome they were much larger in size allowing the sunlight to penetrate into the cathedral. The cathedral had seven domes, and on the interior of the main dome was a depiction of Christ Pantocrator.

St. Sophia in Polotsk became the heart of the state. It served not only for prayer, but also to receive ambassadors, declare war and sign peace, guard the prince's treasury and the property collected by Prince Izyaslav, Rogneda's son, house a library, and enter into and sign trade agreements. It was with good reason that the Prince's state seal read: "Seal of Polotsk and St. Sophia".

Vseslav's contemporaries gave him the nickname Prince Vseslav the Sorcerer. Vseslav's indefatigable energy and his numerous and ever successful endeavours gave rise to the legend that he was born with a magical and enchanting birthmark on his head. Vseslav allegedly always wore a headband which covered the birthmark. His contemporaries saw him as a supernatural with many a legend circulating amongst the people; he was even mentioned in the chronicles and in the first ancient Rus work of literature *The Tale of Igor's Campaign*: "Prince Vseslav was a judge to his subjects, was a ruler to his cities; but at night he would race like a wolf to Kiev. If the morning bells of St. Sophia rang in Polotsk, he could hear the peal in Kiev" (12).

Vseslav continued his father's policy of subjugating other lands to his rule. In 1065 he attached Pskov, and a year later Novgorod. Many were captured, and to further demonstrate his power and humiliate the vanquished enemy the bells of St. Sophia cathedral in Novgorod were removed and melted down.

In early 1067 Vseslav the Sorcerer drove the Kiev retinue from Navahrudak, which from then on became a foothold for the Prince of Polotsk to the south. In response, Grand Prince Izyaslav of Kiev and his brothers Svyatoslav and Vsevolod amassed a huge army and marched on Polotsk. In winter 1067, en route to Polotsk, they besieged Minsk, one of the key cities of the Principality of Polotsk. The residents of Minsk locked themselves inside the city and defended themselves courageously, as they believed that it was the army of Vseslav the Sorcerer on the war path. But they were still unable to withstand the army of the whole of southern Rus, and the Grand Prince captured the city. The city's residents were either killed or imprisoned.

When Vseslav learnt that Minsk had fallen he marched his own army on Kiev. The battle took place in March 1067 on the river Nyamiha. It was still winter, which caused further difficulties for both armies. The chronicles do not relay the details of this battle, but there were many casualties. More than one hundred years later the author of *The Tale of Igor's Campaign* wrote: "The bloody banks of the Nyamiha were sown with Russian bones". The army of Vseslav the Sorcerer was defeated.

According to the traditions of the times, the Kiev princes regularly ravaged the Polotsk lands following this victory. Vseslav the Sorcerer understood that the future independent existence of his principality was in grave danger and he sent a message to Izyaslav of Kiev to ask for peace. The Prince of Kiev was not about to forgive the unruly vassal, but knowing the uniqueness of Vseslav's personality and his popularity among the people, decided to destroy him with cunning trickery. Izyaslav promised to make peace with Vseslav and even to return all of the land he had captured if Vseslav would come to Kiev to ask for this in person. The Prince of Kiev vowed to cause him no harm and kissed a cross in public (which was the strongest possible pledge of his sincerity). Vseslav was informed of this and, believing in Izyaslav's integrity, he and his two sons travelled to Izyaslav. They were immediately arrested, shackled and imprisoned. The situation appeared hopeless to Vseslav: the Principality of Polotsk had not only lost its independence, but the entire dynasty of Prince Vseslav the Sorcerer was threatened with destruction.

However, in keeping with the Russian proverb "Man proposes and God disposes!" Vseslav the Sorcerer was not killed immediately; he was imprisoned for over a year. Perhaps the cross that Izyaslav used to swear that he would not harm Vseslav actually saved him. It was with good reason that he was called Vseslav the Sorcerer. During this time Kiev started to witness civil unrest caused by discontent with Izyaslav's cruelty and oppression. Legends circulated about Vseslav's wisdom and strength, and his name was popular in the lower classes of the city, and at Izyaslav's court. Vseslav's supporters repeatedly called on Izyaslav to release the Polotsk prisoner, reminding him that he swore on the cross and had committed perjury. This dissatisfaction then turned into revolt, and the people of Kiev broke Vseslav from prison and proclaimed him Grand Prince (13). Fearing reprisals, Izyaslav was forced to flee Kiev.

Vseslav only sat on the Golden Throne of Kiev for a short time, reigning for all of seven months. At the time he was the fully-fledged ruler of all of Ancient Rus, that is over half of the Eastern Slavic lands. But the escaped Izyaslav sought the help of the King Bolesław the Brave of Poland, and with the support of the Polish army went to Kiev to win back his throne. It was then Vseslav's turn to run: he decided not to fight and, having picked an opportune moment one night, fled to his home city of Polotsk. Sources differ in their explanation as to why Vseslav came to abdicate such a prestigious throne of his own free will. But the reasons were clear: Vseslav was placed on the throne by commoners, and the Kievan Boyars did not take kindly to this. Furthermore, Vseslav had for a long time fought against the centrist policies of Kiev, and when he took the throne he then had to put them into practice, which was hardly in keeping with his views. Back home, in Polotsk, he had considerable support and his place on the throne was more secure.

The struggle between the two principalities of Polotsk and Kiev for power and influence over Ancient Rus continued throughout the 11th and 12th centuries. From the late 11th century Prince Vladimir Monomakh (1053-1125) entered the fray with the recalcitrant Polotsk princes. Vladimir was an excellent, wise strategist and he had succeeded more than once in uniting the Southern Russian lands and their armies to eventually subjugate the rebellious Principality of Polotsk to a central government. In 1077 and 1078 he launched two military campaigns on Polotsk territory, and was joined not only by the armies of the Southern Russian principalities, but also by the Northern Novgorod retinues. Polotsk was in a hostile environment. The city was occupied and looted. Twice Vladimir Monomakh succeeded in ousting Vseslav the Sorcerer from the Polotsk throne, only for him to return time after time thanks to the support of his people.

In Autumn 1078, in response to Vladimir Monomakh's aggression, Vseslav attacked Russian Smolensk and did to the city what Monomakh had done to Polotsk. In 1084, Vladimir Monomakh went on another campaign to Minsk, which was a well fortified outpost on the southern borders of the Principality of Polotsk. In his older years in his *Teachings for Children* (which was in fact one of the first known "war memoirs" of an individual in history) Vladimir Monomakh proudly wrote: "That autumn I, together with the Chernigov retinue and enlisted soldiers, marched on Minsk fortress, took it and left neither servant nor beast alive in the city...".

Clearly the rich, powerful and sovereign Principality of Polotsk was a constant headache to the Grand Princes of Kiev. The fact that the Vseslav the Sorcerer's undertakings were at the forefront of Kiev's concerns is attested to in a record in the chronicles regarding his death: "In the year 6609 (1101 AD), on Wednesday the fourteenth day of the month of April, at nine o'clock in the morning, Prince Vseslav of Polotsk was laid before the eyes of God." Such chronological accuracy is never encountered for other princes. Even if the Kievan princes did not look upon this news with elation, they were doubtlessly relieved.

Of course, the multi-faceted public and political undertakings of Vseslav the Sorcerer contributed to the prosperity of the Principality of Polotsk and reinforced its independence. The fact that Vseslav, in the final years of his life, never took part in meetings of the vassal princes of Ancient Rus suggests that Polotsk was not dependent on Kiev. When the Eastern Slavic Princes gathered in 1097 in Liubech to announce a new principle: "Let each firmly keep his own patrimony". For Vseslav the Sorcerer this principle had long been implemented in reality. He had nothing to share or discuss with the other princes.

With regard to social policy, Vseslav strengthened the power of his administration and protected the proprietary rights of his people, both the wealthy and the poor alike. Vseslav always managed to reach an understanding with the *Veche*, which traditionally had considerable influence and power in Polotsk. In view of the important role of trade in the economic life of Polotsk, Vseslav issued decrees to regulate trading and tax collection, and ensured that they were strictly enforced. The construction of the St. Sophia cathedral in Polotsk at Vseslav's initiative contributed to the development of education and culture; in order for the cathedral to function it needed educated people, books, religious items and icons. The residents of Polotsk perceived themselves as a unified people and always supported Vseslav's struggle against the central powers in Kiev, even though from an objective standpoint it actually led in the end to the collapse of Ancient Rus.

Sources offer differing opinions on Vseslav the Sorcerer's impact. When viewed from the standpoint of his support for the centralisation and unity of Ancient Rus, Vseslav appears to be something of a separatist and troublemaker. But at the same time, if we consider the collapse of the Ancient Russian state as a natural historical process then Vseslav's merit lies in the fact that he correctly understood the objective conditions required for the development of Belarusian lands and directed his activities towards the protection and reinforcement of state sovereignty.

Following his death, Vseslav the Sorcerer left behind six sons: Boris, David, Gleb, Roman, Svyatoslav and Rostitslav. Hardened from the constant military campaigns against Kiev they all wanted to wield power and have their own dominions. The Polotsk lands were divided amongst them and thus formed separate principalities centred around Vitebsk, Minsk, Drutsk, Lahoysk, Izyaslav and Gorodets. The Polotsk throne was still the most important, and Polotsk remained the main cultural and political centre, but the former centralisation and unity was no more. The brothers constantly fought amongst themselves, and so the history of the Principality of Polotsk at the start of the 12th century was remarkable for its constant warfare, looting and bloodshed. The Kievan princes were however unable to take advantage of this disorder in Polotsk to conquer the unruly city.

In 1103 Prince David of Minsk joined hands with the Southern Russian princes to set off on campaigns against their longstanding enemies, the Cumans. Judging by the records in the chronicles, the campaign was highly successful: "… they returned glorious, grand and victorious…". Such an intimate alliance between David and the southern Russian princes must have made his brothers anxious. David was ousted from the Minsk throne, and Gleb was appointed to take the throne in his place. But a year later, in 1104, David's troops attacked Minsk with the support of Vladimir Monomakh. Despite the fact that the attacking forces greatly outnumbered the Minsk retinue, he failed to take the city, and Gleb remained on the throne.

But in spite of the internal factions, the Principality of Polotsk still pursued a policy aimed at expanding and reinforcing its territory and sovereignty. Thus, in 1102 Prince Boris of Polotsk launched military campaigns against the Yotvingians (a Baltic tribe in the Baltic states) and was victorious on several occasions. In honour of these victories the city of Borisov was founded (now a major administrative centre in the Minsk Province). In 1106 all of the appanage princes of Polotsk led a joint campaign against the Semigallians (nomadic tribes living in the lower Dvina who refused to pay the tribute to the Prince of Polotsk). The chronicles offer the following account: "All of the Vseslavichs were defeated by the Semigallians and 9,000 militia were killed". The failure of this campaign was disastrous in terms of its consequences for the Principality of Polotsk, as the Principality lost influence and control over the lower Dvina for a long time. As punishment for poor preparation of the campaign, the angry *Veche* in Polotsk ousted Boris from the throne.

Following these events Prince Gleb of Minsk came to the fore in the history of the Principality of Polotsk, and with it the affluent Principality of Minsk. Written sources offer considerable information on Prince Gleb, much more than any other descendant of Vseslav. It is likely that Gleb stood out for his remarkable campaigns and was more visible to his contemporaries. He started to actively expand the boundaries of the Principality to the west and annexed new lands around the Dnieper, the Pripyat and the Neman. Access to these major rivers vastly broadened the trading opportunities of the Principality of Minsk and contributed to its economic prosperity. In 1113-1116, the Principality of Minsk already owned the major cities of Drutsk, Kopys and Orsha, and the annexing of these lands brought with it considerable savagery. From the Pripyat to the Dnieper and from the upper Neman to the Western Dvina villages were ablaze. Prince Gleb took thousands of people prisoner and sold them into slavery. Grand Prince Vladimir Monomakh of Kiev reproached and cursed Gleb for his barbarity, reminding him that they were not "pagan nomads, but his own people, Christians", and the head of the church, the Metropolitan of Kiev, excommunicated Gleb.

Gleb's overly aggressive policies and his exorbitant brutality (even for that time) sparked protests across many regions of Ancient Rus.

When Vladimir Monomakh started to prepare a military campaign against Minsk he was joined by numerous princes from Russian and Lithuanian lands. The leader of the campaign against Minsk was the son of Vladimir Monomakh, Yaropolk. The Minsk retinue was wiped out and Prince Gleb captured. Yaropolk then marched on Drutsk where the main slave market was based. The city was taken and razed to the ground; the Russians did not want to remember how they were sold into slavery at that very market. Gleb was taken to Kiev and thrown into the same prison which he once shared with his father Vseslav the Sorcerer. He soon died in prison; the people were told that he was not given any food and died of starvation. Drawing on the events of 1068, the Princes of Kiev realised how dangerous it might be to keep a descendant of Vseslav the Sorcerer in prison, and so they hurried to get rid of him.

Gleb's tragic finale does not in any way diminish his role in the history of uniting the Belarusian lands. He fully dedicated himself to expanding and strengthening Minsk's domain, and his grandiose plans to annex the cities on the Neman, Pripyat and Dnieper are often overlooked in terms of the boundaries of the future state of Belarus with its capital in Minsk.

Having defeated the Principality of Minsk, Grand Prince Vladimir Monomakh (who ruled from 1113 to 1125) intervened more and more in the affairs of Polotsk, ever keen to let the city know that the Principality of Polotsk was nothing but a vassal of Kiev. But Polotsk did not want such subordination and demanded the return of the then annexed Minsk. Vladimir Monomakh repeatedly threatened the princes of Polotsk that if they failed to obey the central powers then they would have to deal with all of Rus' forces. The Polotsk princes resisted, and in 1127 a united Russian militia launched a campaign on Polotsk, led by the son of Vladimir Monomakh, Mstislav. The city was quickly captured together with the cities Logoysk and Isyaslavl. As was customary at the time, the capture of these cities was accompanied by looting and riots. The palace of Prince Bryacheslav of Isyaslavl was entirely ransacked, despite the daughter of Mstislav (who led the attack) being married to Bryacheslav.

The armed forces of the Principality of Polotsk were dealt a massive blow and further fighting was impossible, leading to diplomacy as a result. The Polotsk *Veche* blamed the defeat on Prince David and removed him from the throne, making way for Prince Boris. Mstislav decided to accept the decision of the Polotsk *Veche* as he did not want a long, drawn-out war. This time, the military campaign against Polotsk was over.

However, the Polotsk princes, Vseslav the Sorcerer's sons, differed in their enviable persistence. One year later, when Prince Mstislav of Kiev sent orders to assemble a militia and go to war against the Cumans, they refused and told him to mind his own business. This angered the Prince of Kiev, and in 1129 he sent his plenipotentiaries to the Principality of Polotsk. He ordered that a declaration be made, in all cities in the Polotsk lands, that the common people were not guilty of crimes against the government in Kiev, and so no violence, looting, destruction or bloodshed would be tolerated against the people. But the people no longer had to protect their princes. The Polotsk *Veche*, fearing that the city would again be torn to the ground and destroyed, accepted these conditions, showed obedience and handed over the descendants of Vseslav the Sorcerer to Kiev: David, Rostislav and Svyatoslav. They were taken to Kiev to be tried by the "Grand Prince's Court".

The Grand Prince's Court was made up of princes from all of the vassalage principalities of the Ancient Rus state. The court's judgement was relatively light; nobody was sentenced to death. But in order to finally put an end to the unruly Polotsk dynasty, the court ordered that the captured princes be sent to Byzantium, where they would have to serve in the army of the Byzantine emperor. After arriving in Constantinople, they were sent to war with the Arabs, and for their courage they were repeatedly awarded decorations from the Byzantine Emperor John.

So this was Kiev's third attempt to do away with the recalcitrant dynasty of Polotsk princes which embodied the sovereignty of Polotsk: the first was in 980 with the murder of Prince Rogvolod and his sons, and the second was in 1067 with the capture of Vseslav the Sorcerer together with his sons.

Having deported all of the unruly princes to Byzantium, Prince Mstislav of Kiev (who ruled from 1125 to 1132) came to be the sovereign of the Principality of Polotsk and appointed his son Izyaslav to rule there as prince. But this defeat of Polotsk was in fact the last campaign by Kiev to subjugate other lands. In 1132 Mstislav died and this highly subjective event revealed Kiev's inability to maintain even a semblance of centralisation. The first Ancient Rus empire of Kievan princes separated into numerous feudal principalities amongst which internecine wars flared up with even greater intensity.

Freed from the policies of Kiev, the Polotsk *Veche* appointed Prince Vasilka (ruling from 1132 to 1146), the son of Svyatoslav who was exiled to Byzantium, thereby restoring the Polotsk dynasty.

It is particularly worthy of note that in the 12th century, a republic actually existed for a short time in Polotsk, which was unthinkable at the time under the feudal system. Nonetheless, there is no evidence to suggest any similar occurrence in Medieval Europe. From 1166 to 1180 Prince Vseslav Vasilkovich ruled over Polotsk. Vseslav was a highly respected prince and, according to the chronicles, the people valued his intelligence, kindness and sense of justice. When he died, the *Veche* – which had the right to appoint the prince in Polotsk – was convinced that another prince like him could not be found and so decided to elect 30 elders in his place as the supreme authority. The elders were not just selected from members of the nobility, but commoners too. This republican government lasted for 10 years until 1190. But the people were unhappy with the republic and felt abandoned without a prince as ruler. A prince could love, protect and – when unhappy with something – banish. With thirty rulers it was not clear who was responsible for raising taxes or for unsuccessful military campaigns.

The republic did not catch on, and the *Veche* once again appointed Prince Vladimir, son of Vseslav, to the throne.

By the late 13th century, the political influence of the Principality of Polotsk significantly decreased when the political centre of the Belarusian lands moved to Navahrudak. Around this city a group of Belarusian principalities started to unite: Polotsk, Turov, Minsk, Brest, and Pinsk, which continued the process of forming a Belarusian nation with a common language and mentality.

CHAPTER 2
The Struggle Against the Crusaders

POLOTSK PLAYED AN ACTIVE ROLE (OFTEN MILITARY) IN THE political life not only of the Eastern Slavic region, but also boldly defended its interests in the north and north-west where the deep, navigable Western Dvina river linked Polotsk to the Baltic Sea. In the 10-12th centuries the entire Western Dvina river basin – from its sources to the Baltic Sea – belonged to the Principality of Polotsk, and the two major cities of Vitebsk and Polotsk were key trading centres on the river. There is ample evidence to suggest that the people who lived on the Baltic coast – Livonians, Latgalians, Yotvingians and Semigallians – paid the tribute to Polotsk. They made repeated attempts to rid themselves of this dependence, such as in 1106, when the Semigallians wiped out the Polotsk retinue, but they never fully succeeded. The Polotsk princes installed their own protégés in many Baltic cities and in many cases actually ruled over them. The cities were not just inhabited by Balts, but by Slavs too.

In the 12th century this important strategic Baltic region became a target for expansion for the German, Swedish and Danish rulers. In 1184, the Germans landed at the mouth of the Western Dvina. Shortly after, Monk Meinhard, who sought new land and revenue for the Roman Catholic Church, approached Prince Vladimir Vseslavich of Polotsk to ask for permission to preach in his dominions. The prince agreed, underestimating the importance of this event, resulting in unforeseen consequences both for the Principality of Polotsk and for the White Rus lands as a whole. Having received permission to preach, the colony of German missionaries, merchants and professional soldiers quickly grew in size and started sending its representatives further and further to the east and south-east. The Catholic denomination was keen to expand its influence in the East, as the Western European view was that Catholicism was the only true form of Christianity and that the Orthodox faith was followed by heretics and apostates. This started the process not only of the forced conversion of pagan Baltic tribes to Christianity, but also the elimination of Orthodox churches and followers.

The construction of the Riga Fortress at the mouth of the Western Dvina in 1201 was a serious blow to Polotsk's interests as it closed off access to the Baltic Sea. The next move by the German missionaries was in 1202 when they set up, by order of the Pope, the spiritual order of Brothers of the Sword, whose duty, as the name suggests, was to fight for the one true religion – Catholicism. The new knights wore white surcoats embroidered with a red cross and their black flag bore a white cross, for which they were called "Crusaders". Knights of the Order were both warriors and monks, they were not allowed a family, and had to fully obey the head of the Order, the Grand Master.

The first clash between Polotsk and the Order of Brothers of the Sword came in 1203. Prince Vladimir of Polotsk lay siege to a military fortress to the east of Riga and received a tribute from the Livonians and Latgallians. But on the way back they came across the Brothers of the Sword and the retinue of Prince Vladimir was almost entirely wiped out.

It should be noted that when the local population of Balts were faced with the savage power of the Crusaders and the methods they used to propagate Catholicism and enforce economic oppression, they had to seek protection from Polotsk. In 1206, Livonian plenipotentiaries arrived in Polotsk to ask the prince to protect them and fight the Crusaders. The Livonians complained that they had suffered considerable losses, that their leader Ako had been killed in battle, and that the German knights had given his head as a gift – like a form of trophy – to the Catholic Bishop Albert. But at the same time Bishop Albert sent his own delegation to Polotsk to appease the Prince of Polotsk with gifts and to counteract the Livonians. Polotsk sided with the Livonians and organised a military campaign against the Crusader fortress in Golm. The siege lasted for 11 days. Henry of Livonia described the campaign as follows: "The Rusyns (as he called the inhabitants of Polotsk) were proficient in archery, fought for many days and killed many knights. The Rusyns even made a siege engine following the German design, but without any experience in launching rocks actually injured many of their own soldiers". The campaign was unsuccessful, and the Prince of Polotsk did not succeed in vanquishing one – even small – well-defended knights' fortress.

Koknese and Jersika, both vassal cities of Polotsk, could not resist the crusaders' forces, and between 1207-1214 they were conquered, razed and annexed by the Order. On the burnt out site of Koknese the Order founded a well-fortified German military fortress called Kokenhausen, which henceforth became the main springboard for the crusaders' expansion. As a result, the Prince of Polotsk lost the ability to collect any tribute from the Livonian lands.

Despite these setbacks, the Principality of Polotsk was still relatively strong, and the German knights did not dare set foot on its territory. In 1210 an agreement was reached between the Order of Brothers of the Sword and the Prince of Polotsk whereby Polotsk would renounce any claims to the Livonian territory, but would have the right for its merchants to trade freely in the region and to reach the Baltic Sea through Riga along the Dvina.

In 1216, immediately after the death of Prince Vladimir, on the order of the Pope knights were sent from across Germany to Riga. A massive campaign was launched by the crusaders in the Baltic regions under the black and white cross flag. The Latgallians and Levonians did not have any fortified strongholds; their armies were considerably less well-armed in comparison with the metal-armoured knights opposing them. The knights not only had arbalests but catapults – a new invention in military technology at the time. The territories of Estonia and Latvia were quickly captured, and the crusaders reached the borders of Ancient Rus. If the Russian princes had combined their respective militia at the time, the army could have reached more than 100,000 soldiers and, with all likelihood, would have driven the crusaders back to Riga. But, as reported in the chronicles: "the military standards of the Russian princes were turned towards different countries". The Kiev and Moscow princes and the Polotsk and Minsk princes were constantly at war with one another. But as the greatest danger was threatening the north-eastern lands, Polotsk and Novgorod still managed to reach an agreement, forging a military alliance, and took action together against the crusaders. They sealed their political union with the marriage of Prince Aleksandr of Novgorod to the daughter of Prince Bryacheslav of Polotsk. In 1240 a history battle took place with Swedish crusaders on the river Neva. The Novgorod and Polotsk militia, led by Aleksandr, wiped out the knights, for which Aleksandr received the nickname "Nevsky". Two years later there was a battle on Lake Peipus, and Aleksandr was once again indisputably victorious. These two important victories held considerable historic significance as crusader aggression was halted in the north-west of the Belarusian lands for several decades.

CHAPTER 3
The Principality of Turov

ANOTHER MAJOR EARLY FEUDAL STATE IN SOUTHERN BELARUS was the Principality of Turov, founded in the late 9th century. The city of Turov is first mentioned in *The Tales of Bygone Years* in 980, when it had already established itself as the administrative and commercial centre of the principality. It is assumed that the name "Turov" came from the name of Prince Tur who ruled over these lands. Written references to this prince are few and far between and are highly inconsistent, and so many historians believe him to be fictional.

In the north, Turov's territory adjoined the Principality of Polotsk and, during Prince Rogvolod's rule, belonged to Polotsk. But after Prince Vladimir of Kiev's victory over Rogvolod in 988, Vladimir placed Turov under his control.

The city of Turov had extensive trade links with the Black Sea region, the Middle East, Central Asia and the Baltic states and was a major trade and cultural centre at the time. Turov stood on the banks of the river Pripyat, the waterway from the East to the West. Its close ties with Poland, and with that to the Western Catholic world, had a considerable influence on the material and spiritual culture of the Turov lands, compared with the eastern parts of Belarus which were clearly inclined towards the Byzantine culture.

The Grand Princes in Kiev had always looked on Turov with suspicion: firstly because it was previously Polotsk territory and was forever noted for its recalcitrance, and secondly, instead of turning towards Byzantium for its spiritual and cultural influences, as did Kiev, Turov looked to the west, towards Poland.

The geographical position of Turov was quite different to that of Polotsk: it was not far from the powerful Kiev, and was in fact quite nearby. It was therefore always more difficult for Turov to defend its sovereignty, and it did not do so with quite the same aplomb as Polotsk.

In 988, after the adoption of Christianity, Prince Vladimir of Kiev divided the land among his sons so that they could begin to actively disseminate the new religion – belief in Christ – throughout the dominion. In Turov he appointed his son Svyatopolk as governor (between c.980-1019), who was to contribute to the consolidation of Byzantine influence in the principality. The city also had to unconditionally obey the central powers, pay the tribute to Kiev, and provide troops. In other words, no questions could be raised over its independence. But Svyatopolk, according to the chronicles, did not meet his father's expectations. He married the daughter of King Bolesław the Brave of Poland (967-1025), a Catholic by faith. With Svyatopolk in Turov, she brought over the Catholic bishop Reinbern who made friends with Svyatopolk and was forever pitting him against Kiev, even persuading him to adopt the Catholic faith. The Turov nobility, which still remembered the times when Turov was independent of Kiev, supported his sentiments, and Svyatopolk's wife promised him military backing from her father, King Bolesław of Poland. As a result, Svyatopolk decided to secede from Kiev and began military preparations for the impending battle. Grand Prince Vladimir found out about his traitorous son's intentions and, without waiting for events to unfold any further, attacked Turov in 1013. Svyatopolk, his wife and bishop Reinbern were captured and imprisoned in Kiev. But in 1015, Vladimir unexpectedly died and failed to leave any orders regarding the heir to the throne. Svyatopolk was released from prison by his supporters and easily took the throne in Kiev by right as the eldest son of Vladimir. But this sparked opposition from his many brothers, and a bloody battle for the throne ensued. Svyatopolk gave the order to kill his two younger brothers, Boris and Gleb, but there are no historical records of exactly how this happened. Later, in 1072, Prince Izyaslav of Kiev, the son of Yaroslav the Wise, canonised these two brothers as innocent victims of the monstrous Svyatopolk, making them the first Russian saints. They are depicted on a large number of Russian and Belarusian icons.

Hearing about the death of his brothers, Svyatopolk's brother, Prince Yaroslav of Novgorod, entered the fray. In 1016 he went with his army to Kiev, taking the city with relative ease due to the fact that its people were not at all supportive of (and as a result did not want to protect) the reckless Svyatopolk. Svyatopolk's wife was captured by Yaroslav and Svyatopolk himself fled to Poland.

King Bolesław the Brave of Poland must not have been pleased with the events as they unfolded, and so he gathered an army, called on his allies and marched on Kiev. In addition to the Polish soldiers in his army he also enlisted 300 Germans, 500 Hungarians and 1,000 Pechenegs. The battle took place on the river Bug in July 1017, but it did not start immediately; for two days the opponents faced each other and exchanged pleasantries according to the Chronicles. Yaroslav sent word to the Polish King: "Let Bolesław know that he will be backed into a mire like a wild boar by my huntsmen and dogs". With this Bolesław replied: "You referred to me as a wild boar in a mire, but know this: that mire will flow with the blood of your huntsmen and dogs, your princes and warriors, and I will sully the feet of my horses in that mire…"

Bolesław's words came true, Yaroslav's army was crushed and Yaroslav fled to Novgorod. In August 1018 Bolesław led a second campaign against Kiev, this time taking the city almost without a fight, and captured all of the women in Yaroslav's family – his wife and seven sisters.

In the 14th century it was written in a Polish chronicle: "They say that an angel gave Bolesław a sword which, with God's help, he used to slay his opponents. This sword is still preserved in the church of Krakow, and all Polish kings going to war will forever carry it with them… When Bolesław came to Rus at the angel's admonition, he effortlessly opened the Golden Gates locking away Great Kiev from all its enemies".

Kiev surrendered after an agreement was reached that Bolesław the Brave would not destroy the city. But the King of Poland broke the treaty and allowed his mercenaries to pillage the city. Having shared out the plunder, the Germans, Hungarians and Pechenegs returned home. Bolesław's Polish army remained in Kiev but clearly did not know what to do next and understood that it would not hold on to the city for long. He sent his plenipotentiaries to Yaroslav, who was later nicknamed "The Wise" for his extraordinary talents as a diplomat, to commence negotiations. The negotiations centred around exchanging Bolesław's daughter (Svyatopolk's wife, who was imprisoned for her Catholic faith, which was the trigger for this very chain of events) for Yaroslav's wife. Bolesław wanted to have his daughter back and he hoped that Yaroslav felt the same about his wife. But Yaroslav was not prepared to agree to this and did nothing to free his wife from prison.

As for Svyatopolk, he behaved unpredictably. Despite the fact that it was with the help of Bolesław's Polish army that he returned to the throne in Kiev, he started to call for the people to slaughter the Poles. "No matter how many Poles there are in our cities, slay them" were his exact words according to the chronicles. The people did not take long to be won over and soon they started to slaughter the hated Catholics. Bolesław, having derived no benefit from the capture of Kiev, hastened to leave the hostile city.

Yaroslav the Wise decided that since his wife was in captivity he was now a single man, and set about taking advantage of his freedom in the most advantageous way possible. He sent matchmakers to King Olaf of Sweden with a proposal to marry his daughter. He wanted to use the marriage to increase his influence, bolster the army with Swedes and continue the struggle for Kiev. Before long he was married to Olaf's daughter Ingigerd, who was a pagan, but was baptised into the Orthodox church and took the Christian name of Irena. As dowry she brought Yaroslav the Swedish army, with which Yaroslav immediately moved to Kiev. According to the Ustyug Chronicles he had forty thousand men at his disposal, of whom eighteen thousand were Swedes.

Svyatopolk, no longer able to fight for his precarious throne, was forced to flee Kiev. Again he went to Poland, and en route stopped briefly in the town of Brest, earning the city its first mention in the chronicles in 1019. The fortified city of Brest was part of the Principality of Turov and was the last city on the western borders of the Ancient Rus lands (today, Brest is on the border between Poland and Belarus).

From *The Teachings of Vladimir Monomakh to his Sons* we know that in 1070-1080 Brest was razed and burnt by the Poles. Obviously, this border fortress was the theatre for constant struggles between the princes of Rus and the King of Poland. By the year 1097 Brest was once again mentioned in the chronicles as subordinate to Kiev, together with Turov and Pinsk.

After arriving in Brest in 1019, no further mention is made of Svyatopolk, but clearly he did not seize the Polish crown. There is also no reliable information on the time or place of his death. For all of his shady exploits the people and the chronicles referred to Svyatopolk by the nickname "The Accursed".

After Svyatopolk the Kievan throne was assumed by his brother Yaroslav (ruling from 1019 to 1054), who went down in history as Yaroslav the Wise. Throughout his reign he significantly increased the territory of the Ancient Rus state by annexing new lands, not through military campaigns, but rather by diplomatic and political means.

From Yaroslav the Wise's rule, Kiev firmly held the Turov lands in its grasp due to its prominence as the region through which the Pripyat flows – the most important water course to the West – and as a military stronghold to fight Poland and Polotsk. In contrast to the Principality of Polotsk, the Turov lands did not have sufficient political leverage or material resources to defend its sovereignty in the long term. But this political dependence did not bring about the loss of this region's ethnic identity, which was largely conditioned by western – in particular Polish – influences.

The most prominent leader of the Principality of Turov in the first half of the 12th century was Prince Vyacheslav (1083-1154), the son of Vladimir Monomakh. Under Vyacheslav not only were cities which had previously been taken away from the principality once again annexed, but new cities were conquered, in particular Volodymyr-Volynsky. Subsequently, the Principality of Turov did not suffer the same fate of being split up into small appanages. In 1142 it was split into four principalities in the hands of different dynastic lines.

The situation changed after Yuriy (1112-1168) came to be Prince of Turov in 1158. He completely put an end to the practice of splitting up the principality and allocating the cities to relatives of the Kievan princes and said that he would no longer tolerate any interference from Kiev in the affairs of Turov. Prince Izyaslav of Kiev immediately responded by raising an army and marching on Turov. But he failed to take the city by storm, instead having to resort to a siege. The people of Turov mounted a staunch defence, and the siege lasted for ten weeks, which was unprecedented for military campaigns at the time. The chronicles report that the Kievan troops "imprisoned many and burnt many villages around the city, but they were unable to take Turov city and returned home".

In fact, this victory in 1158 signified Turov's independence from Kiev. In 1162 Prince Yuriy received official recognition of his state's independence from Kiev, and the conflicts ceased for good. Yuriy established a dynasty of Turov princes, and his descendants ruled in Turov for many years to come.

The chronicles describe Prince Yuriy as an experienced diplomat, a skilled and successful military commander, and consistent in achieving his policy objectives. There is no record of any internecine conflicts during his rule.

However, the appanage fragmentation and eminence of cities such as Pinsk, Slutsk, Gomel, and Grodno led to Turov gradually losing its former political significance towards the start of the 13th century.

Slutsk rose to prominence on the turn of the 11-12th centuries, and in 1116 one chronicler wrote: "Prince Gleb of Minsk waged war on the Dregovichs and burnt Slutsk to the ground".

Gomel was mentioned in 1142 in much the same way as Slutsk: "Prince Rostislav of Smolensk attacked the Radimichs and set fire to the city of Gomel".

The city of Grodno, judging by archaeological finds, was evidently first recorded in the chronicles approximately 200-300 years after it was founded. "In 1183 Grodno was burnt to the ground from blazing lightning and divine thunder; even its stone churches burnt down". And it was with these sombre words that the city first appeared on the pages of the chronicles and in the history of Belarus.

Nowadays these three cities are major administrative and industrial centres in Belarus.

On the whole, the political history of the Belarusian lands in the 9-12th centuries is covered only sparingly and in a rather fragmented manner in the ancient chronicles. In essence, this information records struggles between the princes, military operations, and natural disasters. The limited written accounts of certain processes and events during the initial periods of Belarus' history has given (and still gives to this day) historians bases for a wide range of assumptions and theories. The majority of conflicting opinions surround the question of how dependent the Principalities of Polotsk and Turov were on Kievan Rus in the early Middle Ages, and to what extent they can be considered the first Belarusian states. For the last twenty years or so, Belarusian historians have considered Polotsk and Turov to be the first Belarusian states. But Russian historians continue to recognise only the statehood of Kievan Rus, describing it as a bastion of the Russian nation and the protector of all the peoples united under its authority.

As regards the reasons for the collapse of Kievan Rus the following points need to be taken into consideration.

The constant conflicts and wars between the principalities of Rus had deeper inward causes. In political terms, Kiev proclaimed itself the head of the largest state by territory and demanded administrative and military subjugation from its vassals. But the economic ties of the individual provinces were weak. The process of consolidating the Ancient Rus empire was held back by factors such as the ethnic and political traditions of formerly independent tribal associations, and their religious and cultural peculiarities. These peculiarities and differences can be explained by the aspiration for local separatism, numerous attempts to break away from Kiev and the creation of fully independent principality states. At first the strongest and most developed of these states, such as Polotsk, Novgorod and Turov, succeeded in achieving independence, but by the late 12th century Kievan Rus ultimately disintegrated into half a dozen separate sovereign principalities and ceased to exist as a centralised state.

<hr />

Also disputed in the history of Belarus is the question of how and when Belarus emerged as a geographical, national and political concept. An unambiguous answer to such a question is not possible. In modern studies, there is no consensus on this issue. Some researchers believe that Belarusians as an ethnic group began to form in the 8-9th centuries and finally emerged by the 12th century, when Kievan Rus collapsed. The advocates of the *Great Russian* theory argue that the formation of the Belarusian ethnic group actually began after the collapse of Kievan Rus and formed only in the 14-15th centuries.

The modern name of Belarus was previously made up of two words: *Belaya Rus* ('White Rus') in Russian, in Latin *Russia Alba* or *Ruthenia Alba*, in Italian *Rossia Bianka*, and in French *la Russie Blanche*. This was how it was referred to in the historical chronicles of Western Europe. The possible origins of the name Rus are described earlier in this book. But where did "white" come from and why?

Once again, there are differing proposals and theories, with the word "white" being explained in various ways:
- white as a synonym of beautiful,
- white because of the large amount of snow in winter,
- white as a synonym of clean or pure,
- white because it was free of Mongolian and Tatar tyranny (the Mongols and Tatars did not actually reach Belarusian soil),
- white because the population of "White Rus" were fair-haired,
- white because in "White Rus" Christianity was adopted earlier and was spread peacefully, and not through bloodshed, unlike other regions of Kievan Rus.

Evidently, there are ample variants for discussion.

Historical documents first mention the name White Rus from the 12th century onwards in relation to the Vladimir-Suzdal lands. In 1169 Prince Andrey Bogolyubskiy (Andrey "the God-Loving") conquered Kiev, but since Kiev was no longer seen as the capital of Kievan Rus, he had no desire to live there. He believed that Kiev had lost the purity of Orthodoxy as so many representatives of other religions lived there, and so he changed his title, Grand Prince of Rus, to Grand Prince of White Rus, most likely to emphasise that he wanted to rule over White Russia, a land which embraced the purity of the Orthodox faith.

In the 13th century, the Polotsk, Vitebsk and Mogilev regions were referred to as White Rus. This name had fully stuck by the 14th century in documents from the time. In the Hypatian Codex the name White Rus was used in the story of the marriage in 1325 of King Casimir of Poland to Anne, the daughter of Grand Prince Gedeminas of Lithuania. In 1413 the leader of Prussia wrote in a letter that Grand Prince Vytautas of Lithuania was preparing for large-scale war, and so Prussia would soon have to fight the "unit den Weissen Russen" (14). In his military dispatches at the start of the 15th century the Polish Chancellor refers to Polotsk as "the stronghold of White Rus".

On Italian, German and Swedish maps and in numerous 15-16th century chronicles White Rus is used to refer to the eastern lands of modern-day Belarus, as well as originally Russian lands: Novgorod,

Moscow, and Pskov. This is supported by the fact that in 1469 the Russian Tsar Ivan Kalita sent a letter to the Pope which read: "Sixtus, Leader of Rome, writes Ivan, Grand Prince of White Rus, he bows respectfully and asks that you place your trust in his plenipotentiaries".

From the mid-16th century the term White Rus significantly expanded the boundaries of its actual existence, then encompassing Minsk and Grodno, and by the 17th century this name finally stuck for the Belarusian ethnic territory (15). In the 17th century, the German Emperor's ambassador Meyerberg wrote in the book *Journey to Muscovy*: "The name White Rus is used to refer to the territory between the Pripyat, the Dnieper and the Western Dvina… and the cities Navahrudak, Minsk, Mstislavl, Smolensk, Vitebsk, Polotsk and all of their districts".

In the 17th century, alongside the name White Rus, the word Belarus started to be used. In the 19th century the official government of the Russian Empire did not recognise this name, preferring to refer to Belarusian lands in administrative documents as the North-West Russian Territory.

CHAPTER 4
The Religion and Culture of Ancient Belarus

THE CHRONICLES WROTE OF THE EASTERN SLAVS THAT "THEY DO not follow the Law of God, but rather create it for themselves". In other words, this means that the Slavs were pagans. Paganism, as a system of beliefs, developed and transformed over thousands of years, becoming more and more complex. For the Slavs it started as ancestor worship and resulted in a complicated and sizeable pantheon of Gods.

For the ancestors of the Belarusians, the supreme and most powerful God was Perun – the god of thunder and lightning – once of the most ancient of all the Gods. His cult began during the time of the Indo-European in the Bronze Age. Svarog was the god of the sky, and the god of sunlight Dazhbog was his son. Hors was seen as the sun god, and Veles the god of animal husbandry. Stribog controlled the winds that brought rain clouds in times of drought.

Especially important and unfaltering to the ancient Belarusian people was ancestor worship, linked to burial customs. Several times a year they would commemorate the dead; in Belarusian this religious holiday is to this day referred to as *Dzyady* (meaning old people or ancestors) and is still celebrated every year on 2 November. Painstaking preparations were made for this celebration – homes would be cleaned and decorated and special ceremonial food was prepared.

During this period of paganism it is well known that the Eastern Slavs worshiped natural forces: stone, mountains, lakes, trees, and especially fire, the moon and the sun. The ancestors of the Belarusians worshiped stone as a symbol of invincible strength and offered sacrifices to stones. So that the magical power of the stone would give a girl a good husband, the girl would make an offering of her annulet, and to help heal the sick a young calf would be sacrificed. A peculiar custom became widespread along the Western Dvina, that of sailing alongside rocks that presented a danger to boats. People would throw bread and salt into the water, shouting: "I welcome you with bread and salt, take this bread and salt and let me pass!"

The pagans were well aware of what good and evil were, and that the world was engaged in a never-ending struggle between these two forces, between light and dark: evil spirits showered arable fields with stones, took the milk from cows, passed on illnesses to people, but the good were protected from any harm. According to their pagan beliefs, fire had a cleansing force, leading to them burn the bodies of the dead.

Family rituals developed around the three main events in human life: birth, marriage and death. People forever wanted their children to be born healthy, beautiful, strong and intelligent, and so in pagan times they turned to magic to try to programme these qualities into their unborn children. According to Belarusian legends, a lot depended on the midwife delivering the child. Frequently it was experienced elderly women chosen as midwifes, who knew the magical spells and techniques to facilitate childbirth.

Marriage was considered to be the most important event and was accompanied by numerous rituals. Marriage between relatives was strictly forbidden. During the marriage ceremony the bride would be made to sit on an animal skin so that she would be healthy and fertile like animals in the wild. All of the guests would be given a piece of wedding loaf prepared by all of the members of the family clan, and later by members of the rural community.

All of the rites during ceremonies were dedicated to preserving the memory of the deceased and guaranteeing them a good afterlife. It was not just Christians but also Pagans who unquestioningly believed in the immortality of the soul, as well as in a person being able to help after death, or indeed to bring misfortune to others.

The most sombre festival was for the god Perun, celebrated at the end of July. Perun demanded blood sacrifices – bulls, cows, and sometimes even people. It was at this time of year that rye began to be harvested and so the people would ask Perun for good weather.

Christianity started to become widespread in Belarusian lands in the 10th century, after Grand Prince Vladimir of Kiev himself was baptised, marking the Christianisation of Ancient Rus between 988-989.

Grand Prince Vladimir chose Eastern Christianity, which had been developed in the Byzantine Empire. This choice was intentional: the Byzantine Empire held the leading role in the Christian world at the time, and it was with Byzantium and its capital Constantinople that Ancient Rus had maintained long-standing and well-established political, trade and cultural relations.

In 1054 the final split occurred between the Western Roman Catholic Church and the Eastern Byzantine Church. The differences between the Pope and the Patriarch of Constantinople had been growing for a long time and related to the emergence of an even greater number of ceremonial, dogmatic and aesthetic differences in the Western and Eastern branches of Christianity. On the 16 July 1054, papal envoys arrived in Constantinople where they anathematised Patriarch Mikhail Kirullariya and excommunicated him from the Roman Church. The Patriarch responded with his own reciprocal curse. Since then the Eastern Orthodox Church followed its own developmental path, no longer recognising the authority of the Pope. (Incidentally, the anathema declared against Orthodoxy was only lifted in 1965, at a meeting in Jerusalem between Pope Paul the Sixth and Patriarch Athenagoras of Constantinople.)

Unlike the Roman Empire, Christianity in the Russian and Belarusian lands came ready-made with rules polished over the nine centuries of its existence, a finished New Testament and a fully-fledged cult of Christ and the Virgin. There was one significant difference: in the Roman Empire Christianity developed from the bottom up, from the lowest social strata of the population to the government and the elite, and in the Slavic world Christianity came from the top, from the elite (princes) to the people.

Christianity's victory was not fast, and it would still take time for it to dominate Belarusians' minds. For several centuries they, and other Eastern Slavs, followed a peculiar dual faith. This was manifested through a large number of people, who had adopted Christianity, continuing to worship pagan gods and perform pagan rituals. Christianity had failed to dislodge the ancient beliefs from the Slavic mind set, and so the Orthodox Church was forced to embrace them. Many elements of pagan cults, and especially family and agricultural rites, were incorporated into the Orthodox Church calendar of religious festivals.

The first Christians in Belarusian lands appeared long before Grand Prince Vladimir of Kiev declared Christianity as the state religion and started to Christianise all of Ancient Rus. The main Belarusian cities were on the banks of rivers along the waterway "from the Varangians to the Greeks", and it was not only trade which passed along these waterways but also the peaceful dissemination of Christian ideals. For example, the 9th century Icelandic record *The Book of Christianity* writes about the life of the monk Thorvald the Traveller. He Christianised Iceland before visiting the Holy Lands in Palestine. On his return journey he chose to travel through Slavic lands, and in 986 his journey took him through Polotsk. The missionary stopped in Polotsk and was warmly received by Prince Rogvolod. With the support of the prince, who, judging by his attitude towards the Christian missionary, was already a Christian, Thorvald founded the Monastery of John the Baptist, where he was buried following his death in 1002.

When Christianity came to be the official religion after the Christianisation of Kiev in 988, the Orthodox Church maintained a very peaceful and tolerant stance towards the old religion. Paganism still remained the everyday religion of the people for a long time, especially among the peasants with their patriarchal way of life and dependence on the forces of nature.

The non-violent, gradual arrival of Christianity in Belarusian lands had important consequences. Since the time of the first Belarusian state – the Principality of Polotsk – Belarus had always maintained a respectful and peaceful attitude towards other religions. Belarus never witnessed any schisms in the church, as in Russia, or religious wars, as in Western Europe.

For a long time the new faith was called the *Greek* faith, as it had come from the Balkans, and only later, after the official East-West schism of Christianity in 1054, did it come to be known in Russian as *pravoslavnyy* ('Orthodox'), from the phrase *slavim gospoda pravilno*, meaning 'praise the Lord correctly'. Similarly, the English word Orthodox comes from the Greek *orthos* ('Correct' or 'True') and *doxa* ('Glory'), resulting in a meaning similar to 'correct belief' or 'true worship'.

The Church in Belarus fully adopted the organisational structure and principles of the Byzantine Church. Under the rules of the Byzantine Church it had to be governed in the same way as a secular authority. With this in mind, as early as the 10th and 11th centuries Russian and Belarusian principalities started to form ecclesiastical districts in the form of eparchies headed by a bishop. Based on a comparison of various written sources on the history of the Orthodox Church, the first eparchy in Eastern Slavic lands was established in Polotsk in 992.

The head of the church, the metropolitan, was based in Kiev, but the bishops in the eparchies more often than not worked closely with the local prince ahead of the distant metropolitan. The only feature that was rigidly preserved was the religious unity of the Byzantine Church. It was based on strict rules laid down in the Byzantine book *Nomocanon* (a collection of decrees by church councils and laws by Byzantine emperors, compiled in the 6-7th centuries), and its rules were mandatory for all.

The adoption of Christianity was a measure of Belarus' progress. It coincided with the formation of Belarusian statehood and, undoubtedly, had a positive impact on this process. Unlike paganism, the Christian belief in the single Lord Jesus Christ tied in with the absolute rule of the prince over the State, thereby consecrating his rule.

But at the same time, the adoption of Christianity according to the Byzantine tradition, rather than the Roman, significantly complicated relations with Western European nations and laid the foundations for future conflicts and wars. Byzantium, in its prime in the 10-11th centuries, later became stagnant, ending in its total collapse. Western Europe quickly overtook it economically and culturally, and this superiority never waned thereafter. Meanwhile, Orthodoxy continued to hold Belarus in Byzantium's sphere of influence, thereby alienating – and even, in some respects, isolating – the state from Western Europe, which complicated its contact with Western cultural achievements, leading to far-reaching consequences in future. The Orthodox Church started down a path towards isolationism and created numerous ideological barriers that, for many centuries, fenced off the spiritual life of Belarus from Western influences. This caused something of a cultural lag in Belarusian society. Furthermore, even less than two centuries after the Christianisation of Belarus, long-standing aggression from Catholic crusaders against the Belarusian lands started to occur, inflicting permanent and significant economic losses on the Belarusian people.

But in the first few centuries after the adoption of Christianity the state witnessed Christianity's most progressive and positive impact on the development of the spiritual and material culture of the Belarusian people. Churches started to be built, requiring skilled professionals: architects, masons, carpenters, painters, blacksmiths, and many more. A new social stratum – the clergy – was formed from the educated classes. Close contact through religion with high Byzantine culture came to be a stimulus for the rapid development of literacy, education, literature and painting. Monasteries became hubs for the spiritual lives of the people, providing schooling, copying and translating books, and developing the historical genre, in the form of chronicles, where events and historic sequences were recorded, often with philosophical or ethical commentary. These chronicles are now some of the most important sources of information on the early Middle Ages.

In 863 the Byzantine monks (and brothers) Cyril and Methodius created the Slavic alphabet and Slavic writing. The Slavic alphabet *Cyrillic* was in fact named after one of the brothers. This alphabet used in Old Church Slavonic writing later came to be inherited by the Belarusian, Ukrainian and Russian languages.

Cyril and Methodius were the first translators of religious books from Greek into Slavic languages. In the 11-12th centuries such translators, as well as copyists, worked at nearly all of the monasteries in the Belarusian cities of Polotsk, Vitebsk and Brest. Cyril and Methodius were later canonised by the Orthodox Church.

To this day only a few of the handwritten books survive from the early Christian era: the 11th century Turov Gospels (stored in the library of the Lithuanian Academy of Sciences), the 12th century Polotsk Gospels (at the Russian National Library in St. Petersburg) and the 13th century Orsha Gospels (at the Central Library of the Ukrainian Academy of Sciences). These manuscripts are made up of two to three hundred pages of parchment and are decorated with miniature depictions of saints and evangelists and skilfully painted capital letters.

The need for education was gradually understood by society, and the work of talented religious luminaries played a major role in this.

It is worth noting that one of the first well known names of Belarusian luminaries belonged to a woman: Euphrosyne of Polotsk (c.1102-1173).

This Mother Superior, from the Polotsk feudal nobility and the granddaughter of Vseslav the Sorcerer, wholeheartedly embraced the Christian religion. A story of her life has survived, entitled *The Life and Death of the Holy and Blessed and Venerable Euphrosyne, Mother Superior of the Monastery of the Holy Saviour in the city of Polotsk*. This work was probably written in the 12th century, perhaps by one of Euphrosyne's disciples. Over the centuries it was included in dozens of different chronicles and is still our main source of biographical information on the life of this luminary.

With regard to her childhood we read: "There was once a girl very gifted with books, even before she became an adult. And it was the result of her prayers". In her youth Euphrosyne refused all offers of marriage and decided to devote herself to the service of Christ. Still relatively young, Euphrosyne reasoned: "What did the generations that came before us do indeed? They married, reigned and grew rich. But they did not live forever. Life passed them by and their glory vanished with it, without a trace, like a cobweb. But venerable wives, courageously following after Christ, sacrificed their own bodies and heads – their names are now written in the heavens where they praise the Lord with angels" (16).

Euphrosyne ran away to the monastery without her parents' permission. The Mother Superior of the monastery was her aunt, and she pleaded with the young girl: "You are too young to endure all the hardships of monastic life. How can you forsake your princely palace and relinquish your princely powers and luxury?"

It should be noted that monasteries were the centres of society's intellectual potential in the 11-12th century. It was at monasteries that they taught various sciences, developed artistic tastes, and wrote historical chronicles which we now use to study history. Talented youths were able to uncover their abilities as a writer, an artist, or a composer at monasteries. But monks did not sever all their ties with the secular world and actually shared their acquired knowledge with the people.

In 1120, with the bishop's permission, Euphrosyne took up residence in a cell at St. Sophia Cathedral and began to copy books from St. Sophia's library. With her help, over time an entire workshop was set up as a workplace for individuals skilled in bookish trades: Greek translators, scribes, bookbinders, miniature painters, etc. The workshop sold books throughout Belarus, and all the money from the sales was distributed among the poor.

In the late 1120s, Euphrosyne founded the Women's Monastery of Our Saviour. Infatuated by her dreams and aspirations, two of her sisters came to the monastery and brought a large donation with them. These funds were used to build the Church of Our Saviour.

This monastery and church, which is now called St. Euphrosyne, can easily be found by any traveller in Polotsk and is a unique example of the architectural style in Polotsk in the 12th century.

Realising the importance of education, Euphrosyne opened several schools for children, teaching them to read, write and sing religious songs. The highly-educated Euphrosyne broadened the programme to teach the young inhabitants of Polotsk Greek, natural history and history, as well as elocution and rhetoric.

The author of *The Life of Euphrosyne*, who was evidently one of the students of the school, and judging by his style had received excellent lessons in elocution, wrote that Euphrosyne said to her pupils: "Behold, I have gathered you like chicks under my wings so that you can live peacefully and in tranquillity. And with a light heart I will teach you and shower you with knowledge. But I see that your fields are in place, your grain is not growing, and the year is already over. Your shovel lies on the floor, and you are not working to your full potential. I fear that you will end up as empty souls. Try, my children, to avoid this, make your grain heavy-eared, pure, full of seeds of knowledge so that pure and tasty bread may be on Christ's table" (17).

Towards the end of her life Euphrosyne went on a pilgrimage to Jerusalem where she died in 1167.

Euphrosyne of Polotsk was a remarkable representative of the educational movement not only for the Principality of Polotsk, but also for the entire Orthodox world. Her work was a reflection of the fundamental spiritual changes that took place in European culture in the 12th century, when the foundations of a new understanding of the world were being laid and consolidated, and when conditions were being created to approve the new standards of man's spiritual values.

Chrysostom of the 12th Century was the name given to another Belarusian luminary, Cyril of Turov (c.1130-1182), a highly-educated man with a striking personality, and a brilliant writer. Roughly 60 works by Cyril of Turov remain to this day: poetic prayers, canons, teachings, parables, all of which are unique monuments to early medieval literature. His works have been copied and studied in many Eastern Slavic states.

Cyril spent many years in a monastery engaged in literary work and copying books. He did not aspire to higher church roles, but his authority was so great that he was appointed Bishop of Turov. In all his sermons Cyril preached austerity, having fought with alcoholism, which was widespread in Rus at the time: "Christians should not celebrate festivals in a state of drunkenness and gluttony, or by dancing or merrymaking, but by tending to orphans and paupers, and by helping and giving to the poor and infirm". He warned: "Woe betide those who have not observed the wisdom of the scriptures and who have idled, danced and indulged in wine...".

Despite the fact that the position of bishop was a lifelong post, towards the end of his life Cyril stepped down and once again retired to his simple life as a monk at the monastery to continue his literary work and preach on charity.

The Orthodox Church canonised the names of Euphrosyne of Polotsk and Cyril of Turov, making these individuals the first saints of Belarus.

PART 3

THE GRAND PRINCIPALITY OF LITHUANIA

(13-16th centuries)

CHAPTER 1
The Creation of a New State

B Y THE MID-13TH CENTURY ROUGHLY THIRTY SMALL PRINCIPALITIES had been formed on the territory of the once large principalities of Polotsk and Turov, each of which was ruled over by a prince who implemented policies aimed, generally, not only at protecting his own domain, but also at expanding his territory at the expense of his neighbours. As such, every one of the principalities was under threat from external enemies. To the north there was the sinister Brothers of the Sword, to the west the militant Polish princes, and to the south the small but aggressive principalities of the defunct Kievan Rus. The Belarusian princes were flexible in their policy-making and frequently entered into agreements and alliances with Lithuania and Yotvingia (now Latvia). Primarily, it was the danger posed by the Crusaders that brought the interests of these peoples closer together. The internal situation in Lithuania was similar to that of White Rus – there were also a lot of disparate principalities which started to recognise the need for consolidation. Moreover, the Belarusian lands were inhabited by a large number of Lithuanians, and likewise entire Slavic villages had existed in Lithuania since the lands were part of the Principality of Polotsk.

The newly commenced era of state education was closely connected with the complex situation that had developed in Eastern Europe. All of the southern and eastern parts of Ancient Rus and the Ukrainian lands in the 1230s and 1240s were affected by massive conquests by the Mongols, and were ravaged and destroyed. The ruthless army of many thousands of Mongols was a permanent threat to the Belarusian princes, and so they were keen to avoid the tragic fate which befell their southern neighbours. In reality, the question was this: to be or not to be? Consolidation based on the principles of a new state came to be absolutely vital.

The basis for the new state, which went down in history by the name of the Grand Principality of Lithuania, was an alliance between two major regional powers: the Belarusian cities clustered around Navahrudak, and those under the control of militant Lithuanian princes, who were major land owners and leaders of pagan Baltic tribes. The Lithuanian princes divided up the relatively small territory of Lithuania amongst themselves, and when it was seen that it was not enough, they gladly offered their armies and service to their neighbours in Polotsk and Navahrudak.

The most influential of these was Prince Mindaugas (1195-1263), the most powerful feudal lord of Lithuania. After 1237, when Prince Izyaslav of Navahrudak died, Mindaugas was invited by the *Veche* to come to Navahrudak – a city which, based on its significance, had largely Belarusian sympathies at the time – and was appointed Grand Prince.

One would think that the role of unifying the Belarusian lands into a single state ought to have lay with Polotsk, which had already experienced independent existence for some time. However, the feudal wars of the 12th century, the protracted struggle against Crusader aggression and its loss of access to the Baltic Sea undermined its influence and power. From the mid-13th century, the political centre of Belarus shifted from the River Dvina to the River Neman, from Polotsk to Navahrudak, which was at the time the most important city in the region. Founded in the 10th century, and first mentioned in the chronicles in 1044, Navahrudak experienced extraordinary prosperity in the 12-13th centuries. It was a city with extensive international links and a large wealthy social stratum. Navahrudak's main advantage at this time was its distance from the routes used both for Crusader campaigns and for predatory Mongol raids. In terms of its economic and cultural standing, and its material and human resources, Navahrudak and the entire surrounding region, encompassing numerous cities such as Slonim, Svislach, and Volkovysk, was considerably superior to Lithuania both with regard to economy and culture. The Baltic peoples of Lithuania were still pagan, were illiterate, used stone architecture and did not have their own cities. All this added to the political weight of Navahrudak and enabled it to become the centre of the new state.

The fact that, even in the very early days of the Grand Principality of Lithuania, the basis of its economic and military power was bolstered by Belarusian territory, and that Belarusians made up the majority of the population, explains why the Belarusian language, customs and culture gradually started to dominate initially in the Prince's palace, and later among the Lithuanian elite, and subsequently acquired official status across the state.

Prince Mindaugas had a reputation as a capable politician and a successful military leader. Shortly after Navahrudak, the principalities of Polotsk, Minsk and Vitebsk recognised his rule over them. Mindaugas took several military campaigns to the south and, with almost no resistance, was recognised as leader in Turov and Pinsk. The chronicles repeatedly mention that Mindaugas' army was made up of 30,000 soldiers (18). Undoubtedly, his popularity contributed to the fact that he and his entire family soon adopted Orthodoxy; in 1246 he "embraced the faith in Christ from the East with many of his boyars and military leaders" (19).

Later, in 1251, under the pressure of the political circumstances at the time and wishing to consolidate his power over the new young state, Mindaugas adopted Catholicism, as a result of which Pope Innocent IV recognised the new Belarusian and Lithuanian state. By order of the Pope, Mindaugas and his wife Marta were crowned King and Queen of Lithuania in 1253. Through this act the European Catholic world recognised the authority and independence of the new state, putting it on a par with other European nations. Symbolically, this date can be regarded as the year in which the Grand Principality of Lithuania was established.

However, in doing so, Mindaugas was not restricting his religious flexibility. The Crusaders themselves were Catholics, but their increasing claims to more and more land were not to Mindaugas' liking. In 1261 Mindaugas renounced Catholicism and returned to Paganism. The Chronicles write that "his baptism was false, he openly offered sacrifices to his Gods and burned, not buried, the dead, and continued to celebrate all the other pagan rituals" (20). Together with Prince Dimitriy of Novgorod, he was constantly at war with the Livonian and Teutonic Order. In 1263 Mindaugas and two of his young sons were killed under unknown circumstances.

We can assume that by the end of Mindaugas' rule there was already a relatively centralised state called the Principality of Lithuania and Navahradak, at the base of which was Pagan Lithuania (villages of pagan peasants) and Orthodox Belarus (cities with artisans and traders) which joined together under the authority of the Lithuanian princes. As the boundaries of the state were subsequently expanded to stretch from Klaipeda in the north to the shores of the Black Sea in the south, and in the 15th century it became one of the strongest in Europe, in history the state came to be known as the Grand Principality of Lithuania.

The ultimate unification of the Belarusians and Lithuanian tribes can to a large degree be explained by significant political changes in 1230-1240. All of the lands to the south and south-east of Belarus were seized by Mongols and Tatars. They moved over the land like a swarm of locusts, leaving behind destroyed cities and villages. Hundreds of thousands of Slavs were killed or forced into captivity. Belarus itself did not experience the Mongol-Tatar invasion and so its economic and cultural centres were not ransacked (21). This was a major advantage, and the unification of the Belarusian and Lithuanian tribes proceeded very swiftly and peacefully.

As a result of dynastic and feudal strifes, Lithuanian princes succeeded one another relatively quickly in time on the Navahrudak throne, but each of them pursued a policy aimed at expanding the state's boundaries. Under Prince Vytenis (who ruled from 1293 to 1316)

Brest and Grodno were annexed and the Pahonia coat of arms and seal of the state and Grand Prince (which came to be historic for Belarus) were adopted. The *Hypatian Codex* reads: "Having become Prince of Navahrudak he invented a coat of arms and seal for himself and for the entire principality: a knight armed with a sword on a horse, which he called Pahonia". This was symbolic, but also an important step towards consolidating the centralisation of the young state.

Vytenis' rule was marked by constant wars: in 23 years he embarked on 11 campaigns to Prussia, 5 on the lands of the Livonian Order, and 9 to Poland. During these campaigns the leadership of David of Grodno was clearly on display. Coming to the aid of the besieged Navahrudak in 1314, he and his army overpowered the Crusaders' camp, killed its guards and seized all of the horses and supplies. The Crusaders retreated to the Neman, but they found that their food supplies and the vehicles used to transport them had also been destroyed by David's men. Demoralised, the Crusaders retreated *en masse*, and with their retreat they successfully finished them off. Later David of Grodno repeatedly fought the Crusaders in Prussia (1319), at Pskov (1322), and in Bohemia (1324), and led his army to Brandenburg and Frankfurt.

The wars against the Crusaders were successful for the Belarusians. The Livonian and Teutonic Order remained in their positions on the shores of the Baltic sea and, in spite of their aggressive ambitions, were unable to expand their domain into Belarusian lands.

CHAPTER 2
Dynastic Strifes

I F THE PERIOD UP TO THE START OF THE 14ᵀᴴ CENTURY CAN BE described as the era of education and the formation of the Grand Principality of Lithuania, then the subsequent period, the 14ᵗʰ century as a whole, was a period of rapid territorial expansion, which gave rise to an entirely new state among some of the largest European nations.

Prince Gediminas (ruling 1316-1341) continued to pursue the policy of his predecessors. He reigned for twenty-five years and during that time significantly expanded the boundaries of his dominion. Under Gediminas most of the Belarusian lands were incorporated into the new state, and its borders during this period were almost identical to the modern-day borders of Belarus.

Gediminas' political wisdom was manifested in the fact that when annexing new lands he guaranteed them autonomy and territorial indivisibility, he ordered that "the old should not be destroyed", and he preserved local laws, the ownership rights of feudal lords and autonomy in concluding trade agreements. All of this ensured the peaceful growth and consolidation of the Grand Principality of Lithuania.

A great many rumours circulated about the origins of Gediminas. He declared himself to be the son of Prince Vytenis, but many have argued that he was simply his stableman who organised the murder of the prince and seized power. To the rest of the world, such rumours were belittling to the young state, still gathering momentum, and so its enemies – the crusaders in the Baltic, the King of Poland in Krakow, and later the Princes of Moscow – were happy to uphold the rumours. As for historians, Gediminas' origins remain a mystery.

Gediminas founded the new city of Vilno (now Vilnius, the capital of the Republic of Lithuania), reinforcing it as a military fortress before moving the capital there from Navahrudak.

Gediminas' diplomatic successes can be owed to his numerous offspring, seven sons and many daughters. His daughters went off to become the wives of Polish and Russian princes, and his sons were sent to rule in the major cities of the Grand Principality of Lithuania. The Russian Rurik dynasty, from which all of the princes of the Ancient Rus period were selected, was ousted on the Belarusian lands and replaced by Gediminids dynasty.

Gediminas entered into a alliance with the Kingdom of Poland which turned out to be highly profitable for the Grand Principality of Lithuania, but this alliance was preceded by numerous wars and battles. In 1324 Gediminas sent a strong army to Poland led by the invincible Commander David of Grodno, taking the Principality of Brest from the Poles. The campaign resulted in the destruction of 13 villages, 30 churches and the capture of 4,000 people. The King of Poland was not expecting such an attack and was forced to enter into peace negotiations. The end result was a defensive alliance between the two states against their main enemy, the Crusaders. To protect the alliance, the lands of the Principality of Brest were ultimately recognised as being owned by the Grand Principality of Lithuania, and the Prince of Poland married Gediminas' daughter Aldona. In Spring 1325 Krakow received not only a considerable dowry from this marriage, but also 20,000 liberated Poles who were captured during previous battles between the Poles and Lithuanians.

Alongside his diplomatic activities Gediminas developed an active economic approach. In 1323 he went to various European nations calling on knights, merchants, artisans and peasants to migrate to the vast Grand Principality of Lithuania. Resettlers were given possession of land and were exempt from taxes for several years. This resettlement programme was quite prolific, as during Gediminas' rule the government kept its promises and protected and supported the settlers.

Ultimately, the Grand Principality of Lithuania came to be inhabited by people of various different faiths. There was plenty of room: the Principalities of Polotsk and Smolensk to the east, Grodno and Brest to the west, and Turov and Minsk to the south were all inhabited by followers of the Orthodox faith. In the north-western regions were Lithuanians and Samogitians, both pagans. Here lived the survivors from the days of the crusades: Prussians, Yotvingians, Semigallians, all of which clung on to their ancient Pagan faith. Catholics arrived from the Western European nations, mostly from affluent backgrounds, and started to actively consolidate the position of their faith. However, the key position, naturally, was occupied by the Orthodox church. Several Orthodox churches could be found in all cities and towns, and Orthodox monasteries operated, teaching children alongside their other religious work. The official language was Belarusian.

Of constant concern to the state, which increasingly strengthened its positions as a result, were the Crusaders. The military skirmishes with the Crusaders had not entirely ceased. In 1341 Gediminas attempted to liberate the Lithuanian fortress Vilyuenu from the Livonian Order. At the time the Crusaders had already developed firearms – guns firing stone shots. They met the Lithuanian army with unprecedented gun fire and forced them to flee. Prince Gediminas was killed in battle.

The news of his death shocked the country. Despite the fact that Gediminas adopted Christianity in his youth, he was buried according to the Pagan customs. The Chronicles offer us a short description of his burial: "All of the high-ranking knights accompanied his remains to Vilno. There, according to the Pagan custom, they assembled a huge frame made from resinous wood. They dressed the Prince in the festive clothes that he loved the most whilst he was alive. Near him they placed a sabre, a spear, a quiver, a pair of fighting falcons, a pair of greyhounds, a live saddled horse, his beloved servant attached to his body, as well as many other weapons and spoils of war. To commemorate the victories they placed three live imprisoned German crusaders in a line and burned it all. And when it was alight, all of the knights cried with great sorrow, and cast into the fire the claws of lynxes and bears. And when it had all burnt to the ground, all of the bones of the Prince, the horse and the gods were laid in a coffin and buried in the ground".

Gediminas' militant sons could not take revenge upon the crusaders for their father's death. The eldest son Algirdas became Grand Prince (reigning from 1341 to 1377) and took his troops to march on Prussia, a campaign which lasted for several months and was characterised by its cruelty and plundering. Algirdas returned to Vilno with one thousand prisoners and huge spoils. It was with this campaign that his political career began.

Whilst his father was still alive, Algirdas fought not only with the crusaders, but also with the Russian princes to the south and the east. The Principality of Kiev for a long time had not been as strong or as rich a state as it was in the 9-11th centuries. It had been weakened by numerous wars between principalities, and in the 13th century it was finally finished off by the Mongols and Tatars. There was nothing left of the Grand Prince of Kiev's former glory, and so he turned to the smaller southern prince, who paid a considerable tribute to the Mongols and could barely even hold on to his own throne. Under such circumstances, he had no choice but to recognise the supreme authority of the powerful northern neighbour, the Prince of Lithuania. This happened in the 1360s, during Algirdas' reign, and Kiev and the surrounding Ukrainian lands became part of the Grand Principality of Lithuania.

The union of the Belarusian and Ukrainian lands under the control of Vilno and the Lithuanian Princes was generally a peaceful process – the territories recognised the need to unite with one another and the benefits of a centralised government and a strong army to defend against the Mongols and crusaders. For almost a century the Mongols did not encroach on the territory of the Grand Principality of Lithuania, which is more than could be said about the Crusaders. On the orders of the Grand Master of the Teutonic Order, well armed knights flocked from all over Western Europe to Lithuania. They killed the Lithuanian pagans and Belarusian Orthodox Christians with the same ferocity, and looted and destroyed pagan temples and Orthodox churches. Over the 30 years of Algirdas' rule, the crusaders launched more than one hundred attacks, compared with the 30 counter-attacks of the Grand Prince of Lithuania. The most successful of these were in 1345, 1347, 1348, 1352 and 1370. Algirdas ordered his men not to take any prisoners during these attacks; they were ordered to kill, and to only imprison women and children.

The constant fighting went on right up to the border with Poland. Here the army of the Grand Principality of Lithuania was commanded by Algirdas' brother, Kęstutis. In 1350 the Belarusian city of Brest was once again captured by the Polish, before Kęstutis took Warsaw and reached the border with Hungary. King Louis of Hungary amassed a huge army in preparation, and Kęstutis understood that it was not worth progressing further into Europe. Both sides entered into negotiations. Kęstutis was offered a royal crown and soldiers to assist in the struggle with the crusaders. In return, he had to make peace with Poland and Hungary and withdraw his troops from the occupied lands.

Kęstutis agreed, following up his consent with a pagan ritual. In front of the Hungarian army he went up to a bull tied up near King Louis' tent, drew his combat knife and cut off the bull's head. Kęstutis and his closest friends washed their hands and heads in the bull's blood and walked between the animal's torso and severed head three times. After such a vow, the Hungarians could have no doubts that Kęstutis intended to leave their territory. The Lithuanian prince left, but that did not stop him from undertaking new campaigns against Poland in subsequent years. The numerous bloody battles and looting led to devastation on both sides of the border between the Grand Principality of Lithuania and Poland.

Having spent his entire life in battle, Prince Algirdas died peacefully at the age of eighty in 1377, appointing his youngest son Jogaila as his successor before his death. This decision gave rise to protests from his other sons and especially his eldest, Prince Andrey of Polotsk. The family was divided, but many of the more influential family members, including Algirdas' brother Kęstutis, supported Jogaila. Prince Andrey of Polotsk then decided to look for help in Moscow, which was forever at odds with the Grand Principality of Lithuania, laying claim to its eastern lands. Prince Dmitriy Donskoy of Moscow promised to help Andrey; Moscow was not against the idea of stirring up the dynastic strife in its strong neighbouring state. Prince Andrey went to Moscow and joined them at the citadel. He was a great soldier and took part in all of the military campaigns alongside Dmitriy Donskoy, including the famous Battle of Kulikovo in 1381, when the Russian army became the first to win a battle against the Mongols and Tatars (22).

Jogaila knew that Moscow was a strong rival, and so he sought an alliance with its sworn enemy, the Golden Horde, a group of Mongol and Tatar khans. This greatly undermined his popularity among the Orthodox population of the Grand Principality of Lithuania; there were rumours that Jogaila had sold himself to the sworn enemies of the Slavic peoples, the Mongols and Tatars. The situation was immediately seized upon by Jogaila's uncle, Prince Kęstutis, a great military leader enjoying considerable popularity in the state who had dreamed of absolute power since his brother Algirdas' rule. Early in the morning one day in October 1381, he led his personal army on an attack against the Prince's castle in Vilno and took Jogaila, his brothers and his family captive. He demanded that Jogaila abdicate and declare him Grand Prince. Out of desperation, Jogaila agreed to the conditions. Kęstutis showed amazing generosity for the time by not killing Jogaila, instead sending him to rule as Prince of Vitebsk. This charity would later turn out to be damaging for Prince Kęstutis.

Having become head of state, Kęstutis turned around the previous tempestuous activity. Instead of the hostility towards the Grand Principality of Moscow, he led a policy of peaceful coexistence. An intermediary in the implementation of the new policy was Metropolitan Cyprian, making a great contribution to the reconciliation and rapprochement between the two countries over several decades.

Moscow was happy to welcome this policy, as it feared that the Grand Prince of Lithuania could in fact conclude a military alliance with the Golden Horde.

Having made peace with Moscow, Kęstutis returned to his usual affairs – the war with the crusaders. He dealt a crushing defeat on the Livonian Order in 1382 with the people's militia. Several major fortresses were conquered and carts loaded with plunder and thousands of imprisoned knights returned to Lithuania. The crusaders then bribed the most influential princes among Algirdas' relatives. They were exploiting the fact that Kęstutis had illegally ousted Jogaila and took the throne of the Grand Prince, and urged him not to submit. This approach was successful, and many princes cooperated with the betrayal. While Kęstutis was fighting in the field against the crusaders, Jogaila's supporters captured the prince's castle in Vilno in June 1382, slaughtered all the guards and restored Jogaila – who had arrived from Vitebsk – to the throne. To finally dispose of Kęstutis, Jogaila resorted to underhand tactics and deceit: he persuaded his cousin, Kęstutis' son Vytautas, to assist in reconciling with his father. Vytautas believed him and invited his father to Vilno for peace talks. Kęstutis had faith in Jogaila's peaceful intentions and arrived at his castle without protection. Both he and Vytautas were immediately seized and thrown into the cellars of Krevo castle. Several days later Kęstutis was strangled, his wife was drowned, and only Vytautas managed to escape, disguised in women's clothes taken from his wife's maid (23). Later, Vytautas would rise to the Lithuanian throne, and he would come to play one of the most important roles in the history of the Belarusian and Lithuanian state.

CHAPTER 3
The Union of Krevo (1385)
and the Battle of Grunwald (1410)

G RAND PRINCE JOGAILA'S POPULARITY WAS NOT GREAT. IN VIEW of the complex and conflicting political situation he could not reach a final decision on who he should enter into a union with, and who he should continue to fight. Moscow was feasting its eyes on the Grand Principality of Lithuania, as the preceding history of the Ancient Rus state had not yet been forgotten. Poland sought a union with the Grand Principality of Lithuania to strengthen its influence on the European political arena. The Teutonic Order continued to ravage the Lithuanian and Belarusian border lands and put forward more and more new demands. The eldest brother, Prince Andrey of Polotsk was in Moscow where he was actively assisting the militant Dmitriy Donskoy in all of his military campaigns and was still prepared to fight for the right to take the throne of the Belarusian and Lithuanian state.

After the great victory over the Mongols and Tatars in the Battle of Kulikovo in 1380 the authority of the Grand Principality of Moscow drastically increased. Jogaila began to seek a friendship with the Moscow leader, Dmitriy Donskoy. The Orthodox church, aware of the significance of a policy of rapprochement between the two states for the future influence of Orthodoxy on the Lithuanian and Belarusian lands, was keen to assist in the establishment of close ties. Plans arose for a union between Moscow and the Grand Principality of Lithuania. It was envisaged that Jogaila would adopt the Orthodox faith, marry the daughter of Dmitriy Donskoy, and would rule over the state with

Orthodoxy as the official state religion. If these plans had come to fruition then the history of the Belarusian people would have followed an entirely different developmental path.

But the numerous opponents of the Russian project won the upper hand, and the ever doubting Jogaila gave up on the plans.

Realising the weakness of his unconsolidated power, Jogaila was compelled to seek support outside the borders of his state. Having poorly played the Eastern card, he turned his gaze to the West. And the events unfolding in Poland took the history of Belarus' development in a different direction. In 1382, King Louis of Poland died without leaving behind a son. For more than two years there were disputes over who was the rightful heir to the throne. Finally, it was announced that the Polish state would be ruled over by the 10 year old daughter of Louis, Jadwiga. The question immediately arose over who would become her husband, as that man would take the Polish crown. Under the insistent pressure of the Vatican, which feared the creation of a powerful Orthodox bastion in Eastern Europe, Poland agreed to hand the royal throne to Jogaila in return for extensive Orthodox Belarusian and Ukrainian lands, with a view to the subsequent imposition of Catholicism.

So quite unexpectedly, the unpopular Jogaila, who had not even proven himself worthy of being leader, except for the betrayal of his own uncle, had the good fortune of wearing the crown of Poland, one of the most influential Catholic states at the time. It was convenient for him that he was 35 years old and was not yet married. To the majority of the Polish nobility, especially the anti-German part, he seemed the best candidate. Poland and the Grand Principality of Lithuania shared a common enemy, the Teutonic Order, which covered both countries' exit onto the Baltic Sea and was constantly ravaging and plundering their border lands. By joining forces, the question could finally be raised not only of ending the Order's aggression, but of switching to the offensive. For Jogaila personally a major plus was the fact that upon entering into the union with Poland and taking the Polish throne, the prolonged dynastic strife for the throne would end, and his brothers

Andrey and Vytautas would no longer pose any danger. Jogaila was happy and was prepared to accept any conditions. And there were a lot: before taking the crown Jogaila, and all of his family, pledged to adopt Catholicism, to pay money from the income of the Grand Principality of Lithuania to the Polish treasury, to pay 200,000 florins to the former fiancé of Jadwiga, Prince William of Austria, and to eternally incorporate the Belarusian and Lithuanian state into Poland. In return for all this, Poland promised to support Belarus and Lithuania in the fight against the Crusaders (24).

Thus, it can be argued that in the 1380s there were two realistic ways to further the development of the Grand Principality of Lithuania: in a union with the Orthodox Grand Principality of Moscow, or in a union with Catholic Poland. If Jogaila had been the son-in-law of Dmitriy Donskoy he would have adopted Orthodoxy, he would have received the Orthodox name Yakob Olgerdovich and would have Christianised the still pagan Lithuania according to the Orthodox faith. But Jogaila chose the West over the East. The consequences of the choice Jogaila made to favour the Polish crown and Catholicism were only truly felt in the 16th century when the conflict between the Belarusian and Lithuanian state and Muscovite Rus gradually came to acquire not only a political, but also a markedly religious dimension.

The situation which was to emerge after the marriage of Jogaila and Jadwiga required official legal formalities. It was therefore agreed that a Union would be signed with Poland. The main argument for such a Union was primarily the threat from the hostile Teutonic Order. Over the period 1345-1395 the German knights attacked the border lands of the Grand Principality of Lithuania on 96 occasions. But at that time there was also another equally important reason for the Union: by the end of the 14th century the political position and might of Moscow had strengthened as a second power aspiring to a union of the Belarusian, Ukrainian and Russian lands as a single state. Something had to oppose this claim. The Grand Principality of Lithuania, weakened by its internal dynastic struggles, was keen to consolidate its position with the assistance of Poland.

Through the Union the Polish feudal lords expected not only to protect their property, but also to extensively broaden their domain at the expense of the Lithuanian and Belarusian territory. The Polish nobility was confident that Jogaila, in thanks for his coronation as King of Poland, would increase Poland's rights and privileges. The Catholic Church hoped to increase their profits through the new tithes that it would receive from the Christianisation of Lithuania. None of them were wrong.

Immediately after the 15 October 1384, when the 12 year old Jadwiga was crowned as monarch, in Krakow and Vitebsk, which was Jogaila's residence at the time, intensive talks about marriage and the Union started to take place. At the start of the summer in 1385 three of the largest embassies – Poland, the Grand Principality of Lithuania, and Hungary – met in Krevo, where they finally worked out the conditions of the Union and Jogaila's obligations that he would have to fulfil in return for the Polish crown. The Grand Prince of Lithuania, who ruled over a state where three quarters of the population were Orthodox, promised to adopt Catholicism and to convert all of his relatives, and agreed to White Rus, and all the other lands up to the Black Sea, being eternally attached to the Polish Crown. Amongst the agreements was also another stating that Jogaila was ready for anything. The problem was that Princess Jadwiga was already married. In 1378, at the age of seven, she was betrothed to the ten year old Austrian Prince William Habsburg. After the ceremony the newlyweds were released to their homes, with Jadwiga's marital duties not due to start until she was 13. If either of the two rejected the marriage they had to pay 200,000 florins compensation (which was more than 700 kilograms of gold). Although this payment should have been paid by the Poles to her might-have-been husband, the happy groom Jogaila took care of this payment himself.

The conditions of the Union included a requirement that the two united states had to be ruled over by a single person, combining the duties of the King of Poland and the Grand Prince of Lithuania. First this would be Jogaila and then the heir apparent of Jogaila and Jadwiga.

The foreign policy and defence of the territory would be collaborative, and the internal governance in each of the countries separate. And the Grand Principality of Lithuania and Poland each had to have their own government, their own treasury and their own army. The Belarusian population was allowed the liberty of the Orthodox faith (25).

On 11 January 1386 the Polish embassy handed Jogaila a document confirming that he was appointed as "king and custodian of the Kingdom of Poland". The Grand Prince, well aware of the Poles' former deceit, demanded that he be recognised as King "in public", rather than just on paper. On 2 February there was a "gathering of gentry" organised, and representatives of the people declared in turn, in the presence of Jogaila's many relatives and the Lithuanian nobility, that Jogaila was the King of Poland. Only after this pageant did the new king travel to the capital Krakow to marry Princess Jadwiga.

En route Jogaila welcomed Polish nobles with assurances of faithful service and obedience. Among them was a secret envoy of Queen Jadwiga, whom she had entrusted to closely examine the "Eastern savage and monster" – such was the way that Jogaila had been characterised by his opponents. But Jogaila's secret informants found out about this and told their master. Jogaila then invited the Queen's spy to bathe with him in the bath-house, after which the agent reported to the Queen that "Jogaila's body is slender, well-built and becoming, he has cheerful eyes and a thin face; he is not at all nasty, like others have told you – in his manner he is important and looks like a ruler" (26).

The huge convoy loaded with riches that accompanied the new King brought about admiration among the nobility and the commoners, and there were rumours of his fantastic wealth. But Jogaila did not begrudge giving gifts to the Queen and her court, generously endowing them with gold, jewels and rich fabrics. These gifts bore testament to the wealth of the Belarusian lands that made up the economic foundation of the Grand Principality of Lithuania.

Having arrived in Krakow, Jogaila and his entire court and relatives were baptised according to the Catholic customs and he took the name Władysław Jagiełło. After this, the long-awaited marriage ceremony took place.

Władysław Jagiełło was King of Poland until his death in 1432 and was the founder of a new dynasty of Jagiellonian kings which ruled over Poland until 1572.

———◆———

The Union of Krevo laid down the foundations for the gradual expansion of the political and religious influence of the Grand Principality of Lithuania and Orthodox culture on Poland. Prior to 1385, the development of the Belarusian-Lithuanian state was of course dominated by Belarusian origins and Belarusian culture, which was manifested primarily in the official status of the Belarusian language. It was not only used by the chancellery and court of the Grand Prince, but was also used by all other social classes from feudal lords right down to the poorest of peasants. After the Union of Krevo, a process was initiated to displace the Belarusian culture, known as Polonisation. But this was a slow process: until the second half of the 16h century Belarus and Lithuania continued to live according to their own customs, and the Union remained largely an "on-paper" construct only.

It was not an easy task however to fulfil one of the main conditions of the Union of Krevo on the conversion of the population of the Grand Principality of Lithuania to the Catholic faith. Orthodoxy had existed on Belarusian, Lithuanian and Ukrainian lands for more than three centuries, all of the cities were Orthodox, and the rural populations of Lithuania were still largely Pagan. It should be noted however that Lithuania was the last European country to adopt Catholicism. In particular, Žmud, a Lithuanian province around Kovno (now Kaunas), only officially adopted Catholicism in 1415, and before that was the last Pagan territory in Europe.

In 1387 Władysław Jagiełło issued a decree on the privileges that landowners would receive if they converted to Catholicism from Paganism or Orthodoxy. Among the benefits were the right to dispose of their estate without restrictions, an indisputable hereditary ownership right, and exemption from numerous taxes and duties. The Orthodox feudal lords did not have such privileges. It was actually the very first attempt to discriminate against Orthodox believers on a legal level.

———◆———

No sooner had Jagiełło succeeded in consolidating his position as the new ruler of the two powers did his rebellious cousin Vytautas once again enter the political arena. He maintained his pro-active relations with Moscow and continually threatened Jagiełło with the prospect of an uprising. In 1389, on the initiative of Queen Jadwiga, Vytautas entered into negotiations with royal envoys and promised not to challenge Jagiełło's authority. But immediately after making such promises, Vytautas and his Lithuanian and part-Muscovite army first attacked Lutsk, before then moving on to Vilno. But Vytautas failed to take these well-fortified cities and was forced to flee with his family and his numerous retinue to the Crusaders, which accepted him – not for the first time – and supported him as they were never against supporting dissidence and confusion in the neighbouring state. In exchange for their support, the Teutonic Order demanded that Vytautas take a solemn oath and make assurances that after gaining power in the Grand Principality of Lithuania he would be a loyal subject of the order and would repay debts for any support, arms and provisions that he may receive. Vytautas agreed to all the conditions, swore on the Holy Scriptures and signed the papers.

Vytautas' separatist aspirations had the support of a significant part of the Belarusian and Lithuanian population. He was associated with the desire to restore the state's political significance which had been, in some respects, infringed upon by the Union of Krevo. Those who were unhappy with the strengthening of Poland fell in line behind Vytautas, even though he was only pursuing his own personal goal – to gain power exclusively for himself.

In August 1390, a forty-thousand strong army made up of allies of Vytautas and Crusader Grand Master Konrad Wallenrod went on the offensive against Vilno. Not far from the city they met Jagiełło's army, made up of Belarusian, Lithuanian and Polish soldiers. Luck was on the side of the rebel Vytautas whose army was victorious, opening up the way to Vilno. But defenders in the city of Vilno – a well-fortified city ever since the days of Gediminas – showed extraordinary courage. The three-month siege of the city resulted in failure for Vytautas, and he was forced to withdraw with the looted goods and prisoners to Prussia.

After analysing the situation, Jagiełło and his allies reached the conclusion that the armed struggle with Vytautas could continue for years, and that save for ruin, and in the worst case the subordination of the borderlands to the Crusaders, nothing would give. The King, perhaps out of pretence, but certainly wisely, said to his opponent: "Do not destroy more of your land, it is your motherland and ours; join us and we will seek an accord and great brotherly love. Reign on the throne of Vilno – it was the throne of your great uncle Algirdas, the brother and friend of your father Kęstutis". Thus he was voluntarily offering power to Vytautas in Lithuania (27).

Vytautas immediately agreed. First, he went to his own castle in Kovno, killed all of the German Crusaders and merchants there to clearly demonstrate through his deeds his refusal to support them, and went to the capital Vilno. In July 1392 he approached the city walls and sent his messengers into the city to inform everyone that Vytautas had returned home of his own accord. When they saw the white flags of Vytautas' messengers, the residents of the city were astounded: these people, who had two months ago devastated everything in Vilno, killed, taken prisoners and ransacked the city, were all of a sudden coming with peaceful intentions!

In the end, the long and drawn-out dynastic struggle ended in compromise. In spite of the protests of many members of his family – Algirdas' descendants – Jagiełło handed Vytautas – Kęstutis' son – the throne in Vilno and appointed him Governor in Lithuania. As for Jagiełło, he continued to rule on the Polish throne in Krakow.

Vytautas held the throne from 1392 to 1430 and was nicknamed 'The Great' during his lifetime. Thanks to his uprising and lust for personal power the Belarusian and Lithuanian state received its own fully independent governance and had little regard for the will of the King of Poland. The objective situation at the time contributed to Vytautas' desire to create a Grand Principality of Lithuania – not on paper, but in reality, as a strong centralised power to weaken the role of Poland in the region. Vytautas consolidated his power, implementing centralisation reforms and pursuing an active foreign policy. As a result, the Grand Principality of Lithuania extensively broadened its borders and came to hold considerable international authority. During Vytautas' rule the Grand Principality of Lithuania covered the entire territories of modern day Belarus, Ukraine, Lithuania and parts of Russia right up to cities only 100 kilometres from Moscow – Mozhaysk, Kaluga and Tula (28). To the south the border of the state ran along the Black Sea and Azov Coast, and in the south-west along the Dnieper. Protecting and defending such a large dominion was not a simple task, even for the determined, resourceful and savage ruler that Vytautas had shown himself to be. But he managed. In the 1420s Vytautas became the political leader of the whole of Eastern Europe. He even held authority over the Polish feudal lords who promised not to put themselves forward for the Polish throne without his consent if Jagiełło were to have no direct descendants.

At the end of the 14th century the Mongols and Tatars once again started to threaten the south-eastern borderlands of the Belarusian and Lithuanian state. The situation became dangerous when in 1395 the Golden Horde came to be controlled by the aggressive Timur. Faced with this situation, Vytautas attempted to create a sort of buffer Tatar state as a barrier to protect against Timur. He welcomed into his home in Vilno the exiled Tatar Khan Tokhtamysh and in 1398 helped him to conquer the Crimean population and establish control over fortresses along the Azov sea. It was clear that these actions would certainly lead to war with the Golden Horde, and so Vytautas sought the help of the Grand Principality of Moscow and western European nations. Moscow refused to give any positive response, and from the west only a few troops of German, Poles, Hungarians and even several groups of Crusaders came to assist. Even the Crimean Tatars promised to take up arms in the event of a war. But the underlying strength of the coalition lay with the troops of the Grand Principality of Lithuania, with even those princes who Vytautas had stripped of their possessions after coming to power showing a willingness to fight against the Mongols and Tatars.

In August 1399 a unified international army under the command of Vytautas himself left Kiev for the capital of the Golden Horde, the city of Sarai. In the very first battle, Vytautas' army was crushed. The Mongols and Tatars seized the entire convoy of the Grand Prince, and Vytautas himself barely managed to escape with a small group of soldiers. The Mongols and Tatars chased him back to Kiev. More than 20 Belarusian princes, grandsons and great-grandsons of the great Algirdas, were killed in the battle. It was doubtlessly a heavy loss, one which affected Vytautas' credibility and slowed the process of consolidating and strengthening the state. But at the same time the Mongols and Tatars were made aware of the might of the Grand Principality of Lithuania, and for several decades did not dare to trouble its borders.

The victory over the Teutonic Order at Grunwald brought Vytautas his greatest military honour. Back in 1392, during the intensifying struggles between Jagiełło and Vytautas, the Teutonic Order was already preparing to divide up the discordant Grand Principality of Lithuania and entered into an agreement with the King of Hungary on who was to receive what. It was planned that Hungary would receive Poland, a large part of Ukraine and the Belarusian stronghold of Brest. The Teutonic Order would get all of Belarus, the territories of Lithuania, Latvia and Estonia, as well as Pskov and Novgorod. The fact that such an agreement existed was never forgotten by Jagiełło or Vytautas.

For more than two hundred years the Belarusians, Poles and Baltic peoples had been faced with a strategic issue, not only holding back the constant expansion of the Crusaders, but also eliminating this military threat. Some possibility of achieving this goal was seen in the Union of Krevo, when Poland and the Grand Principality of Lithuania entered into a political and military alliance, and were able to stand united against the Crusaders.

In 1408 King Jagiełło and Grand Prince Vytautas started making preparations for a great campaign against the Crusaders. In Winter 1409, the Belarusian regiment began to amass in the Belovezhskaya forest. They brought cannon and shots specially adapted to the storming of castles. This was complemented with huge convoys of arms and provisions. The Crusaders learned of these preparations and decided to neutralise the brothers Jagiełło and Vytautas by taking them prisoner. They formed a detachment of the strongest and most experienced knights (which we would now call "special forces commandos") and sent them in to seize the castle in Volkovysk where, according to the knights' secret information, the two rulers were currently based. The castle was seized for several minutes, but Jagiełło and Vytautas were not there. In a fit of fury the Crusaders burned the city to the ground and took the entire male population of the city prisoner.

On the eve of the Battle of Grunwald Vytautas' Belarusian army was made up of 40 regiments, each with more than 500 soldiers. There were also 5,000 Tatar mercenaries and one regiment of soldiers sent from Novgorod. From Poland, under the command of Jogaila himself, 50 regiments had been amassed, each of which with 200-300 soldiers. The total allied army consisted of more than 40,000 soldiers.

The Teutonic army, led by the troops of Grand Master Ulrich von Jungingen, was somewhat fewer in number but was better armed and trained. By way of example, it had 100 cannon, compared with the 32 of its opponent.

The battle took place on 15 July. The Belarusian light cavalry started the onslaught. After two hours the Polish regiments entered the fight. Approximately one hundred thousand soldiers from both sides fought on the field near Grunwald almost until sunset. The upper hand moved from one side to the other. The land was covered in blood. More and more new reserves were thrown into the fray. Finally, the Crusaders began to retreat, but they were surrounded before being brutally slaughtered to prevent their escape. By evening, the fight was over with the complete defeat of the Crusaders. Their camp, with herds of spare horses, provisions, weapons and hundreds of barrels of wine (presumably for the Teutons to celebrate their victory), was seized.

The entire leadership of the Teutonic Order had been killed: Grand Marshall Wallenrode, Grand Komtur Lichtenstein and Grand Master von Jungingen.

Approximately half – twenty thousand soldiers – of the Grand Principality of Lithuania's army had been lost, the majority of which were in the Belarusian regiments. Losses in the Polish regiments were minor, as reported by Jagiełło in one of his letters the day after the victory.

After the defeat at Grunwald centuries of German aggression had been brought to an end. The balance of power had shifted in favour of the Slavic nations in Central and Eastern Europe. Belarus enjoyed nearly 100 years of peace. The victory at Grunwald convinced Europe that to the east lay a strong state, the Grand Principality of Lithuania. This victory also helped the ethnic consolidation of the Belarusian lands. Regiments from Polotsk, Smolensk and Navahrudak all went into battle, and they returned united as a united Belarusian people.

On 1 February 1411 the Peace of Thorn was signed with relatively soft terms imposed on the Order. The Order gave Samogitia to Lithuania, the Dobrzyń Province and the mouth of the Vistula to Poland, and paid war indemnities. However, the actual destruction of the army and the death of all the leaders of the Order undermined the power of the Teutons. A number of Hanseatic cities in Europe immediately withdrew from alliances with the Teutons, and the flow of money, knights and mercenaries fell sharply. This signified the gradual disappearance from the political area of the struggle with Belarus' long-standing enemy.

———————◆———————

After the death of Vytautas in 1430, with the support of the Belarusian princes Švitrigaila, brother of King Jagiełło, became Grand Prince of Lithuania. It was these princes that Švitrigaila relied upon in his anti-Polish policy. He declared that he would withdraw from the Union with Poland, remove power from the Catholic barons, and the Orthodox Belarusian aristocracy would take on powerful stately positions and gain the right to sit in the *Rada*, the state's parliament, a right which had been denied by Vytautas. In reality the monopolistic power held by the Catholic feudal lords, which they quickly seized following the Union of Krevo, shifted to the political elite in Belarus. This evoked considerable dissatisfaction and conspiracies among the Lithuanian nobility, who were enthusiastic supporters of Poland. In the night of 1 September 1432, the conspirators, led by Vytautas' brother Sigismund, attacked Švitrigaila's castle and captured his family. Švitrigaila managed to escape to Polotsk and the conspirators elected Sigismund as Grand Prince (ruling from 1432 to 1440). Lithuania and Poland recognised him as the rightful ruler, whereas the Belarusian Polotsk, Vitebsk and Minsk provinces remained loyal to Švitrigaila. A Civil War broke out between 1432 and 1440.

Švitrigaila was notable for his unpredictable nature and his alcohol addition. In Smolensk he ordered that the Orthodox Metropolitan Gerasimos be burned at the stake having got infuriated with him over something. This act damaged his popularity. In spite of the fact that he had a much more numerous army than his opponent, he lost battle after battle. In the summer of 1435, he suffered a major defeat at the Battle of Wilkomierz. Approximately 20 Belarusian princes were killed and 42 captured.

It was, in reality, a war fought for the throne. But the involvement of large swathes of the Belarusian population in support of Švitrigaila because he supported Orthodoxy, and not Catholicism, gave this civil war a nationalistic and religious dimension. This war did not determine, but rather reveal the existence of significant political and religious differences in the Grand Principality of Lithuania.

As a result, Švitrigaila suffered defeat, but Sigismund's power did not last long. He immediately removed all Belarusians from power and started to implement an acutely pro-Catholic policy. Belarusian patriots led by Czartoryski princes organised a plot killing Sigismund in 1440 in his own castle in Trakai. The Polish party placed the younger brother of King Jagiełło, Casimir, on the Lithuanian throne (from 1440-1492). Following this, the domestic policy of the Belarusian and Lithuanian state witnessed a long period with no conflict whatsoever.

CHAPTER 4
The State and Class Structure

THE GRAND PRINCIPALITY OF LITHUANIA WAS A FEUDAL MONARCHY in which the feudal lords had the right to own the population dependent on it – the peasants. The land, the main means of production in the feudal era, belonged to the state, feudal lords and church organisations. Large private landowning feudal lords only made up less than 10 per cent of the population, and the rest of the population was divided into classes: the gentry, the middle-classes, and the clergy.

The feudal lords were the privileged part of the population and their exclusive right to land ownership formed the basis for their power and wealth. This class was however not uniform. Most of the land was owned by former appanage princes and family members of former ruling princely dynasties – the descendants of Rurik, Rogvolod and Algirdas. These landowners created a stratum of barons comprising some of the most powerful princes holding stately positions and whose right to land ownership came about through inheritance. The other feudal lords were minor princes and boyars who came to be referred to as the gentry or nobility. They owned land only conditionally, if, for example, they had been employed by a baron or the Grand Prince. As a reward for their service they would receive land, but it could also be taken away from them. Since the Belarusian and Lithuanian state was in a near constant state of war the value of this class of military servicemen was forever growing. The gentry had fairly well consolidated its position and played a significant role in the governance of the state, primarily through the *Sejm*, an elected body attended by representatives of the gentry from all of the districts and provinces.

For a long time the Grand Principality of Lithuania was not governed by a single set of legislation. The Grand Princes regularly published Privileges governing rules on land ownership and the payment of taxes. The Grand Prince could adopt them at his own discretion, and something that would apply to one feudal lord, a Catholic, for example, would not be allowed for other Orthodox lords. The first orderly and common code of laws was adopted in 1468 during the reign of Grand Prince Casimir IV, referred to as Casimir's Law. It consisted of 28 articles containing rules on civil, criminal and procedural law. According to Casimir's Law the age of criminal responsibility was seven. For petty theft committed for the first time the punishment would be in the form of a fine, whereas for grand theft the offender would be sentenced to death by hanging. In addition, Casimir's Law refers to offences such as robbery, pillage and witchcraft as theft. Article 19 of the Law authorises the use of torture. From the articles defining the laws on land ownership it became clear that peasants gradually come to be dependent on the landowner. For example, they would be exempt from the many payments to the state treasury, as between the peasants and the state was a feudal lord, their master. The peasants only paid payments to the master. Thus the government started to regulate its economic relations through the only legal entity that was important to the state – the feudal lord; peasants in reality ceased to have any legal status.

The legal culture of the Grand Principality of Lithuania made a huge leap forward in the 16th century when it adopted Statutes (codes) offering organised collections of laws. The decision on how to organise previous laws and decrees into one collection was made at the *Sejm* in 1522. After this decision, work started which would last for seven years. It was overseen by a committee of officials, academics and representatives of the clergy, headed by Grand Chancellor Albrecht Goštautas. If we consider the fact that such a systematic collection of laws was not present anywhere else in Europe at the time we can make some assumptions as to the number of practical and theoretical issues facing its contributors.

In 1529 the collection was submitted for review by the *Sejm* in Vilno and approved. At the heart of the Statutes were concepts such as state sovereignty, the unity of law for all, and the preference for written laws, all of which were highly progressive for the time. In the thirteen sections, consisting of 282 articles, the foundations of the state system, the composition and powers of public bodies and the courts, and the legal status of the various classes and social groups were laid down in law. The first section defined the prerogatives of the Grand Prince's power and the rights of the barons, the second was dedicated to state defence, the third dealt with the personal and class rights of the gentry, the fourth and fifth were devoted to land ownership laws, the sixth concerned the organisation of the courts and judicial process, etc. The Statutes were written in the official Belarusian language and existed only in numerous handwritten versions, but were never published.

However, the first Statutes should not be idealised as many of the articles were merely declarative, on account of the weaknesses of the executive and judicial bodies.

The next 20-30 years after the adoption of the Statues were a time of considerable change in all spheres of public life in the Grand Principality of Lithuania. For example, the remit of the *Sejm* took definitive shape as the supreme legislative body of the state, and the influence of the gentry was greatly increased in the political arena. As a result a need arose for new laws. In 1551 a committee made up of 10 members – 5 Catholic and 5 Orthodox – was created alongside the *Sejm* to expand the code of laws. Ten years later, in 1561, the committee provided the *Sejm* with new draft Statutes. Many of the articles of the new laws were widely discussed at *Sejm* meetings, and some were not accepted. The second Statutes entered into force in 1566.

The new Statutes consisted of fourteen sections and 367 articles. The first three sections covered state law, section four was devoted to the courts and judicial process, and sections five to ten were on criminal law. For the first time, the separation of the courts from the legislature and the executive was proclaimed. And even more clearly stated than in the first statutes were articles prohibiting foreigners from holding public office. The Statute was written in Belarusian and later translated into Polish and Latin.

With the adoption of the second Statutes in 1566 the codification and systematisation of laws was far ahead of similar projects in other countries. Its closest neighbours Poland and the Grand Principality of Moscow did not have such a refined code of laws. This suggests that the Belarusian and Lithuanian state's social relations were on a higher level, and that there were legal experts who were both theoretically and practically trained well enough to reflect on and consolidate these relations in a code of laws.

The third edition of the Statues was drafted and published after the adoption in 1569 of the Union of Lublin to unify the two states. Under the terms of the Union the Kingdom of Poland and the Grand Principality of Lithuanian would maintain their own laws within their respective territories. The new collection of the Statutes contained 488 articles. It was written in Belarusian, and was only translated into Polish in 1614 (29).

———————◆———————

The majority of the population of the Grand Principality of Lithuania were peasants. Right up to the mid-16th century this class was not uniform. There were those peasants who had personal freedom, carried out their military service, and whose status was nearer to that of the gentry. But this stratum was relatively small. The bulk of the peasants were to a greater or lesser extent dependent on the feudal lords and had virtually no civil rights whatsoever. In fact, these peasants existed only to meet the needs of the feudal lords and the state.

In the 14-16th centuries there was a significant growth in the cities and the urban population. The largest of these cities at the time were Polotsk, Vitebsk, Mogilev, Minsk, Brest and Grodno. Polotsk had a population of approximately 50,000 inhabitants, whereas Vitebsk,

Vilno and Minsk had roughly 20,000. The medium-sized and smaller cities, of which there were more than 500 in the 16th century, had about 2,000-3,000 inhabitants each. In terms of their socio-economic status, cities were subdivided into state (Grand Principality) and private cities – namely those owned by powerful barons.

The urban commoner population was subdivided into three groups according to their property. The upper rung included large-scale merchants and artisans. Often they owned land which brought those nearer the top of the urban ladder closed to the gentry. The middle group included small-scale traders and artisans who owned a property.

The legal status of commoners often depended on the city in which they lived. The inhabitants of Vilno, Polotsk, Brest and Minsk had far more rights as these cities had the right to self-governance, "Magdeburg Rights" following the example of the German city of Magdeburg which in the 13th century was the first ever to receive such rights. According to this right, trading activities, property rights, the social statuses of citizens, and socio-political life was governed by the city's own system of laws. The city's population was exempt from all feudal obligations and instead introduced a single money tax. The governing body of the city was the city council which was made up of two parts: a *Rada* elected from the city's citizens and a court appointed by the *Rada*. To house the city council each city built a special city hall. Needless to say, these Magdeburg Rights were very progressive for the time as a system of governance incorporating elements of democracy, and it should be noted that the Belarusian cities were most easterly boundaries of this form of democracy in Eastern Europe: the Russian lands to the east of Belarus never came to adopt the Magdeburg Rights.

More than 80 per cent of the population in major cities were Belarusian. But they were also inhabited by Russians, Ukrainians, Lithuanians, Poles, and from 14-15th centuries Jews and Tatars.

The state capital had been Vilno since 1323. It was here that the government bodies and residence of the Grand Prince were based and the meetings of the state *Sejm* took place.

The *Sejm* was convened at the request of the Grand Prince or the *Rada*. Meetings of the *Sejm* required the participation of the entire *Rada*, Catholic and Orthodox bishops, senior priests, government officials from all levels, and selected delegates from the gentry of all the provinces. It was not strictly defined which issues fell under the remit of the *Sejm*; it depended on what was most pressing and important to the state at the time. The main role at the *Sejm* fell to the *Rada* and the feudal barons, as they would determine which decisions would be adopted.

The central authority in the country was the Grand Prince. He controlled the executive activities of the higher state bodies and the administration, and served as commander-in-chief of the army. It was with his signature and seal that the legislative acts of the government would be enacted. In accordance with tradition, the Grand Prince was selected by the representative body of the feudal nobility: initially the *Rada*, and from the 16th century onwards, the national *Sejm*.

The *Rada* (council) was initially a supplementary body to the Grand Prince's authority. The Grand Prince himself would invite those he deemed useful or necessary, from the point of view of the people, to attend the *Rada*, and was at liberty to accept or refuse its advice. In 1492, before electing Grand Prince Aleksandr to the throne, the gentry put forward demands to increase the powers of the *Rada*. Aleksandr issued a constitutional charter which greatly expanded the powers of the gentry and the lawful rights of the *Rada*. The *Rada* started to choose between 30-40 permanent representatives of the nobility and the clergy. The 1492 Charter stated that henceforth all laws and orders handed down by the Grand Prince should only be implemented with the consent of the *Rada*.

The coat of arms of the Grand Principality of Lithuania – named "Pahonia" (literally "Pursuer") – first appeared in the 1270s during the reign of Grand Prince Vytenis. The 1566 Statutes enshrined it as the national coat of arms of the Grand Principality of Lithuania. Each province and principality had its own seal bearing the coat of arms.

The coat of arms showed a white knight with a sword and shield on a red baroque shield.

Under the new administrative divisions of the 15th century the Grand Principality of Lithuania was split into 6 administrative divisions called provinces: Vilno, Trakai, Kiev, Polotsk, Vitebsk and Smolensk (30). The provinces were ruled by governors of the Grand Prince, but he could not appoint them without the consent of the local feudal lords and townsfolk, and if the city had Magdeburg Rights he had to obtain the consent of the City *Rada*.

The governments of the Polotsk and Vitebsk provinces each had their own peculiarities. Ever since the days of the first Belarusian state the Principality of Polotsk had maintained its own traditional *Veche*. The appointment of the prince, the approval or rejection of governor candidates, and even the recognition of the Grand Prince's power were all decisions adopted by the *Veche*, the people's assembly. If the *Veche* expressed clear opposition then the Grand Prince had to make concessions to tie in with local interests. The right to the *Veche* was maintained until the late 16th century.

Thus, in the 15-16th centuries the Grand Principality of Lithania was a form of constitutional monarchy. Representative bodies such as the central *Rada*, and the local *Radas* which existed in each province, placed significant checks and balances on the powers of the Grand Prince. In this regard, the Grand Principality of Lithuania was considerably different to the Muscovite state which had clearly developed as an absolute monarchy.

CHAPTER 5
The Struggle with Moscow

FROM THE VERY OUTSET OF ITS EXISTENCE THE GRAND PRINCIPALITY of Lithuania set itself the goal of uniting into a unified political entity the disparate principalities of Eastern Slavs occupying large swathes of territory following the collapse of Kievan Rus. In the 13th century and the first half of the 14th century it was the only possible candidate for the role and had no rivals. City after city and territory after territory gradually – and generally peacefully – came to be part of the Grand Principality of Lithuania. In the second half of the 14th century the unifying state was confronted with an opponent – the Grand Principality of Moscow, which had grown quickly and differed in its ambitions and aggression. And then, this other state, gathering together new cities around itself and broadening its own territory, finally, touched upon the borders of the Grand Principality of Lithuania.

The hostilities began in the 13th century over the relatively small Principality of Tver, in which there were both Lithuanian and Muscovite groups. Algirdas twice fought the armies of Dmitriy Donskoy, winning once but losing on the other occasion. Algirdas, busy fighting with the Teutonic Knights, ceased his claims to the principality and Tver fell to Moscow.

During Vytautas' rule, a struggle started for Novgorod and Smolensk, and in 1404 these two strategically important principalities became part of the Grand Principality of Lithuania.

In the 14th century Moscow was not yet a strong state. Having grown from a small appanage principality, it worked its way up to prime position step by step. A victory over the Mongols and Tatars at the Battle of Kulikovo in 1380 played a considerable role in its rise to eminence.

The process of unifying the principalities of north-eastern Rus around Moscow ended in the second half of the 15th century. By this time all of the disparate principalities had lost their independence and were incorporated into the Muscovite state. The Grand Princes of Moscow began to see themselves as the masters of all the Slavic lands that were once part of the Ancient Rus state. So historically, two centres were emerging, Vilno and Moscow, each laying claim to the leading role in the region. But on Belarusian soil the unification process had taken place almost three centuries earlier, and so the Belarusians were not about to hand over their dominion to Moscow. In the end, the two centres could not help but clash with one another. The Grand Princes of Moscow had once ruled over their own ancestral lands and still continued to uphold the same governing principles of holding on to their ever increasing power. "By the will of God all of the Russian lands have been our dominion ever since ancient times", declared Dmitriy Donskoy. The Grand Prince had forgotten that "since ancient times" his dominion was only the relatively small Moscow and was not the richest compared with other cities. But the Grand Princes of Moscow made their great ambitions for power clear and presented themselves as the representatives and owners of "all of Rus". "All of Rus" was understood to mean White Rus and Little Rus (now Ukraine) – territory which had long ago established its own statehood and was not in any way prepared to subjugate itself to Moscow.

In 1472 Grand Prince Ivan III (1440-1505) married a Byzantine princess called Sophia Palaiologina who had been baptised by the Pope. This stoked his ambitions and he set out to return all of the former lands of Kievan Rus to Orthodox hands, thereby positing Moscow as the Third Rome. Ivan III referred to himself as none other than the "sovereign of all Rus" and in the years 1483-1484 in a number of documents the title "Tsar" appears for the first time (a Russian version of the Latin "Caesar", the emperor). His heir would already be married to the throne according to all the rules of the Byzantine emperors (31).

From 1487 he was no longer Grand Prince, but rather Tsar Ivan III, and he started an undeclared borderlands war for his "ancestral lands" (which he had never seen himself, and nor had his ancestors) – the Belarusian lands. For this he even sought to collude with the long-standing enemies of the Slavs, the Mongols and Tatars, for whom Belarus had always been something of a chimaera. With the assistance of Khan Mengli Giray he wrought havoc on the Belarusian lands along the eastern and southern borders. Many cities were destroyed and thousands of prisoners were sent to Moscow and the Crimea. Grand Prince Aleksandr of Lithuania was forced to seek peace, and to make the peace agreement more durable, he sent his matchmakers to visit the daughter of Ivan III, Elena, whom he then married.

But this "marriage with Moscow" did not make the peace any more solid. In one of his messages Grand Prince Aleksandr did not refer to Ivan III as the "ruler of all Rus" and the angered Russian leader immediately sent Aleksandr an official declaration of war. In June 1500 there was a battle near the town of Dorogobuzh, killing more than 8,000 soldiers. The Belarusian army was entirely wiped out and their commander, Prince Konstantin Ostrozhskiy, was taken prisoner. After the battle, the Muscovite army plundered the eastern Belarusian lands for three years until they began to starve on the territory that they had entirely destroyed. In 1503, the two sides finally signed a peace treaty under which the exhausted Belarusians were forced to give Moscow the cities of Gomel, Rogachev, Chernigov and Bryansk – in total 19 cities and their surrounding land. Thus, Moscow took control over territory stretching along the entirety of the eastern border of the Grand Principality of Lithuania inhabited by Belarusians and Ukrainians. This made up one quarter of the state's entire territory. Belarus had lost everything that Grand Prince Vytautas had gained in the battles to annex them to the Grand Principality of Lithuania.

In 1505 both leaders in the Grand Principalities of Lithuania and Moscow died, to be replaced by Aleksandr's brother Sigismund in Vilno and Ivan III's son Vasilyy III in Moscow. Once again they began to fight amongst themselves having taken advantage of a minor skirmish. In 1508 Prince Glinsky, an opponent of Sigismund, fled to Moscow from Vilno and Moscow granted him political asylum. Sigismund was extremely unhappy that his enemy had welcomed an honoured person in Moscow and sent a letter of protest. Taking advantage of this conflict, Moscow's army stormed Belarus once again, but Sigismund had foreseen the onslaught and was waiting at the Muscovites' border with a well-prepared Belarusian army. The army was victorious in the first battle and chased the Russian army back towards Moscow. Tsar Vasilyy III (all Grand Princes of Moscow started to refer to themselves as Tsar after Ivan III), having seen that the situation had become too dangerous, requested peace, this time promising that the peace would be "eternal". With this Prince Konstantin Ostrozhskiy and other Belarusian military leaders were released from prison.

The "eternal" peace promised by Moscow lasted for all of five years. In 1512 the Muscovite army attacked Smolensk but failed to capture the city. A new attempt to take the strategically important and rich city was undertaken in 1513, but again, to no avail. After destroying all of the villages around Smolensk the Russian army returned to Moscow. The third assault on the city began on 16 May 1514 and finally, on 30 June, the city was captured. The Muscovite army, having won this important battle, marched deep into the country. In September 1514 they were stopped near the town of Orsha where there was a great battle. The eighty-thousand strong Russian army was defeated by the thirty-thousand strong Belarusian army commanded by Konstantin Ostrozhskiy. Through skilful manoeuvring he managed to deceive the vigilance of the Russian commanders and lead their army into a Belarusian artillery ambush. The Muscovite army was forced to flee, and the pursuit of the fleeing army turned into a massacre. The Battle of Orsha resulted in the deaths of thirty thousand soldiers.

But even this did not bring an end to the war. The cities of Vitebsk, Polotsk, and Orsha were destroyed by Russian troops on several occasions and scores of villages perished. The homeless and ruined peasants went into hiding in the woods to escape the killing and plundering. Seeing that there was no end to the war, they began a mass exodus to the south, to Ukraine. Only in 1522 was an agreement signed, but not for peace, for a armistice for 5 years. The Belarusians did not succeed in winning back the lost ground and Smolensk remained with Moscow.

In 1533 Tsar Vasilyy of Moscow died and his successor was the young Ivan IV, who later came to be known as "The Terrible" (1530-1583). Under the young successor's rule dynastic plots started to emerge, and Vilno decided to take advantage of the weakening power in Moscow, to take revenge and to regain the territory it had lost. The convened *Sejm* approved the decision to go to war, and even agreed to treble the war tax. After two years of localised hostilities an armistice was once again signed, but the Belarusians did not reclaim the lost land.

Since all of the battles were fought on Belarusian territory, Grand Prince Sigismund of Lithuania knew that without the support of the Belarusian nobility he would not succeed. So he had to implement measures to involve the Belarusian aristocracy in the governance of the state. In the 1530s he increased their rights and privileges considerably and the aristocracy were allowed representatives in the *Rada*. The noble Belarusian princes Glebovich, Drutsk, Sapieha, Vyazhevich and Khodkevich were appointed as members of the *Rada*.

In the years 1558-1582 Tsar Ivan the Terrible of Moscow led a protracted war with the Livonian Order. Livonia (now Latvia and part of Prussia) asked for help from the Grand Prince of Lithuania and became protectorate of the state. A war with Moscow was once again inevitable and the borderlands of Belarus were again forced to suffer. In early 1563 the Moscow army, totalling two hundred and fifty thousand soldiers, laid siege on Polotsk. Prince Mikołaj "The Red" Radziwiłł used his Belarusian army to close off the road to Vilno, but he was unable to help Polotsk. In February 1563 Polotsk was captured by the troops of Ivan the Terrible. On his orders all those who refused to adopt Orthodoxy were to be severed with swords or drowned in the river Dvina. Thousands of prisoners and a convoy of hundreds of carts filled with loot from Polotsk went east, to Moscow. None of these Belarusians ever returned to their hometown, and Polotsk was populated with migrants from Moscow. When, after 15 years of war, Stefan Báthory finally liberated Polotsk and the surrounding villages from the Russian army, this once rich and economically developed land was a young forest and overgrown wilderness.

Thus, during the 15-16th centuries the relationship between the Grand Principality of Lithuania and the Grand Principality of Moscow was hostile. This was not only down to their respective claims to the leading role in superpower politics, but was also due in part to religious differences. The Muscovite rulers saw themselves as protectors of the Orthodox population in Belarus and Ukraine which had been harassed the Poles and Catholic church. At the same time, the Orthodox population had not entirely cut itself off from the population of the Muscovite state in terms of its national religion. These peoples did truly have common historical roots and were united by their traditional culture and common religion. In spite of the on-going military battles and fierce aggression, the pro-Moscow separatist sentiments amongst the Belarusian nobility had relatively strong support. In the late 15th century there was a real wave of dissent when the Belarusian princes Bielski, Vorotynskys, Vyazemskys, Meretskov and Shemyatichi left for the Grand Principality of Moscow, and in 1508 when the influential Prince Glinski fled. He dreamt of liberating Belarus from Poland and restoring the Kievan monarchy to rule over all of the Orthodox peoples. The anti-Polish sentiments of the Belarusian population gave Moscow an excuse to continue its aggressive policies which Moscow itself called "liberatory".

In the 15-16th centuries the Grand Principality of Lithuania went through a period of civil war and a protracted war with Moscow. The difficult international position, the loss of eastern territory and economic collapse forced the ruling elite to once again seek help from Poland and enter into the Union of Lublin in 1569 which resulted in the loss of the Grand Principality of Lithuania's independence and sovereignty.

CHAPTER 6
Religion and the Reformation

RELIGION STILL PLAYED A LARGELY CRUCIAL ROLE IN THE spiritual and cultural life of the 14th and 15th centuries. As previously, Belarus was dominated by the Orthodox church. At the same time it had an impact on Lithuanian Paganism and opposed the active dissemination of Catholicism. Until the late 14th century the Orthodox church was the only centralised church organisation. The rulers of the Grand Principality of Lithuania, the Grand Princes, supported the church as it, in turn, consecrated their power and smoothed out various social issues. The number of Orthodox churches can only be estimated on the basis of the data available from the mid-16th century: in the capital Vilno there were 17 Orthodox churches, in Pinsk 14, in Navahrudak 10, in Polotsk 9, and Vitebsk, Grodno and Slonim each had 7.

Monasteries served as centres for education, culture and spirituality where both religious and secular schools were based, libraries were set up and historical chronicles and records were kept. Almost all of the monasteries had art workshops where they created icons. The entire territory of Belarus had approximately 30 Orthodox monasteries, of which 17 were in the Principality of Polotsk, which had remained a centre for cultural and spiritual life since ancient times.

Until the 15th century Belarusian metropolitans were Greeks or Bulgarians as they were considered to be more educated theologians, but then this supreme spiritual position came to be held only by members of the Belarusian church hierarchy.

In the late 15th century a collection of documents entitled *The Scrolls of Yaroslav* were compiled, defining the legal status of the Orthodox church and its relationship with the secular powers. Church property was proclaimed untouchable by the secular government and the metropolitan was given full powers of church affairs: "The metropolitans and bishops shall have the right for perpetuity to judge and ordain, and to celebrate all things spiritual for Christians under Greek law". Since then, the Orthodox hierarchy had to be members of the Grand Principality's *Rada* and took part in meetings of the Belarusian barons.

Together with the Orthodox denomination Catholicism came to define the culture of Belarus. In the 13th and 14th centuries attempts to disseminate the Catholic faith in Belarus did not have much success, but after the conclusion of the political and military alliance with Poland (Union of Krevo, 1385), the Catholic religion became the official religion of the state's rulers. This could not lead to any changes in policies regarding religious tolerance, which had until this point been characteristic of Belarus as a state. Having signed the Union and taken the Polish crown, Jagiełło had to turn the entire Pagan population of Lithuania to Catholicism, and he implemented this promise with violent methods. For example, when two Lithuanian Pagan feudal lords refused to adopt Catholicism, he sentenced them to death.

The number of Catholics grew rapidly in Belarus precisely because of the conversion of Pagans within the state, and over time, as the Catholics became more and more numerous, the Orthodox population began to suffer all kinds of discrimination. Members of the Belarusian nobility could not be elected to the state *Rada* and could not take part in elections for the Grand Prince. An Orthodox believer, upon marrying a Catholic, had to immediately adopt Catholicism or face punishment. In 1437, 43 years before the Spanish Inquisition, the Grand Principality of Lithuania created its own inquisition "with the right to seek out and punish heretics and Russian apostates". The word "Russian" here was defined as all followers of Orthodoxy. However, it should be noted that this inquisition was largely on paper only, as the inquisition never started to take any decisive action on Belarusian territory.

The organisational structure of the Catholic church was set up in record time. Within the space of a year after the Union of Krevo, Jagiełło ordered the creation of a Vilno episcopacy, covering Minsk, Navahrudak and Vitebsk. The Lithuanian barons played an active role in the creation of the economic foundations of the Catholic church. By the mid-16th century 90 per cent of all of the land that made up the Vilno episcopacy had been handed over to it by the feudal lords. With the active support of the supreme powers the 14th and 15th centuries saw the foundation of Franciscan monasteries (Pinsk, Lida, Oshmyany), Bernadine monasteries (Polotsk), and Augustinian monasteries (Brest, Bystrica). They all quickly came to be major landowners.

The contribution of the Catholic church and monastic orders to the culture of Belarus was considerable. Above all else, this contribution was reflected through the dissemination of moral values and the development of education.

———————◆———————

In the first half of the 16th century Western Europe witnessed the start of a process to improve the Catholic Church in its own way, which went down in history under the name of the Reformation. It was a broad socio-political and ideological movement pitted against the old dogmas of the Catholic Church and its influence in all spheres of political and social life.

This process did not bypass Belarus.

The first pieces of information on the emergence of Reformation ideals in Belarus came from the 1520s. The first seditious ideas on the true faith in God started to be heard in the court of King Sigismund I in 1521 from an Italian preacher by the name of Francisco Lismanini. He was a leading figure of the Reformation, an Italian humanist and a shrewd politician. His efforts with the King's court resulted in the creation of a huge library with works by the likes of Luther, Calvin,

Melanchthon and Zwingli. At the same time in Vilno monk Stanislav Rapegellan of the Franciscan order started to preach the ideas of Martin Luther. He soon left for Wittenberg, where for a long time he was a pupil of Luther himself before receiving a doctorate in theology. After returning to Belarus he continued to preach Lutherism with considerable success.

The first to take an interest in the ideas behind the Reformation were the upper classes in Belarusian society. Nobles and merchants started to familiarise themselves with the new views on religion and the word of God during trips to Western Europe, having acquired controversial literature and listened to Protestant teachings on their travels.

In 1539, a graduate of Wittenberg University, Abraham Kulva, opened the first Lutheran school in Vilno with the assistance of the queen, the wife of Sigismund I, Bona Sforza. The school took in 70 students, primarily the children of barons and nobles. The graduate also preached the ideas of Martin Luther in Vilno's St. Anne's Church. Abraham Kulva's sermons so inspired the residents of Vilno and expanded their knowledge of the gospels that Bishop Pavel Golshanskiy had to turn to King Sigismund for assistance in the fight against heresy. In 1542, the frightened King issued an decree stating that any nobles recognising and disseminating Protestant ideas (namely those disagreeable to the Catholic Church) would be deprived of their property and noble status. In the same decree he forbade young people from going to study in Germany and banned schools from inviting teachers and educators from Germany.

But the decrees and repression could not halt the desire for a spiritual renewal. One year later the law banning study at German universities was repealed.

In Brest, Symon Zak, a master of theology and graduate of Krakow University, started to preach the beliefs of the Swiss Protestant John Calvin. Residents of Brest as well as nobles from all around came to hear his sermons. Bishop Valerian Protasevich decided to give the apostate a run for his money and summoned him before the episcopacy court. In his order to appear at the court the bishop kindly informed him that he would give the defendant the opportunity to renounce his seditious views and to return to the true Catholic faith. So as to have a witness at the hearing, the bishop suggested that the accused appear in court alongside four friends. But on the day of the judgement Symon Zak was not accompanied by four of his friends, coming instead with roughly three hundred supporters. Bishop Protasevich did not even dare start the court proceedings, and simply walked away. Symon Zak was sentenced in absentia to exile from the country and to have his property confiscated.

A striking figure in the history of the Reformation in Belarus was Prince Mikołaj Radziwiłł (1515-1565). He was born into a noble family in Nesvizh but was brought up among the court of the King of Poland in Krakow. He graduated from Krakow University in preparation for becoming a statesman. He went down in history by the name of Mikołaj "The Black" Radziwiłł, due to his black beard, to distinguish him from his cousin, Mikołaj "The Red" Radziwiłł, who also occupied a prominent position in the history of Belarus.

King Sigismund I, ruling in Krakow, was already getting old, and Mikołaj Radziwiłł and his supporters insisted that power in Vilno be given to the son of the aging King, Sigismund II Augustus. In Autumn 1544 the *Sejm* ratified this decision, and the thirty-year-old Mikołaj Radziwiłł became the first advisor and right-hand man of the new ruler, with whom he had enjoyed a long friendship since his days at the Polish court. He was promoted to marshal, or as we now know it, foreign minister. Mikołaj Radziwiłł's influence on state policy increased further after Sigismund II Augustus married Mikołaj's cousin Barbara Radziwiłł. This marriage was done in secret, as the heir to the Polish crown was supposed to gain the approval of the father and the Polish *Sejm* for their marriage beforehand, but he knew that they would never agree to such an unequal union. Only in 1548, when King Sigismund I of Poland died, and Sigismund II had taken the Polish crown, did he let on that he was not single and was already married to a princess from a noble bloodline rather than a royal one. The Polish nobility, and especially the mother of Sigismund II, the ambitious Bona Sforza, flatly refused to recognise the new queen and demanded the dissolution of the unequal marriage. Princess Bona was an ardent Catholic which, however, did not prevent her from frequently selling positions in public office to supporters of the Reformation when they paid her enough for it (32). But the King remained adamant, and two years later, Barbara Radziwiłł was solemnly coronated in Krakow. However, fate had it that this Belarusian noblewoman was only destined to be queen for a short time, dying suddenly one year later, reportedly having been poisoned by her husband's mother.

In 1551, Mikołaj Radziwiłł was appointed state chancellor – the highest position in the Grand Principality of Lithuania. The King granted him the right to keep documents on the domestic and foreign policy of the Grand Principality of Lithuania in the archives of his palace in Nesvizh, having converted it into the state archives. Given that Sigismund II Augustus was now permanently based in the Polish capital Krakow, the real power in the Belarusian and Lithuanian state was held by Mikołaj Radziwiłł.

But Prince Mikołaj was not purely concerned with his political career. The well-educated and forward-thinking Radziwiłł could not remain indifferent to the ideas of the Reformation that had captivated 16th century Europe. He first became acquainted with them during his studies in Germany, and in Vilno he came to be involved with the Protestant Abraham Kulva, whose powerful preaching evoked admiration for his faith and conviction in the young Radziwiłł.

The ideas of the Reformation spread relatively quickly and attracted intellectuals with their simplicity and purity. A living faith and a direct relationship with God was exactly what was sought after by the public consciousness at the time.

In 1552 Mikołaj Radziwiłł met with Symon Zak and allowed him to preach in his castle in Brest where hundreds of people could hear Calvin's follower. In 1553 Radziwiłł was visited by Emperor Ferdinand of Germany, and this trip finally convinced him that he had made the correct choice of religion. When he returned to Vilno, the Chancellor of the Grand Principality of Lithuania and commander of the state army Mikołaj Radziwiłł publicly announced his conversion to the Evangelical faith, free from the Pope and idolatry. He also spoke about the opening of a Calvinist Church in Brest Castle and invited all those seeking the true faith in Christ to visit.

In the same year, Radziwiłł opened his own printing house where he began widespread publication of Protestant and educational literature. At the same time, in his vast dominion he started to build a new Calvinist church and was not sparing in its construction. After Vilno and Brest Calvinist churches opened their doors in Orsha, Nesvizh, Kletsk and Vitebsk. In each of these churches a primary school was set up. Virtually all of the future elite of the Grand Principality of Lithuania, people who decided on state affairs right up to the start of the 17th century, studied in these schools. The Calvinist schools had a fundamentally new educational system, offering a much broader education than the Catholic schools, and also helped to spread the ideas of the Reformation. The Vilno Calvinist school founded by Mikołaj Radziwiłł sought to declare itself an Academy at the end of the 16th century, but it was only due to strong opposition from the Catholic hierarchy and the violent new Catholic King Sigismund III coming to power that this project was not carried through.

Radziwiłł exchanged personal correspondence with Calvin, Wolf, and Melanchthon and consulted with them on practical and theological issues. Prince Radziwiłł was well aware of the need for publishing activities in order to successfully develop the Reformation. He saw that it was through the printed word that the ideas of Calvin and Luther would become known throughout Europe and would influence the thinking of thousands of people. In his printing houses in Brest and Nesvizh he started to publish Catechisms, textbooks on various aspects of science, and polemical works. In 1563 Mikołaj Radzivill started an ambitious printing project – the translation of all of the books of the Bible into Polish. The translators he invited worked on the translation of the Bible from its original languages: the Old Testament from Hebrew, and the New Testament from Greek.

In the late 1550s the Glebovichs, Saphiehas, Wiśniowieckis, Aginskys, Pronskys, Narushevichs and Shemets – the families of some of the most powerful barons – announced their commitment to church reform. The barons and gentry, followers of both Catholicism and Orthodoxy, started a mass shift to Calvinism, and the teachings of Martin Luther came to be more popular among the urban middle class.

Before its very eyes Belarus became a Protestant country. By the late 16th century the Grand Principality of Lithuania had more than 300 Protestant churches. At the Cathedral in Brest in 1596, at the time of the church union, the Catholics began to reproach the Orthodox church for having entered into an alliance with the Calvinists, and put forward the example that in the Navahrudak District the reformers "took for themselves" 60 Orthodox churches, and out of the 600 Orthodox noble families only 16 did not accept Calvin's teachings (33).

It should be noted that the nobility in Belarus, unlike may countries in Western Europe, accounted for approximately 10 per cent of the population (in 16th century France, for example, they only made up 1.5 per cent, and in Germany 2.3 per cent). The fact that the vast majority had sided with the Reformation was the reason for the Protestant churches spreading so quickly.

So Calvinism came to be the most popular religion in Belarus. The families of powerful Catholic barons such as the Radziwiłłs, Sapiehas and Hadkevichs happily adopted the doctrine, aimed at the development of individual consciousness and responsibility. Calvinists were ardent supports of the words of the apostle Paul: "He who does not work shall not eat". But the most important thing for the nobility that had adopted Calvinism was to do away with the interference of the church in secular affairs. The representatives of the Belarusian and Lithuanian nobility, supporters of full sovereignty of the Grand Principality of Lithuania and its separation from Poland, saw in Calvinism an ideological justification for such independence, which neither Catholicism or Orthodoxy could offer, reflecting as they did the interests of either Poland or Moscow.

Mikołaj "the Black" Radziwiłł, who was called the "uncrowned king" on account of his wealth and huge political influence, built in Vilno, directly in front of the Catholic Church of St. John, a magnificent temple for the Calvinist community, and invited Calvinist preachers from Belgium and Switzerland. Calvinist communities were established in Vitebsk, Zaslawye, Minsk and many other cities. They set up highly popular schools as well as shelters for orphans and the elderly and hospitals. In the 16th century Belarus had seen the creation of roughly 100 Calvinist communities, and by the end of the century the organisational and territorial structure of the Calvinist church had already been fully created. A Lithuanian province was created which contained six districts headed by superintendents. The central district was that of Vilno. Ideological and organisational issues were submitted for discussion by local synods in meetings attended not only by church ministers but also secular folk.

In the 1560s a more radical movement started to emerge in Belarus out of Calvinism: Arianism. This ideology received its name from the Bishop of Aleksandria, Arius, who lived in the fourth century. He opposed the divine nature of Christ and the Holy Trinity. In the Middle Ages Arius' ideas were developed by scholars, Russian heretics and Anabaptists. With the advent of the Reformation Arianism flared up with renewed energy. The ideologist behind Aranism in the 16th century was the Spanish scholar Miguel Servet. In the 1540s the majority of Spanish and Italian followers of Arianism were forced to flee from the Inquisition, first to Switzerland and then on to Poland and Belarus. The Arians not only sought a partial reform of the religious world view of Christianity, but also a change in social living conditions. They refuted private land ownership, the privileges of the feudal lords and their dominance over peasants, and opposed the wars and national and religious inequality. The Arians developed a large number of utopian plans to reconstruct society, teaching equality, a classless society, justice and brotherhood. These ideas could not divide the representatives of the nobility, or even the barons, so Arianism in Belarus was more 'popular' in nature and created small pockets of communities in many cities. The radicalism of the Arian ideologists, and their practical attempts to implement their social slogans was met with considerable anxiety by those in power. The Arians were persecuted not only by the Catholic church but also by the state. In the early 17th century there were several trials of Arians ending in a death sentence. The final blow to Arianism was a resolution by the state *Sejm* to banish Arians from the Polish-Lithuanian Commonwealth. They were given three years to settle their property affairs and then anyone who dared to profess and propagate Arianism was sentenced to death (34).

Naturally, this reformist approach developed the cultural and spiritual life of Belarusian society. In the mid-16th century ten printing houses were opened in Belarusian cities where they published polemical, educational and pedagogical literature, rapidly increasing the number of literate people in the state.

Reformation ideas spread relatively peacefully in Belarus. In 1563 the barons and nobles, led by Mikołaj Radziwiłł asked the King to repeal a 1413 decree forbidding non-Catholics from occupying the highest public offices. Sigismund II Augustus, knowing that there were hardly any Catholics left amongst the noblemen who had approached him, issued a decree whereby anyone who believed in Christ, regardless of whether or not they recognised the Pope as the head of the church or not, were equal before the state government and could serve their country on an equal footing. It should be emphasised that by this time no other country in Europe had adopted such a progressive law with regard to Protestants.

The fact that the ideas of the Reformation spread throughout Belarus in a peaceful atmosphere of religious tolerance bears is supported by the Warsaw Confederation adopted in 1573, one year after the St. Bartholomew's Day massacre in France, which proclaimed and guaranteed religious peace and freedom in the Polish-Lithuanian Commonwealth and the Grand Principality of Lithuania (35). It was the first legal act in European history to pronounce the equality of people of different religions. For Europe, engulfed at the time in bloody religious wars, the Warsaw Confederation was an example of how to address the issues of freedom of conscience and religion. Just five months earlier in Paris a very different document was adopted: a royal decree banning all kings of meetings, sermons and Protestant services, on penalty of death.

In 1588 the Warsaw Confederation was translated from Polish into Belarusian and was incorporated into the code of laws making up the Statue of the Grand Principality of Lithuania, providing official legal protection to the Protestants.

Only one class, but nonetheless the most populous class of all, was virtually unaffected: the peasantry. The Reformation held no interest amongst the broad masses of the Orthodox rural population and as such did not spread at all (36). The peasants in Belarus were illiterate, impoverished, and questions about the essence of Christianity were far removed from their daily life. The main points of the Reformation – denying the supreme authority of the Pope, dogma and relics, and doing away with the celibacy the clergy – did not make sense in the eyes of the illiterate peasants as they did not even recognise the Pope, and Orthodox ministers had always been able to marry even before the reform. Some barons tried to force the peasants to adopt the new faith, rounding them up to listen to the sermons, but this was entirely unsuccessful. The new ideas fell on deaf ears in the peasant communities, and so the Reformation movement in Belarus was not so widespread and popular as it was in other European countries. Belarus did not have the right socio-economic footing, as the bourgeoisie had not yet developed in the 16th century in comparison with other countries such as Germany or Holland.

Developments in spiritual life in the second half of the 16th century coupled with the Reformation contributed to the development not only of culture but also the economy. The teachings of John Calvin paid considerable attention to human identity and particularly emphasised the importance of honest performance of one's duties. In 1556, under the leadership of Mikołaj "the Black" Radziwiłł, an agrarian reform was implemented which gave each peasant family a plot of land measuring 21 hectares. The plot of land was called a *voloka*, whence the name of the reform – *volochnaya reforma* – was derived. Every peasant family had enough land to feed themselves and were able to sell any surplus harvest. The new system of economic management gave positive results, yields increased, and rye and barley began to be exported in large quantities for sale abroad.

The economy was not only of interest to politicians, but to poets too. Prince Jan Abramovich, one of the proponents of the reform movement in Minsk, wrote a book "Perspectives on the Cheap Purchase and Expensive Sale of Grain", in which he wrote about the benefits of the free market. The philosopher and poet Yazep Damanevsky (37) wrote in his works about labour as a source of human happiness, and laziness and inactivity as the reason for poverty. Not surprisingly, with such ideas in circulation, the country was experiencing good economic growth.

Thus, the Reformation, which began as a protest against the legacy of Catholic dogma, brought about changes in all walks of public life, no matter how far removed they were from religion: politics, economics, education, etc. One could call the 16th century the golden age of Belarus, the best period of its history.

In spite of its subsequent defeat, it is hard to overestimate the value of the Reformation for Belarus. The ideas of the Reformation contributed to the development of Belarus' civil and national identity and led to the penetration of Renaissance ideas into spiritual life and education, drawing the Belarusian and Lithuanian state into the pan-European historical process.

———————◆———————

Soviet historical works have always claimed that the main reason for the mass adoption of the Reformation by Belarusian barons and nobles was their desire to seize the property of the Catholic and Orthodox churches, and the desire to exert control of a new cheaper church which would no longer be able to extort wealth from their own personal riches. Such a purely materialistic view of history has no basis whatsoever. The land ownership of by no means the most powerful of the Belarusian barons, such as the Hadkevichs, Glebovichs and Radziwiłłs, far exceeded that of the Catholic bishops, let alone the those of the Orthodox church, which was many times poorer even than the Catholic church. Therefore the gentry could not possibly have coveted their wealth. Conversely, the construction of new reformation churches and printing houses, aimed at the dissemination of the new ideas, and the opening of schools and shelters for the poor all required huge financial resources, and the newly-converted were by no means sparing in funding these investments. Documents from the time, including extensive personal correspondence between Belarusian nobles, indicate that the main reasons for their move towards the Reformation were a personal sincere belief in the new ideas and a desire to see the church renewed and cleansed of its centuries-old hypocrisy.

CHAPTER 7
Literature and Printing

THE EMERGENCE OF LITERARY CREATIVITY IN THE BELARUSIAN
lands was associated with the adoption of Christianity in the 10th
century and the influence of the high literary culture of Byzantium
and Bulgaria. Most of the literary genres in Belarus were religious in
nature: the lives of saints, prayers, sermons for reading or for church
services, all of which were written in Old Church Slavonic.

Out of all the genres of truly Belarusian literature from the time,
the genre that witnessed the most dynamic growth was the chronicle
– a historical work giving descriptions of events over a series of years.
They combined a documentary basis with an emotional, figurative, and
fictionalised understanding of the past.

In terms of their content and form the chronicles can be divided
into four main groups:
- *The Chronicler of the Grand Princes of Lithuania*
- *The Belarusian and Lithuanian Chronicle of 1446*
- *The Lithuanian and Zhmoytskaya Chronicle*
- *The Bychowiec Chronicle*

The Chronicler of the Grand Princes of Lithuania was the first work of
Belarusian historical literature. It was written by an unknown author
around 1430 in Smolensk in the form of a single work, similar to a
long novel, but without the use of dates, which distinguishes it from
traditional Russian chronicles. The story describes the history of the
Grand Principality of Lithuania from the death of Gediminas in
1341 up to the end of the 14th century, covering the struggle between

Jagiłło and Kęstutis and Vytautas, before then describing in detail and praising Vytautas as the ruler of the Belarusian and Lithuanian state. The author managed to create an interesting an entertaining narrative, describing real life political and military events. It can be assumed that the author was a member of the ruler's court, as he is highly familiar with the events taking place and the intrigue surrounding the dynastic confrontations. In his story, the author clearly supports the centralised policy and the idea of a strong centralised government, as well as exhibiting support for activities directed at eliminating the fragmentation of the splintered feudal state. Later, the work was incorporated in parts into other chronicles, including Polish chronicles. The book also reached Moscow where it provided Russian readers with a vital source of knowledge on the history of their neighbouring state.

The Belarusian and Lithuanian Chronicle of 1446 is so called because the last events that it recounts date from 1446, and it begins its chronology from the mid-9th century, a century before the adoption of Christianity. It contains a lot of information about the history of Kievan Rus, but also a number of separate sections on local Belarusian origins, such as the *Smolensk Chronicle* and *Praise Vytautas*. The very name *Praise Vytautas* is particularly apt in view of the content of the work, which describes Vytautas' conquest to expand the territory of the Grand Principality of Lithuania, his wise policies and love for the people.

The Lithuanian and Zhmoytskaya Chronicle describes the course of history from the legendary Roman nobleman Polemon right up to Prince Gediminas of Lithuania. In this work, written in the style of a novel, it asserts that the Lithuanian princes are descended from Roman emperors. Legend has it that the Roman aristocrat Polemon belonged to the family of Emperor Nero. The cruel Nero hated Polemon for his beauty and courage, and Polemon was forced to flee to save his life. All of his family and friends fled together with him. They settled on the banks of the river Neman in Lithuania and founded the first cities there. And it was from these first settlers that the line of Lithuanian princes was alleged descended.

This chronicle was compiled in the 16th century and contains many stories to evoke a sense of patriotism and pride among the Lithuanian people for their country, and to underline the higher origins of the Lithuanian princes over the Eastern Slavic princes. The work contains numerous errors and inaccuracies, and is somewhat biased in portraying the history of Lithuania in the form of a legend and fairy tale with a view to glorifying its past.

The Bychowiec Chronicle is the most comprehensive and reliable of the Belarusian chronicles. Its name came from its owner, Aleksander Bychowiec, a nobleman from Vawkavysk, who owned the only surviving manuscript copy of the Chronicle. The chronicle describes in detail the political history of the Grand Principality of Lithuania since its creation in the 13th century, right up to the 16th century. *The Bychowiec Chronicle* was written in Belarusian, in a form close to the spoken language, and was published twice: in 1846 it was published by the Belarusian scientist Teodor Narbutt, and in 1907 it was published in the 17th volume of *The Complete Collection of Russian Chronicles*. Both of these works are now incredibly rare.

The Belarusian chronicles not only recount the chronological order of historical events but also contain legends, sagas, proverbs and secular and war stories. Their authors both historians and writers with considerable artistic skill, aesthetic taste and a creative imagination.

In the 16th century chronicles were hardly ever written, as they came to be replaced by other literary and historical genres.

Out of all the genres of church and religious literature, the one which underwent the greatest development in Belarus in the 14-15th centuries was travel writing. They were not directly linked to canonical literature. This genre originated as a result of pilgrimages to Palestine. The first pilgrim from Belarus was Princess Euphrosyne of Polotsk, who made her journey in the 12th century. In the 14th and 15th centuries pilgrimages to Jerusalem became very popular, especially among the nobility. Out of the many written descriptions of these journeys the best known are *Agrafena's Pilgrimage* (14th century), *Varsafoniya's Travels* (15th century), and perhaps the greatest *Journey to Tsargrad and*

Jerusalem by Ignatius of Smolensk. (Tsargrad was what the Belarusians called Constantinople.)

Ignatius was a monk from Smolensk, and in 1389 he went to Constantinople to visit holy sites and St. Sophia's Cathedral, the most magnificent Orthodox cathedral of the era. His journey took 15 years, and over the years Ignatius made notes about the places he visited and the political events that took place at the time. In 1406 Ignatius of Smolensk died in a monastery on Mount Athos in Greece, and his *Journey* has been rewritten many times, becoming popular throughout Eastern Europe.

One notable contribution in the history of Belarusian literature was the work of Gregory Tsamblak (1364-1450) (38). He was born into a Bulgarian noble family, but most of his life was tied to Belarus. In 1406 he met with Grand Prince Vytautas of Lithuania, who at the time was in a period of conflict with the Metropolitan of Moscow. Prince Vytautas no longer wanted the head of the Orthodox church to be a protégé of Moscow and insisted that Tsamblak be appointed as Metropolitan of the Grand Principality of Lithuania. Tsamblak took up residence in the city of Navahrudak, Belarus, where he lived until his death. More than twenty of his works survived. In general they were sermons, speeches at funerals, or biographies of saints. They are written in a highly figurative language style, rich in metaphors, similes, antitheses, and rhetoric, and the funeral speeches were unusual at the time on account of their interest in the psychology and character of the deceased, who were for the most part leading public figures.

———————◆———————

Belarusian culture was not spared the pan-European Renaissance – the heyday in the flourishing of culture in the new Bourgeois democratic nation states. A characteristic feature of the Renaissance period was the formation of national languages and literatures in almost all European countries. The 16th century in Belarus was the time of its greatest cultural and intellectual developments when some of the greatest cultural and public figures lived. In the 16th century many of the most important events in the history of Belarus took place, eventually giving the Belarusian people definitive form as a nation.

The Renaissance in Belarus was of course different to the Renaissance in Italy or Germany and had its own unique features. The economic gap from Europe and the dominance of mediaeval feudal relations held back the development of secular forms of culture. And while the Renaissance ideas penetrated their way into Belarusian literature and art, the development of Renaissance culture was left unfinished.

Francysk Skaryna (c.1487-1551) was a leading representative of Renaissance culture in Belarus (39). His name came to be almost a symbol of the Belarusian Renaissance, as he is associated with the publication of the first books in the Belarusian language. Streets in many cities in Belarus, as well as various cultural establishments in the 21st century, bear the name of this important cultural figure.

The exact date of Francysk Skaryna's birth is not known, but in 1504 he became a student at Krakow University, so it can be assumed that he was born in the second half of the 1480s. The future luminary was born in Polotsk into the family of the rich merchant Luka Skaryna.

At home there were always a lot of discussions about the distant and exotic countries that his father had visited and the customs and rituals of other peoples. Young Francysk easily memorised these stories and soon learned to read, learning Latin with ease, which gave him the opportunity to significantly expand the very narrow sphere of reading that was common for young men at the time. With his knowledge of Latin he was able to read books on history, theology and philosophy.

In 1504 Skaryna went to Krakow and enrolled at the university, which was a rarity for Belarusian youths, even those from a wealthy family. He chose to study at the faculty of "the seven free arts", where he read grammar, rhetoric, dialectics, arithmetic, geometry, astronomy and music. In 1506 he graduated from the faculty and was awarded a bachelor's degree. He decided to continue his studies at the faculty of medicine, where he was later awarded the title of licentiate in medicine and doctor of the "free arts".

Many books on Skaryna say that after Krakow he went to study in Padua (Italy), at one of Europe's oldest universities, the University of Padua. But this is not true. Skaryna did not study at Padua University; he only went there to sit an examination and receive his doctorate in medicine. This is noted in a record dated 5 November 1512 preserved in the university archives: "… a highly erudite, poor, young man – a doctor of arts – came from a very distant nation, perhaps four thousand miles or more away from our glorious city, to increase the renown and splendour of our Padua, as well as our flourishing collection of philosophers and our holy College. He appealed to the holy College to allow him, as a gift and out of a special sense of kindness, to undergo, with God's mercy, tests in the field of medicine at the holy College. If you will allow me, Your Excellency, then I will introduce him. The aforementioned young man goes by the name of Mr Francysk, son of the late Mr Luka Skaryna of Polotsk…". The next day, on 6 November 1512, Skaryna was allowed to take the entrance tests, and on 9 November he passed the examination with flying colours and received recognition of his medical merits.

In 1517 Skaryna founded a printing house in Prague publishing the first ever printed book in Belarus, the *Psalms* in the Cyrillic alphabet. During the course of 1517-1519 it translated and published 23 books of the Old Testament in Belarusian. The Belarusian Bible, published by Skaryna, was far ahead of similar publications in neighbouring nations, for example, the German translation by Luther, and in the Slavic world it was second only to the Czech translation of the Bible. The first book published by the first Russian printer Ivan Fyodorov came 47 years later. What this meant for Belarusian culture is best demonstrated by an example. Currently, the library of the Academy of Sciences in St. Petersburg stores the only monument of Belarusian literary art from the early 16th century: the Bible in Old Church Slavonic. It was copied by the monk Matthew, and he carried on making copies for 5 years from 1502 to 1507. This volume is about the same as the 23 books of the Bible published by Skaryna in Prague from 1517 to 1519. Thus, in half the time taken by Matthew to copy one book of the Bible, Skaryna published several hundred copies of the Bible. Since each print run of each part of the Bible was made up of 500 copies, in just two years more than 10,000 books left Skaryna's printing house. Such a collection could not even be created by 100 copyists in 10 years.

Skaryna's patrons were the Belarusian barons Bogdan Onkov, Yakub Babich, and Prince and Commander Konstantin Ostrozhskiy (40).

Skaryna intended to publish the entire Bible, as noted on the title page of his books in the preface to the first edition, however his work remained incomplete. But the vast majority of the Old Testament was published by him. It should be noted that when they were published Francysk Skaryna was effectively the creator of a new literary genre, the foreword. Before him, no publishers dared to write a foreword to the Bible. Giving a brief and succinct description of the content of the published work, Skaryna at the same time expressed his own civil, political and pedagogical views. These prefaces by Francysk Skaryna came to be classic examples of this genre and served as a model for future writers in the 16-17th centuries.

Skaryna looked on the books of the Bible as a source of knowledge on history, geography and astronomy. In some cases he even dared to shorten the text, or explain obscure words and phrases to make the biblical texts more accessible to a wider range of Belarusian readers.

By publishing the books of the Bible, Skaryna dared to go one step further: in every copy he inserted a small portrait of himself. It is worth noting that at the beginning of his publishing days typography had been around in Europe for more than 70 years, and during this time more than sixty thousand books had been printed. Not one can be found where there is a portrait of the publisher or printer. Putting his portrait in a book, let alone the Bible, took considerable resolve. Having done so, the Belarusian luminary emphasised the role of the publisher and his cultural and educational mission, the importance of which most people did not understand at the time.

In 1525 Skaryna moved to Vilno and founded the first printing house in Eastern Europe, where he published *The Small Travel Book* (1522) and *The Apostles* (1525).

The Small Travel Book was a collection of religious and secular works. The book was aimed at people who, by the nature of their occupation, had to travel frequently and needed to have religious and astronomical information for their journey. Like *The Apostles* it was published in a small format on thin paper, making it cheap and accessible to a wide audience.

After Yuriy Odvernik, one of the sponsors of the Vilno printing house, died in 1525, Skaryna was forced to cease his publishing activities. But every cloud has a silver lining, as they say. Francysk Skaryna fell in love and married Odvernik's widow Margarita and was happily married, admittedly only for a short time until Margarita's death in 1529.

In 1525, the last Grand Master of the Teutonic Order, Prince Albrecht of Brandenburg, secularised the Order and made the secular Principality of Prussia subordinate to the King of Poland. The Prince of Brandenburg was renowned for his progressive views, was highly passionate about reformist ideas, and decided to actively involve himself in the book publishing industry. For this he invited Francysk Skaryna to Königsberg, arriving there in 1529 or 1530. The Prince of Brandenburg wrote: "…we recently welcomed into our dominion, the Principality of Prussia, the glorious man Francysk Skaryna of Polotsk, a doctor of medicine, your subject, a nobleman, and now our beloved faithful servant…".

In 1529 Francysk's elder brother Ivan died and after his death a protracted court case was initiated against Skaryna due to the fact that his brother left behind a lot of debts and his creditors brought claims against Francysk Skaryna as his heir. It was fairly disturbing and a dark period in Skaryna's life; he could not stay and work in Königsberg for long and was forced to return to Vilno. The creditors even managed to have Skaryna arrested on the pretext that he had received and was concealing his brother's inheritance. Skaryna spent several months in prison in Poznan while his nephew Roman chose not to intervene in this complex case. Roman managed to arrange a meeting with King Sigismund I of Poland and convinced him that the inheritance had actually been received by himself, his nephew, and not by Skaryna. Sigismund I, believing Roman, issued a royal decree on 24 May 1532 releasing Francysk Skaryna from prison, and then, hearing from his advisors about Francysk Skaryna's educational work and becoming interested in Skaryna as a person and his book publishing work, he continued to look into his case and played a hand in his ultimate fate. Six months later, in November 1532 King Sigismund I issued two official deeds in which Skaryna was finally acquitted of the inheritance charges, but also received all manner of benefits, so-called "royal privileges", namely protection from any prosecution (except by the king's orders), protection from arrest as well as sanctity of his property and exemption from city duties and services.

Francysk Skaryna was not only one of the first publishers in Europe, but also a luminary of the Renaissance period. His political ideal was one of an enlightened, humane and strong monarchical power. In many of his writings Skaryna wrote that the ruler should be pious, wise, educated, compassionate and fair to his subjects, arguing that he should rule the country in accordance with the law and oversee the justice system. Skaryna believed that a society could progress and develop only in a peaceful and harmonious environment: "hardship brings all kingdoms to ruin". Born a Belarusian and living in the European borderlands, he ingeniously incorporated the traditions of the Byzantine East and Latin West into his works.

For his time Francysk Skaryna was definitely a "man of peace". He graduated from university in Poland, sat his doctoral examination in Italy, met and debated with Martin Luther in Germany, and worked together with the alchemist and physician Paracelsus. In Vilno he spent several years as the personal secretary of the Bishop of Vilno, and was knighted by the Grand Master of the Teutonic Order. He also took part in the preparation of the first code of laws, the Statutes of the Grand Principality of Lithuania, published in 1529. His journey to the Grand Principality of Moscow in 1534, however, ended in misfortune. Skaryna wanted to distribute the books he had published in Belarusian in Moscow, including the Bible, as he was convinced that they would be of interest to brotherly Belarusians and the Orthodox community. But relations between Moscow and the Grand Principality of Lithuania at the time were extremely hostile following several decades of incessant wars. Moscow had always looked with suspicion upon everything that was happening in the neighbouring Belarusian and Lithuanian state. In terms of its cultural and spiritual life it was significantly behind Vilno, where the Renaissance currents had had some impact, albeit relatively minor. The reason for Moscow lagging behind was largely due to its centuries-old Tatar bondage and the rooting of many Asian traditions in the Russian way of life. Francysk Skaryna's Bible, published in the Belarusian language and accessible to common folk, caused much resentment among the hierarchy of the Orthodox church in Moscow. Their unshakable creed was that the holy book should not be translated, and should be published, as it had been for centuries before, in Old Church Slavonic. In addition, conservative church leaders were generally suspicious of all forms of printing and saw no benefits to the process. A striking illustration of this is the fact that several decades later the first Russian book printers Ivan Fyodorov and Petr Mstislavets were banished from Moscow and took refuge in the more progressive Belarus.

In all of Skaryna's works there was never any trace of any religious fanaticism, nor any hostility towards any other faith. His views, free from religious constraint, and accepting of the European ideas of the Renaissance and Reformation, did not fit into the dogmatism of the Muscovite society and despotic Russian autocracy of the time. Therefore it is not surprising that he was met with extreme hostility. The clash between these two worlds ended with bonfires in squares in Moscow where Skaryna's books were burnt. Deeply disappointed, Skaryna was forced to leave Moscow quickly for fear of even greater persecution.

Evidently, the barbaric East made a lasting impression on Skaryna, and for the rest of his life he chose to live in the western Slavic lands in peaceful Prague, where he practiced as a doctor. The exact date of his death, much like his birth, has not been ascertained by scholars, but it is estimated that he died around 1551, as in 1552 his son, Symon, came to Prague to collect his inheritance.

To this date only about four hundred copies of Francysk Skaryna's books have survived. All editions are extremely rare, especially those from Vilno. These rarities are now in the archives of libraries in Minsk, Moscow, St. Petersburg, Vilnius, London, Prague, Copenhagen and Krakow.

Francysk Skaryna's humanistic ideas developed from figures from the Belarusian Renaissance such as Nikolay Gusovskiy (1470-1533), Symon Budny (1530-1593) and Wasyl Ciapiński (1535-1600).

In the years 1520-1522 Nikolay Gusovskiy (41) was in Rome as part of a diplomatic mission. Pope Leo X was intrigued by the poetic talent of Gusovskiy and commissioned him to write a poem about the strange far-flung land of Belarus. This *Poem about the Bison* (1523) was Nikolay Gusovskiy's most famous work. In it he glorified the nature of his native Belarus with great patriotism and humanism, called for the unity of all the peoples of Europe, condemned war, and depicted the hard work of the peasantry and the daily lives of the poor. He found an admirer of his talent in Grand Princess Sforza of Lithuania, who offered him financial support. Thanks to her, his poems *The New Victory over the Turks* (1524), *The Life and Deeds of St. Hyacinth* (1525) and *Consolation* (1523) were published in Krakow.

Symon Budny (42) was a well-known European preacher, church reformer and humanist. In 1562 he wrote and published a clever polemical book *On the justification of sinful men before God*, and in 1572 printed the Old Testament. In the edition of the New Testament in 1574 he provided numerous comments and remarks that were the first attempt in world literature to make radical rationalist criticisms of the Gospels.

Symon Budny shared the beliefs of John Calvin, and later became attracted by a more radical trend in Protestantism – Arianism, whereupon he started to actively disseminate his ideas. Catholic priests were angry and reproached Symon Budny for having expanded or shortened the texts of the Gospels at his own discretion in order to corroborate the ideas of Arianism. For example, he selected 26 quotations from the Gospels to prove that Jesus Christ was not only God, but also that his birth was no sacrament, and as a result he should not be paid such divine homage. These ideas, unacceptable to Catholics, were described and justified in his final work *On the most important aspects of the Christian Faith* (43). Being gifted with speed and clarity of thought, well-educated, having knowledge of a lot of ancient and modern languages, and renowned for his writing talent, Symon Budny enjoyed extraordinary popularity among reformers not only in Belarus and Poland, but also across Western Europe.

Symon Budny's views were shared and supported by Wasyl Ciapiński (c.1540-1603) (44). In the 1560s in the town of Tyapina near Polotsk he founded a printing house where he began to publish his own works and religious literature, which he had translated into Belarusian himself. His house had an excellent library. In 1570 he published the Gospels, printed in two columns, one in Old Church Slavonic and the other in Belarusian. Wasyl Ciapiński found it distressing to learn of the Union of Lublin in 1569 as he knew that it would adversely affect the further development of Belarusian culture. He had a negative attitude towards the process of Polonisation and the imposition of Catholicism on the Belarusian people which increased considerably after the Union of Lublin. Ciapiński wrote a lot about the need to develop science and literature in the native Belarusian language. One of his greatest services to Belarusian culture was his translation of the Gospels into Belarusian.

As mentioned above, the Russian pioneers Ivan Fyodorov and Petr Mstislavets were expelled from Moscow, as the Muscovite clergy refused to recognise and use the printed books. They fled to the more progressive Belarus and settled on the estate of the baron Georgiy Khadkevich. It was from here that they published the *Instructive Gospels* (1569), the *Psalms* (1570) and several other works.

In the second half of the 16th century there were dozens of printers operating in Belarus. The truly diverse forms of literature – religious, theological, secular, legal – were published in Polish, Belarusian and Latin. In 1588, the Mamonich printing house in Vilno printed the code of laws (Statutes) of the Grand Principality of Lithuania. Translations of novels from Western European languages were a major breakthrough in secular literature. Very popular were translations of the French courtly romance *The Tale of Beauvais*, and the image of the adventurer Beauvais even entered into Belarusian folklore. The works *The Story of Attila*, *Troy* and *Alexandria* were also translated from Italian and German.

The period of the Grand Principality of Lithuania's existence from the 13th to the 16th century was doubtlessly of fundamental importance in the history of the Belarusian people in shaping its spiritual culture and national identity. It resulted in the development of the Belarusian language, the creation of their own highly developed legal system, and the flourishing of socio-political and philosophical thought. Belarusians still love to look back on this former period of the Grand Principality of Lithuania. The residents of the state, which was the Eastern border of the pan-European Renaissance movement, without a doubt had far more rights and spiritual freedoms than their eastern neighbours in the Grand Principality of Moscow. To Belarusians this period largely meets the modern democratic standards used as a guide to this day. If pride can be derived from warlessness, the lack of subjugation of other peoples, and the closeness of the public and political systems of the past to modern standards and values in a nation's history, then Belarusians truly have something to be proud of.

CHAPTER 8
The Belarusian Language

THE BELARUSIAN LANGUAGE BELONGS TO THE INDO-EUROPEAN language family which started to diverge approximately 3000-2500 B.C. The majority of common features in terms of the phonetics, grammar and vocabulary of the Slavic and Baltic languages, which are uncharacteristic of other European languages, suggest that after the collapse of the Indo-European language, the Balto-Slavic linguistic group existed for quite a long time.

The penetration of Eastern Slavs into the Baltic environs led to the development of Balto-Slavic bilingualism. The Slavic linguistic element on Belarusian territory was first established in the southern and eastern parts. In the northern and central areas of Belarus the Baltic linguistic components prevailed and existed for longer than in the south.

The Eastern Slavic tribes had poor contact amongst themselves and spoke in their own tribal dialects which represented a spoken version of the Ancient Rus language. The relative unity of this language survived until about the 11-12th centuries. Despite dialectal diversity around the 12th century regional language features started to be outlined which would later form the basis for the formation of the Ukrainian, Belarusian and Russian languages. The phonetic and grammatical features of Belarusian were clearly visible in written sources from the 12th-13th centuries from Polotsk, Vitebsk and Smolensk.

The vocabulary provides convincing evidence of the linguistic characteristics of Belarusians. After the unification of the Belarusian lands in the 13th century into the Grand Principality of Lithuania there were significant changes in political and economic life, within the context of which intense changes in language started to occur, with a large growth in new words for example. This rapid enrichment of the language's vocabulary took place using the existing characteristics of the Belarusian language as a basis and built on them. In the new state the Belarusian language gained official status and this certainly contributed to the enrichment of the new lexicon. New terminology was created which quickly spread and came to be used by everyone. First of all there were common names for tools, forms of land ownership, agriculture produce, trade goods, social groups, types of feudal duties and taxes, artisanal specialities, etc. – in short, everything that reflected the everyday economic and social life of Belarusians. Belarusian phonetic sounds and loan words were acquired, for the most part from Latin, Polish, German and Lithuanian.

The vocabulary of the Belarusian language was based on three historical layers: common Slavic lexicon, Belarusian neologisms, and loan words from other languages. The common Slavic lexicon was the core of the language's vocabulary and so the majority of roots still link Belarusian to Russian and Ukrainian, whereas some features were closer to Western Slavic languages, primarily with Polish.

The Belarusian language's official status for nearly four centuries – from the 13th century to 1696 – served as a basis for its progression. It was used in the court of the Grand Prince of Lithuania, and by the feudal nobility and gentry regardless of their ethnicity, Lithuanian or Belarusian. The state institutions – public offices, courts, various chancelleries – all worked in Belarusian. Sessions of the *Sejm*, diplomatic negotiations and contracts were all in Belarusian. The language was used to create chronicles, fictional, promotional and journalistic works. Francysk Skaryna published the first Bible in Belarusian in 1521. The Reformation of the 16th century contributed to the rapid spread of the Belarusian language in canonical literature of the time: the reformer and educator Symon Budny wrote his works only in Belarusian. The Uniate church, which was formed after the

Union of Brest in 1599, made Belarusian the language of its church services over Old Church Slavonic of Latin. Admittedly however, this was done for its own selfish purposes: to attract as many Orthodox peasants and other lower classes to its services.

The Belarusian language was also adopted by other ethnic groups: Jews, Gypsies, Lithuanians, and Tatars, for whom it was a means of inter-ethnic communication within their state of residence.

But having reached a high level of development, from the late 16th century the Belarusian language started to lose ground to Polish. The first to move *en masse* to Polish were the Belarusian nobility, who saw it as a way to emphasise their loyalty to the Polish king. In a decree from 1696 the Polish *Sejm* declared Polish an official language of Belarus. So for several centuries Belarus enjoyed a period of bilingualism: the Belarusian language was the language of the peasants and the poor, and Polish came to be the language of the nobility and official documents.

PART 4

BELARUS WITHIN THE POLISH-LITHUANIAN COMMONWEALTH

(1569-1795)

CHAPTER I
The Union of Lublin
(1569)

IN 1569 AN EVENT OCCURRED IN THE LIVES OF THE BELARUSIAN people that would in many ways determine the future history of the nation. A new agreement, in principle at least, was signed between the two politically united states of the Grand Principality of Lithuania and the Kingdom of Poland to bring the two nations together into a single state. In legal terms the Union of Lublin gave rise to a new federal state, the Polish-Lithuanian Commonwealth (in Polish: *Rzeczpospolita*, meaning 'public matter', a literal translation of the Latin *Res Publica*, whence the term 'Republic' is derived). So what made the government of the Grand Principality of Lithuania sign up to this agreement, thereby entirely losing its own independence?

It should be noted that over the last two centuries the Polish government had exerted more and more pressure on the Belarusian and Lithuanian state (which was already in an alliance with Poland) so as to acquire new land and positions in Belarus and Lithuania. It was not only the government but also the Polish Catholic Church too which sought to expand its influence in the Orthodox east. The Belarusian people – both the poor and nobility – were relatively successful in resisting these advances and defending their territory and religion. Poland had failed to quickly "swallow up" the Belarusian and Lithuanian state, but it was waiting for the right moment.

Within the Grand Principality of Lithuania in the mid-16th century the situation was difficult as there were politicians with various different foreign policy stances. On the one hand, among the gentry, there was a group with pro-Polish sentiments. In terms of narrow-minded morals the Polish way of life, fashion, literature and language seemed like the most attractive option Belarusian nobility who had not been spoilt with life's luxuries. These sentiments were widely supported and disseminated by the Poles themselves, large numbers of which had moved to the Belarusian lands over the past two centuries after the signing of the Union of Krevo. But on the other hand, some of the older Belarusian princely families were pro-Russian and sought to use Moscow's influence together with Orthodox rhetoric and the memory of the former unified state with the Russians: Kievan Rus. The barons used all of their powers to prevent the negotiations on the Union from starting and tried to find support across the various strata of society (45). But there was also a third pro-German party. It was led by state chancellor A. Goshtold, a supporter of a rapprochement with the holy Roman Empire of the German Nation.

The political conditions were fully ripe for the new Union when, as a result of the Livonian War waged by Moscow, there was a direct threat to the very existence of the Grand Principality of Lithuania. The Russian Tsar Ivan the Terrible openly declared that he intended to reclaim "all of Prince Monomakh's Rus", referring to all of the Belarusian and Ukrainian lands. In February 1563 the Muscovite troops laid siege to and took the most fortified city in Belarus, Polotsk, and the road to the capital Vilno lay wide open for the taking. If we are to believe the Muscovite writers of the time, Tsar Ivan the Terrible took an army of two hundred thousand horsemen, eighty thousand infantry and one thousand guns to Polotsk (46). The Russian Tsar's soldiers committed terrible atrocities in the city. The *Pskov Chronicles* read: "All Jews and their families were thrown into the cold river in the city and drowned". The same fate befell the Catholics: Bernadine and Dominican monks were killed one by one, and their monasteries burnt to the ground. Ivan the Terrible, who called himself "the liberator of Orthodoxy from the heretics" ordered his soldiers to kill on the spot anybody who had not been baptised in the Orthodox manner. The war with Moscow was costly to the entire population of the Grand Principality of Lithuania. For instance, in 1542 the entire state's tax was only about twenty-two thousand kopeks, whereas in 1567, due to the need for military expenditure, it was almost five times more: one hundred and five thousand kopeks (47).

The Belarusians were forced to seek defence against Moscow from their long-standing and closest ally, Poland. For the negotiations on the new Union in 1563 a Belarusian delegation arrived in Warsaw headed by Prince Mikołaj "the Black" Radziwiłł. The draft Union prepared by them was not accepted by the Poles as it made provisions for preserving the independence of the Grand Principality of Lithuania under the rule of the King of Poland. The ideal situation for the Polish rulers was the incorporation of the Belarusian and Lithuanian state into Poland.

The negotiations resumed in 1566 with the Poles in Lublin and representatives of the Grand Principality of Lithuania in Brest. Contradictions and disagreements protracted the negotiations. But finally, it was decided that a national *Sejm* would meet in Lublin, starting its work in January 1569 and lasting for six dramatic months. Each party put forward its own conditions which were rejected by the other party. Neither party wanted to give in. The ambassadors of the Grand Principality of Lithuania ultimately left Lublin as they believed it impossible to continue to negotiate the Union on the conditions put forward by Poland. Poland then chose to demonstrate its strength. King Sigismund II Augustus issued a decree on the Polish annexation of Ukrainian territory covering Kiev and Volyn, which was almost half of the territory of the Grand Principality of Lithuania. At the same time, on Belarusian soil, the Muscovite army of Ivan the Terrible was still in charge. The Muscovites had not only plundered the Belarusian lands but they had also actively built up their own military fortresses in the cities of Ulla, Usvyaty, Sitno and others. Lithuanian and Belarusian ambassadors had tried to negotiate with Ivan the Terrible and even offered for his son Fyodor to take the throne in Vilno, but other than humiliating themselves, they achieved nothing. Moscow wanted more. But the Belarusian and Lithuanian state could not afford to fight on two fronts, with Poland on the one hand, and with Moscow on the other.

Faced with such a difficult situation, the delegation returned to the talks in Lublin. The delegates did not hide the fact that only a very difficult situation had forced them to make concessions. One of the delegates, Prince Mikołaj Razdiwiłł said: "When we were on our way here we were on our backs with the enemy driving us on" (48).

On 1 July 1569 the Union of Lublin was signed. On the day of its signing the Belarusian Prince Khadkevich spoke in front of the delegates, asking the Polish king to preserve all the laws of the Grand Principality of Lithuania and to not bring any harm to his people: "We ask of you a most humble request: make it so that this union will not result in humiliation and oppression for us and our descendants". With these words, all of the Belarusian and Lithuanian ambassadors got down on their knees. King Sigismund II Augustus assured all present that the Union would only serve to benefit all the people of the new state.

The Union stated that the two countries would henceforth be united forever as one indivisible state, proclaiming: "From this time both countries are one united Polish-Lithuanian Commonwealth, in which both states and both peoples will be united in a single people and a single government" (49). The King of Poland was to rule over the state and he was to be elected at the national *Sejm* in Krakow. The election of the Grand Prince of Lithuania and the *Sejm* in Vilno was repealed. The Polish king pledged to preserve all of the rights, privileges, public offices, princely titles and the inviolability of land holdings and property for the annexed Belarusian and Ukrainian lands. Henceforth the state had a single currency and eliminated customs services on the former border between the two states.

One of the conditions of the Union was the formation of common laws. A commission set up in Vilno had to adapt the Belarusian laws to the needs of the Union and existing Polish laws. But it was relatively difficult to do so, as the Belarusian laws, as set forth in the Lithuanian Statutes, were much larger and more substantial than the underdeveloped Polish legislation. The Poles did not have such an expansive and voluminous code of laws as the Lithuanian Statutes, and so the Belarusian legislation came to be the principle code in the Polish-Lithuanian Commonwealth.

In spite of all of its peaceful promises, Poland – which was stronger in economic terms than Belarus – actually had unrestricted opportunities to exercise great-power policies against the Belarusian population. It became impossible for the Belarusians to legally stand in the way of policies to Polonise and impose Catholicism on the state.

Thus, the independent and strong mediaeval state of the Grand Principality of Lithuania disappeared from the political map of Europe. Its annexation into the Kingdom of Poland was the result of the complex political position of the Belarusian and Lithuanian state in the mid-16th century, its weakness after the war with Moscow, and the centuries-old divisions between Catholics and Orthodox within the Belarusian society. For too long Belarus had been in the middle of two opposing forces: the Catholic West and Orthodox East, and sooner or later, one of the parties was bound to pull the country under its sphere of influence. In 1569, Belarus chose the West and became a Polish province for two centuries until 1775 when Moscow was able to take its revenge and unite Belarus with the Russian Empire.

The history of Belarus as part of the Polish-Lithuanian Commonwealth is one of the most exciting and complicated periods in its history. This period has forever interested the historians of those countries closely affiliated with the historical destiny of Belarus: Poland, Lithuania, Ukraine and Russia. Numerous studies have been written which express sometimes entirely opposing views on the religious relations of the peoples of these countries, political history, the struggle for independence, and who represented this independence and how it represented itself.

CHAPTER 2
Religious confrontation and the Union of Brest (1596)

A FTER THE SIGNING OF THE UNION OF LUBLIN A NEW STAGE IN the religious conflict between Catholicism, Protestantism and Orthodoxy broke out. The 17th century can arguably be referred to as a period of Counter-Reformation. At its head was the order of Jesuits, who sought to propagate Catholicism around the world.

Just one month after the signing of the Union an event occurred which perhaps appeared relatively insignificant to its contemporaries, but which played a key role in the future history of Belarus. A group of twenty Jesuits arrived in Vilno, headed by Magee, the former head of the Austrian Jesuits. In 1570 they opened a college made up of five classes, with a special department to school Jesuits. They took in youngsters from all social classes and religions; the education was free and lasted for 6 to 7 years. At first, nobody wanted to learn there: Protestant schools had gained considerable experience by then and were very popular, but the foundations had been laid. The Jesuits had extremely highly developed methods to impact on the hearts and minds of people of different ages, social classes and religious beliefs.

The Jesuits attracted the attention of King Sigismund II Augustus through his sister Anna, a devout Catholic. Then several rapid changes took place on the Polish throne. Following the death of Sigismund II, who had no descendants, in 1572 the French prince Henry of Anjou Valois was appointed as King. But he was only in Warsaw for

6 months and returned to France as soon as he found out that his brother, King Charles IX of France, had died. Henry Valois hated the Polish crown and sought the more prestigious throne in France. There were disputes for some time over who the future king should be, and this "interregnum" lasted for three years. In 1576 the baron and talented military commander Stephen Báthory was appointed king (reigning from 1576-1586). The Jesuits quickly managed to win over his favour thanks to the Livonian War. In 1579 the Jesuits and Báthory were involved in the military campaign against Polotsk, which, after fifteen years of occupation, was finally liberated from the Muscovite army. They bravely endured military hardships, treated the wounded, and took the confessions of the dying. Stephen Báthory greatly appreciated their service and discipline, and would often say: "If I were not King, I would have become a Jesuit". In gratitude for their dedication Stephen Báthory promised to build a college in the liberated city of Polotsk. This promise was carried out in royal fashion. In 1580 the Jesuits received eight Orthodox churches and seven monasteries in Polotsk, together with all of their associated buildings and property. The Orthodox population in Polotsk had only one cathedral left. In the decree handed down by Stephen Báthory it stated: "I do this so that the Jesuits shall have a college to educate the youth in the Catholic faith, disseminate the Catholic faith among the Orthodox by every means, open up new Latin Roman Catholic parishes in Belarus and thereby do away with Orthodoxy in these lands".

The next king, Sigismund III Vasa (reigning 1587-1632) was not only a supporter of the Jesuits, but was actually an alumnus of the Jesuits. He was the son of King John III Vasa of Sweden and Catherine, the sister of Sigismund II. Throughout his long reign he never once abandoned his yearning to make Catholicism the only religion in the Polish-Lithuanian Commonwealth. All of his domestic and foreign policies were based on this overriding principle.

The Jesuits always managed to find a way to the heart of other kings, and the Polish king's court forever remained at the centre of their attention.

There is no need to give an account of the Jesuit order in this book as they are already well documented in the history of Western Europe. But it should be noted that the Jesuit order as an organisation was very similar to the parties of totalitarian regimes in the 20th century. The order had its own "maximum" programme (the global kingdom of God), "minimum" programme (the expansion of Catholicism and the authority of the Pope), and its own practical – and not idealistic – ethic that allowed and even prescribed murder if it was necessary for the church. Add to this the almost military-like discipline and perfect acts of conspiracy. The activities of the order, wherever they took place, were always of a religious nature, but were also, to a greater extent, political (50).

In Belarus the Jesuit order did not use the methods used by the Inquisition, limiting themselves only to propaganda. The Jesuits directed their propaganda primarily at barons and the nobility that had adopted Protestantism, and this propaganda had a relatively swift impact on this group of people. Among the first to return to Catholicism was a descendant of Prince Mikołaj "the Black" Radziwiłł. His son, nicknamed "the Orphan" by Mikołaj Radziwiłł, dedicated his entire life to uncovering and destroying the copies of the Bible published by his father. He spent a total of five thousand gold coins doing this and found almost all of the copies, burning them all. He closed all of the printing houses in the domain left to him by his father. Nobility was extended to all the major princely homes. The "Prodigal Sons" who had adopted Protestantism started to return to the bosom of Catholicism.

Representatives of the urban class, merchants and artisans gradually renounced Arianism and Calvinism. The Jesuits had won the sympathy and confidence of the people through their active work in the field of philanthropy. They not only opened schools and colleges, but also pharmacies, hospitals, and homes for the sick and the homeless. During an outbreak of plague in Vilno in 1580 Jesuit monks did not leave the city, but stayed to care for the sick, take confessions and oversee burials. All of this contributed to their enormous moral authority.

Influencing the young was easiest in schools following the excellently prepared Western European model for educational programmes. After Polotsk Jesuit colleges were open in Vitebsk, Nesvizh, Pinsk, Brest, Grodno, Navahrudak, Minsk and Orsha. In 1618, 3,165 pupils and students studied at Jesuit schools in Belarusian cities. It was this high-level educational activity that was the policy of the Catholic church, looking forward to the future. The Jesuit colleges initially taught theology based on the mediaeval scholasticism, but students also actively studied the philosophy of Aristotle, logic, physics, and astronomy. The Jesuits paid particular attention to subjects and sciences needed by the nobility for a career in politics: Latin, law, rhetoric, etc. Thanks to generous donations from the Vatican, tuition at the Jesuit college was free. Soon the Jesuits' students started to fill out the administrative apparatus and influence decisions on state and civil matters.

In 1579, the Academy of Sciences was opened in Vilno, the first higher education institution in Belarus. It was set up following the model of Western European universities and had the power to train bachelors, masters and doctors in the liberal sciences, philosophy and theology. The programme included history, foreign languages, philosophy and theology. At the Academy the professor of theology was Marcin Śmiglecki (1564-1618), whose works were translated into many different languages. He received particular celebrity in the academic world through his work *Logica* which was widely used right up to the 19th century at the Sorbonne and Oxford, where his works were repeatedly reprinted. The professor of philosophy Matvey Sarbevskiy (1595-1640) was not only a scientist, but a poet, and in 1623 he received the Pope's laurel wreath, much like the famous poets Dante Alighieri and Francesco Petrarch. The Academy of Sciences started to furnish schools and colleges with teachers, allowing them to maintain their high standard of teaching. The Vilno Academy of Sciences was the easternmost university for two centuries right up to the establishment of Moscow University in 1755.

The Jesuits that had arrived in Belarus actively taught the Belarusian language and used it in churches for sermons. To forge closer ties with the local population they went to teach the Belarusian language at the Polotsk Jesuit College. They translated and published religious literature in Belarusian. This was a wise policy at the time for the Orthodox church declared any attempt at translating the Bible from the Old Church Slavonic into Russian or Belarusian as heretical despite the fact that Old Church Slavonic had long been out of use and was not understood by common Belarusians.

In France in 1589 King Henry IV expelled all Jesuits as "demoralisers of youths, destroyers of civil order, and enemies of the king and state". The Jesuit Order was forbidden in France. Whereas, in the Polish-Lithuanian Commonwealth, the Jesuits were supported in full by the monarchy. Landing any public office was only possible with its support and patronage.

In the early 17th century Belarus started to see a change in generations. The generation of the Reformation was taken from the world, and their children did not follow in the footsteps of their fathers; they made a different choice. Studying the biographies of the statesmen of the time, what is striking is that almost all of them were Calvinists and Lutherans, educated in Reformation schools; but in the first two decades of the 17th century there was a mass shift to Catholicism or the newly formed Uniate Church.

The Counter-Reformation in Belarus was part of the pan-European process, but had its own unique features. We have already described how the ideas of the Reformation, mainly Calvinism, were widely adopted among the higher strata of Belarusian society: the barons and gentry. But as soon as ideas of social protest and social equality started to appear in the Reformation movement, and especially in Arianism, the feudal elite lost interest. The signing of the Union of Lublin played a role, for as a result of it there was a realignment of the political forces, and the most sensitive to the state of affairs – the barons and gentry – quickly returned to the mainstream Catholicism and were always consistently followed by the Polish royal court and government authorities.

Let us not forget that for several centuries there had been two Christian churches in Belarus, the Orthodox church and the Catholic church, and in the second half of the 16th century two more had appeared, the Protestant church and the Uniate church. The peaceful coexistence of these various branches of Christianity brought with it solid norms of tolerance in society, and so the Counter-Reformation did not take such terrible and detestable forms in Belarus as it did in Western Europe, and religious persecutions were not as severe as they were in the Muscovite state where a single-church ideology still dominated. The Jesuits wisely ingratiated themselves with the Belarusian gentry, as they understood that the gentry was opposed to the Polish royal court and was not especially interested in the strengthening of the King's power on their territory. The leader of the Counter-Reformation, the Jesuit Piotr Skarga, promised the Belarusian gentry some liberties: "We do not want a monarchy," he declared, "like the Turks have, like the Tatars have, or like the Russians have in Moscow, one which has no consideration for any rights or laws. We want a monarchy which is based on fair laws and wisdom of authority…" (51). Thanks to this diplomacy and considerable flexibility, the Catholic church managed to gradually win back former Protestants by peaceful means, and through the Union of Brest brought Orthodox believers closer to Catholicism.

During the course of the 17th century in Belarus, there were approximately 70 to 80 Protestant communities. The most long-lasting of them was the Polotsk Protestant Church which was burnt to the ground in 1632, not by the Jesuits, but by the Russian army. In 1636 the church was restored and remained until the 18th century. In 1658, the Polish *Sejm* decided to expel Arianists from the Polish-Lithuanian Commonwealth; they were only able to stay in the country if they adopted Catholicism. Gradually, the number of Protestant communities steadily decreased and by the mid-18th century there were only about forty communities on Belarusian territory.

Orthodox believers were the second main enemy after Protestants in Belarus in the eyes of the Catholic church and the Jesuit Order. But what was there of the Belarusian Orthodox church at the time?

By the mid-16th century the Polish kings had practically taken complete control of the Orthodox church, having appropriated its right to manage the church.

Firstly, the king originally only approved the Orthodox bishops and abbots appointed to the church council, but then started to appoint them of his own initiative without any coordination with the church authorities. The main suitability criteria were not the high spiritual and moral qualities of the candidate, but rather service to the Polish Crown and the king. There were even instances when the monasteries were headed not by monks, but by the laity. This inflicted a crushing blow on the credibility of the Orthodox church.

Secondly, the king assumed the right to transfer churches and monasteries to be managed by lay persons. The royal decree to this effect allowed the trustee to use the property of the churches at their discretion. As a result, the Orthodox church became something of a "feeding trough" for those people that were pleasing to the king. Without using any funds from his own treasury, the king allowed these people to get richer and richer.

Thirdly, the king ruled that the laity had authority over Orthodox priests, which paved the way for all sorts of denunciation and abuse.

All of this undermined the Orthodox organisation from within; it lost its credibility, and believers turned over to Catholicism or Protestantism. But despite such harsh conditions from an objective standpoint, the Orthodox church remained steady on its feet. It was the mainstay of the Belarusian peasants and the urban middle and lower classes who remained steadfast to their faith, traditions and language.

The policy of imposing Catholicism in Belarus came not only from the Polish king, but primarily from the Pope, who wanted to control not only Belarus and Ukraine, but also Moscow. The Pope even instructed his legate Antonio Pasevana to try to win over the Russian Tsar Ivan the Terrible to Catholicism. The papal servant replied that it would be pointless to travel so far for this as it would be hopeless, at which he advised going as far as the Grand Principality of Lithuania to concentrate all of their efforts on the state. In his opinion they should not attempt it immediately, but rather spend a long time ring-fencing the state, not yet touching on issues such as dogma and rituals. They needed to reach an agreement between the two churches on the establishment of an intermediate Uniate church, and only then, after the Uniate church had been set up could they start to promote Catholic doctrine little by little. This plan was thought out over many years as they had taken account of the fact that the broad masses of the Belarusian population had strengthened and consolidated the centuries-old traditions of Orthodoxy. They would have to raise and educate a new generation tolerant of the Catholic faith, and then start to propagate the faith using more resolute methods. If they did not do this, warned Antonio Pasevina, the Orthodox people would revolt against the Pope's authority.

In line with this plan the Jesuits started ideological and psychological preparations for their special union or agreement between Catholicism and Orthodoxy. Initially, it was necessary to win over the barons and gentry, as well as to convince the Orthodox priests of the historical necessity of the union between the two Christian churches.

The Jesuit Piotr Skarga was particularly active in promoting the new Union. He was born in Poland, educated in Rome, and took four monastic vows of the Jesuit Order there before being sent to the Polish-Lithuanian Commonwealth in 1570. He quickly became the heart and soul of the Union propaganda movement, became close friends with King Stephen Báthory, becoming his right-hand man, and after his death was a faithful servant of Sigismund III Vasa. On his initiative the college in Vilno became the Academy of Sciences, and for several years he managed the Polotsk college, writing and translating religious works there. In 1577 he published the book *On one church for the one God* in which he justified the position that the Christian church should be united and under the Pope's control. He saw the cause of the schism, namely the division of the Eastern church from the Western in 1054, as having its roots in the excessive pride and stupidity of the Patriarchs of Constantinople. Piotr Skarga believed that the Orthodox church had become overly dependent on the Russian Tsar in Moscow and was currently in a period of crisis and in need of rescue. He argued that it could be saved if it returned to the faith of its predecessors and subjugated itself to the Pope in Rome. Piotr Skarga called for a Union, a basic condition of which would be that Orthodox believers could retain their customs and rituals, religious holidays and saints, and traditional church decorations, but only if they recognise the supremacy of the Pope over their church.

Piotr Skarga was a talented debater and writer, as well as, of course, a Polish patriot. He sincerely believed that the church union could be achieved through persuasion, without recourse to rebellion or violence. He devoted a lot of effort to bringing the authoritative commander Konstantin Ostrozhskiy on side to accept his ideas. He was the most powerful baron in Belarus, owning more than 100 towns and 1,200 villages with an annual income of more than one million gold coins. From his guards and retinue he could muster an army of 30,000 people; even the King of Poland could not amass such an army. He was courageous, independent and had enormous political influence and authority over the people. Piotr Skarga managed to convince him of the truth behind his ideas, but Konstantin Ostrozhskiy insisted on an explicit condition that the decision on the Union would only be taken at a meeting of the general church council. The chances of the Orthodox believers at the council agreeing to such a union were practically non-existent.

Meanwhile, a number of Orthodox bishops – Ipatius Patsey in Brest, Cyril Terletsky in Lutsk, and others – sent a letter to King Sigismund stating: "We, the undersigned bishops, wish to recognise as our head and pastor the priest of St. Peter on earth, the most holy Pope of Rome, as a result of which we expect the glory of God to increase. But, in wishing to subjugate ourselves to the Pope, we want all of our ceremonies, liturgies and rituals that had long been held by our holy Eastern church to be left in place, and we want His Royal Highness to guarantee, through official documents and decrees, our freedoms and all of the articles that we will be presented with. We pledge ourselves to the authority and blessing of the Pope" (52). But this was understandable: they received their position from the secular king, and in order to preserve the position they had to abide by his wishes. Metropolitan Mikhail Razoga received a directive from the Jesuits: "With regard to your followers, especially those common folk among them, you should be very careful not to give them the slightest reason to learn of your intentions and plans, else you can come to expect overt action and military uprisings from them. We will introduce new rites to the church, not immediately, but gradually".

In 1595 bishops Ipatius Patsey and Cyril Terletsky secretly went to Rome to sign an agreement on the Union. Prince Konstantin Ostrozhskiy learnt of this mission and was outraged that this was all done in secret without the people knowing, and published and disseminated a *Message to all districts* in which he called on the Orthodox believers to come together and defend their faith. State Chancellor Lew Sapieha ordered the prince to stop the dissemination of this message under the pretext that his text had not been agreed with the king or approved with the state seal. Ostrozhskiy disobeyed the orders and the as yet unsigned Union sowed the seeds of civil war.

For two years there were uprisings in Belarus and Ukraine led by Severin Nalivayko, one of the commanders of Konstantin Ostrozhskiy's army, a devout Orthodox follower and hater of all that was Polish. During the rebellion his mother, sister and brother stayed at Konstantin Ostrozhskiy's castle, and thanks to this were still alive after the execution of Nalivayko himself. The rebel forces took to doing what was the norm for insurgents, attacking and robbing from their opponents. Among other things Cyril Terletsky's castle, as well as the castle of his brother, were razed to the ground, having taken all of the valuables and scattered all of the documents found regarding the preparation of the Union. But the uprising was suppressed and Severin Nalivayko was brought in chains to Warsaw and, after excruciating torture, was finally executed.

After the rebellion had been suppressed there was nothing more to wait for, the all-out attack was possible, and so Pope Clement VIII issued a papal bull declaring that the two churches should be joined as one. Fearing a renewed armed uprising, King Sigismund III Vasa of Poland was forced to agree to convene the general Orthodox council. It was held in the Belarusian city of Brest in October 1596 and immediately split up the supporters and opponents of the Union. In fact, there were two council sessions, one for Uniate followers and another for Orthodox. The Orthodox council removed Metropolitan Mikhail Ragoza and all of the bishops from their positions and excommunicated them from the church. The Uniate council in turn excommunicated all of the remaining Orthodox priests.

But the power was on the side of the government, and the government certainly supported the proposed Union put forward by the Pope. The agreement on the creation of a new Uniate church, which was named the Greek Catholic Church, was signed. Two books by Piotr Skarga are devoted to this council session: *The Brest Council* and *In Defence of the Brest Council*, published in Krakow in 1597.

There then began a long period of confrontation within the Orthodox church. The churches that recognised the Union and the authority of the Pope continued to function, hold services and follow the Orthodox liturgy and were strongly supported by local authorities. The only aspect that they had to change in their religion was the recognition of the supreme authority of the Pope as God's protégé on earth. This trend came to be named the Uniate Church, or the Greek Catholic Church. But hundreds of churches in Belarus did not recognise the authority of the Pope; they still remained true Orthodox churches. The tactics of the Uniate church were aggressive and offensive, but the Orthodox churches stubbornly defended themselves and continued to exist.

———————◆———————

In the early 17th century Cossacks – armed detachments of peasants and petty gentry – started to form in considerable strength. These groups started to defend the resentful Orthodox church. The King in Warsaw was forced to take this power seriously and in the 1620s gradually abolished all royal decrees aimed at persecuting Orthodoxy and passed a law making it illegal to loot and take Orthodox churches. In 1620, the Orthodox hierarchy was restored in Belarus and Ukraine. It must be recognised that the policy of implanting Catholicism by this time had somewhat relaxed its tough approach. But not all of the violent Jesuits chose to adhere to this. In Vitebsk, the Jesuit Iosif Kuntsevich still closed Orthodox churches, stripped priests of their dignity, and ordered the execution of several Orthodox followers, choosing to have them drowned in the river Dvina. In response to his cruelty a rebellion broke out in the city on 12 November 1623. A mob of angry townspeople and peasants from nearby villages rushed to the home of the detested Kuntsevich, killing him and throwing his corpse into the river Dvina. All of Kuntsvich's assistants were also killed. All of the Orthodox churches in the city rang out their bells in triumph. Rome came to hear of the uprising and Pope Urban VIII ordered a massacre in Vitebsk. An investigative committee was set up headed by State Chancellor Lew Sapieha. 75 people were sentenced to death and had their property confiscated. Vitebsk was deprived of Magdeburg rights (the right to self-government), the city hall building which housed the local authorities was destroyed, and all of the cupolas of the Orthodox churches were removed and sent off to be melted down.

CHAPTER 3
The False Dmitriy Affair
(1604-1613)

IN THE EARLY 17TH CENTURY THE MUSCOVITE STATE UNDERWENT A period of turmoil. The dynasty of Ruriks, who had ruled from the 10th century, had come to an end as Ivan the Terrible did not have a single heir. Crop failures led to unprecedented famine: in Moscow alone over two years – 1600-1602 – almost 120,000 people died of starvation (53) and grain prices increased thirtyfold. In 1598 the influential boyar Boris Godunov was appointed Tsar, but he was not a member of a royal dynasty. He was the best candidate for head of state at the time, as an intelligent, energetic and far-sighted politician. But the question of his legitimacy continued to haunt the royal court, where intrigue and conspiracy continued to reign, while the war-torn country was overrun with poverty and famine. The people saw it as "God's punishment for the sins of the Tsar"; there were rumours circulating that Boris Godunov was guilty of murdering the son and heir of Ivan the Terrible, the young prince Dmitriy, who died under mysterious circumstances in 1591. The boyars, disgruntled with Boris Godunov, supported the rumours and even claimed that Dmitriy had miraculously survived and should now take the throne.

The troubles in Russia prompted the Polish authorities to take action. The circumstances were perfect for an imposter to step onto the scene. In such uncertain times there was always somebody willing to take advantage of the turmoil. Such a man appeared in Poland. He disguised himself as the surviving prince Dmitriy, the youngest son of Ivan the Terrible, who had allegedly died under suspicious circumstances. This pretender to the Russian throne, monk Grigoriy Otrepev, had escaped from Moscow to Poland. He was born in Belarus, was an Orthodox monk and was so pious and devout that at a young age he rose to the position of secretary of the Patriarch of Moscow, and attended sessions of the State Duma in the royal court as a scribe. Before he fled to Poland he had lived in the Kremlin and therefore was very familiar with the life, customs and intrigues of the royal court there. Still in the Kremlin he began to tell his co-workers mysterious stories about his descent, as if he were a noble, which would one day lead him to sit on the Russian throne. Such an adventurous personality came as a gift to the Polish leadership, and so it began a political game aimed at seizing power in Moscow. King Sigismund III Vasa of Poland and State Chancellor Lew Sapieha assembled an army led by "False Dmitriy" ready to go to Moscow. The organiser of the False Dmitriy campaign on Moscow was Senator Yuriy Mnishek who believed so strongly in the success of this political venture that he had no fears over giving over his daughter to the sham tsar.

Of course, there were strict conditions set for the future Russian tsar: as soon as he took the throne he would have to give Poland Smolensk, Pskov and Novgorod together with all of their territory, and Moscow would establish Catholicism and offer the Poles extensive trading benefits. By the time of the Moscow campaign Grigoriy Otrepev was already engaged to the Polish Catholic noblewoman Marina Mnishek, who was destined to become tsarina for a short time.

In October 1604 False Dmitriy's troops arrived in Russia. His army was made up of 1,600 soldiers recruited from Poland and 2,000 Cossack mercenaries from Ukraine who were ready to fight anytime, anywhere, and for any side. Most of the cities met "the miraculously saved, kind and true tsar" hospitably. Only rarely was the Russian army involved in clashes with the army. The unexpected death of Boris Godunov contributed to the success of False Dmitriy in 1605. More and more militia from the Russian cities that they had occupied joined False Dmitriy's army, increasing its numbers almost threefold. On 20

June 1605, with a festive ringing of bells and the cheers of the crowds he entered Moscow. The fifteen-year-old Tsar Fyodor Godunov and his mother had been strangled in his palace in the Kremlin.

Otrepev's advisors told him how he could be crowned as soon as possible, but he said that he first wanted to see his mother. The widow of Ivan the Terrible had for many years lived in exile in a monastery, but messengers were sent to her. The meeting between the so-called son and supposed mother took place in front of a huge number of people. From surviving descriptions of the meeting False Dmitriy dismounted his horse and ran to the carriage, his mother stepped out, and they both wept and hugged each other. This idyllic scene convinced all those present of the authenticity of the now alive prince.

On 30 July 1605 Grigoriy Otrepev was proclaimed Tsar Dmitriy I. The people were split between those who believed him to be the true king and those who thought of him as an imposter and a criminal.

If Grigoriy Otrepev was really going to rule Russia as tsar then his behaviour in Moscow was extremely short-sighted. On the one hand he brought back many princes and boyars from exile who had been out of favour with Boris Godunov in an attempt to gain their support. But on the other hand he, in every way possible and everywhere he went, proclaimed his disdain for the Russian customs, organised dances and celebrations, and on holidays allowed music and dances that were once unthinkable in the Russian court. He allowed his large Polish entourage and army to behave aggressively and with open contempt towards the Muscovites. He ordered the court boyars to learn to play cards and chess, which again caused profound condemnations and almost mystical horror. His number of supporters quickly started to diminish.

The new tsar also had a keen interest in precious jewels. Despite the fact that all of the valuables that had been amassed by the Russian royal court over the years were now his he still yearned to acquire more. Queen Anna of the Polish-Lithuanian Commonwealth, who was in need of money, sent her envoy Stanislav Nemoevskiy to Moscow, bringing a collection of Anna's jewellery to sell. The tsar bought them for the incredible price of 69,000 Polish zlotys. Two years later this jewellery was returned to Queen Anna of Poland by the new tsar Vasiliy Shuyskiy with a categorical demand that the money be returned to the Russian treasury.

In April 1606 the tsar's fiancée Princess Marina Mnishek arrived in Moscow with great pomp and circumstance. She had 2,000 Polish officers and 200 servants among her entourage. On 8 May the couple were married and the coronation of Marina Mnishek took place. Descriptions of this celebration suggest that such a magnificent coronation had never taken place in Moscow before, and similar luxury would only be witnessed again with the coronation of Empress Catherine II the Great.

The lifestyle of the young couple immediately came to be resented. The Russian tsar was married to a Catholic who had absolutely no intention of adopting Orthodoxy. According to the Russian custom, the young married couple should visit the bath-house every morning, but the tsar and tsarina did not do this; in other words they simply did not wash after they had spent the night together... Western Europeans were not really aware of the bath-houses as such and only washed once every couple of months. But False Dmitriy and Marina were true Europeans and wanted to live in the Russian court as Europeans. There were whispers around the court that the tsarina, who did not wash, smelt like dead rats, and the tsar stank worse than a poor peasant knee-deep in manure. At dinner times False Dmitriy and Marina would bring an unfamiliar and strange object to the table: a fork. At the time Russians had never encountered forks and ate either with a spoon or their hands. The fork was immediately referred to as the "devil's pitchfork". During services at the Orthodox church, the tsarina, seeing that Russians would sometimes approach icons and kiss them, set about doing the same, but to the great indignation of those present actually kissed the Mother of God directly on the lips instead of humbly kissing the corner of the icon. All of this gave rise to a huge feud in the court and rumours quickly started to spread.

The young couple's reign only lasted one week. On 17 May a mass uprising started in Moscow under the boyar Vasiliy Shuyskiy. The prisons were opened up and the people were issued with weapons. A veritable massacre was set in motion in the city with thousands of Poles being killed. An angry mob stormed the palace of False Dmitriy and he was brutally murdered. Marina Mnishek managed to escape, but with this her involvement in the history of Russia, unfortunately, was not over, and an even more dramatic fate awaited her in future.

The body of the murdered False Dmitriy was profaned by the crows. His naked body was dragged out of the Kremlin through Spassky Gate to Red Square. There he was placed before his supposed mother Maria Nagaya. She was again asked to say whether he was really her son or not. According to the memoires of her contemporaries she gave an ambiguous response: "You would have had to ask me when he was alive; now that you have killed him he is not mine". Other sources say that she only gave a short response: "Not mine!" For three days Muscovites were allowed to jeer at the corpse as they pleased as it lay on a table in Red Square: filth was poured over him, he was sprinkled with sand, and a pipe was stuffed in his mouth, evidently, due to his former great love for music. His body was then finally buried outside the city in the cemetery for the poor, drunks and the nameless. Despite it being May, immediately after the funeral frosts suddenly struck, destroying all of the already-sprouting seeds and corn, and turning all of the May grass in the meadows grey. False Dmitriy's supporters whispered that it was God's punishment for murdering the true tsar and that his opponents argued that they could not rid the city of his evil and that now "the devil would take revenge on us all". All of these rumours continued to haunt society in Moscow, and so the body of False Dmitriy was dug up and burnt on Red Square, mixing his ashes with gunpowder and firing the mixture out of a cannon in the direction whence he had come – to the west, towards Poland.

In Western literature, Tsar Dmitriy I was depicted in Lope de Vega's play *The Grand Prince of Moscow or the Persecuted Emperor*, but the famous Spanish playwright took some liberties with the Russian history. He portrayed False Dmitriy as the true pretender and tsar who had suffered at the hands of conspiracies by Russian Barbarians. The American historian and writer Harold Lamb dedicated his work *Master of the Wolves*, written in 1933, to False Dmitriy. In this novel, written as an alternative history, the demonic False Dmitriy avoided death and mockery on Red Square and fled to the Ukrainian steppes. The poet Marina Tsvetaeva dedicated her *Marina* cycle of poems to Marina Tsvetaeva, writing lyrically about the love of the Russian adventurer and imposter to the Polish beauty Marina.

When "troubled times" have set in in history, unfortunately they do not end quickly. Peace did not come to Moscow with the death of False Dmitriy. Vasiliy Shuyskiy was made tsar, but the situation remained volatile. In the summer of 1607 yet another prince Dmitriy turned up, but this time history tells us nothing about his origins. Rumour had it that he was not killed in Moscow, but was miraculously saved. With the remnants of False Dmitriy I's army the new pretender to the throne took the small town of Tushino just outside Moscow. The Russian language still has the expression "Tushino villain" (*tushinskiy zlodey*) to mean a dishonest man or criminal. Tushino was set up as a second administrative centre of Russia headed by the Poles, where all of the forces opposed to Tsar Vasiliy Shuyskiy flocked. In Summer 1608 Marina Mnishek arrived in Tushino with her father. They recognised "this Tsar Dmitriy" as the new pretender to the Moscow throne and called on him to go to Moscow and overthrow Vasiliy Shuyskiy. It should be noted that prior to this period, despite the arrival of the Polish army in Moscow with False Dmitriy I, the Polish government consistently professed its neutrality and non-intervention in the disorder reigning in the Russian state. In September 1609 the Polish King Sigismund III Vasa openly declared war on Russia and the Polish army began a siege on Smolensk. False Dmitriy II was no longer needed by Poland; he brought only confusion to the balance of the political forces. No longer supported by the Poles he fled Tushino, and behind him Marina Mnishek too was forced to flee.

In the summer of 1610 Moscovite boyars overthrew Vasiliy Shuyskiy and handed him over to the Poles. In order not to provoke Skuyskiy's supporters to attempt to rescue him, the imprisoned tsar was taken to Warsaw where he soon died in prison. In Moscow, the Polish ambassadors and Russian boyars signed an agreement inviting the son of Sigismund III Vasa, Władysław, to take the Russian throne, also allowing Polish troops into Moscow. The ambassadors of King Sigismund III Vasa were sent to Marina Mnishek and False Dmitriy, who were in Kaluga at the time, with a demand to abdicate. There were no longer needed by the Polish King and were only getting in the way, as the goal of taking the throne in Moscow had been achieved. A proud refusal followed, and so Marina and False Dmitriy were now not only the mortal enemies of the Russians, but also their former allies the Poles. As a result of a secret plot the "Tushino Villain" was killed, and Marina continued to live under protection in Kaluga with her newly born son and her small detachment of Polish officers. Marina declared her son to be the rightful heir to the Russian throne.

The Catholics were unable to accept the fact that a Pole was sitting on the Russian throne. In 1611-1612 at the instigation and under the leadership of the Muscovite merchant Kuzma Minin a national militia was amassed from across Russia. Everyone who was able to bear arms went willingly to fight the "cursed Poles", as it was clear even to the most illiterate peasants that their country was dying and the time had come to set things straight. Prince Dmitriy Pozharskiy led the army. A monument to these two outstanding personalities still stands to this day on Red Square in Moscow.

In August 1612 the militia regiments besieged the Polish garrison in Moscow. The Polish army which came to Moscow to provide reinforcements and brought numerous supplies and weapons was completely destroyed by the Russian army. The Polish garrison in Moscow had no choice but to surrender. Marina Mnishek knew that her days were numbered, but she had nowhere to escape to; even the road to her native Poland was now closed to her. With a small group of Polish officers she fled to the south of Russia, but was captured and taken in chains to Moscow. Here her three-year-old son was hanged and, according to communiqués from Russian ambassadors to the Polish government, she "died in prison from her longing for freedom". According to other sources, she was hanged in secret.

In January 1613 the Zemzkiy Sobor – the first Russian parliament – in Moscow appointed a new tsar – Prince Mikhail Romanov. And so a new royal dynasty had been established in Russia, ruling until the revolution in 1917. The troubled times came had come to an end.

CHAPTER 4
The Anti-Polish Cossack and Peasant Uprising (1648-1651)

I N THE 1530-40S A NUMBER OF SPONTANEOUS POPULAR UPRISINGS and protests took place against the Uniate Church. In Polotsk in October 1633 an attempt was made on the life of the Uniate Archbishop Selyava. The Archbishop was wounded but the shooters were captured. However, the residents of Polotsk were not allowed any reprisals against them, so they raided the prison and released the prisoners.

In May 1648 Ukraine witnessed the start of an uprising against the Poles and the Uniate Church which quickly spread to Belarusian territory. The main forces behind this uprising were Cossacks and peasants with the petty gentry and Orthodox clergy also taking part. One of their main demands was the dissolution of the Uniate Church and independence from Poland.

In August 1648 an elder in Pinsk reported to the Polish government that "peasants, from Valishevichey to Mozyr from all of the however many villages and towns there are here, as well as the residents of Gomel, Turov, Loveya and their surrounding districts all joined the Cossack detachments and vowed to fight to the last drop of blood".

In the Summer of 1648 the Cossack and peasant army led active campaigns, crushing the commonwealth army of the Polish Crown and occupying the cities of Pinsk, Gomel, Brest, Mozyr, Turov, Kobrin, Loev and many other villages in southern Belarus. The residents of these cities, mostly Orthodox, offered no resistance, and all of the Catholic and Uniate priests were forced to flee.

Buoyed by the victories the Cossacks tried to take the city of Slutsk, a well defended military fortress belonging to the Radziwiłłs. But here they were faced with failure: the resolute, but not especially professional Cossacks lost more than a thousand people and never even got close to the fortress.

Bogdan Khmelnitskiy (1596-1657) took over as ideological and military leader of the rebels. He was a noble from a Ukrainian Orthodox background, educated first at an Orthodox school and later in the Jesuit College in Kiev. Khmelnitskiy had perfectly mastered the art of rhetoric, and knew Ukrainian, Belarusian, Polish and Latin. But in his memoires he wrote: "The Jesuits have not succeeded in reaching the very depths of my soul; I easily ousted their teachings from my soul and saved the Orthodox faith of my ancestors". When the popular uprisings started Bogdan Khmelnitskiy was made hetman of the Zaporozhye Cossacks, several thousand troops amassed from peasants and the petty gentry.

To fight the rebels the Polish King sent an army of fourteen thousand men with artillery. The Catholic church subsidised the recruitment of German, Hungarian and Swedish mercenaries. The first city to be captured from the rebels was Pinsk, where rebels were massacred *en masse*. More than three thousand residents of the city, their wives and children were murdered, and documentary sources indicate that out of the 6,000 homes in Pinsk more than 5,000 were burnt to the ground. Even State Chancellor Albrecht Radziwiłł blamed his relative Janusz Radziwiłł for destroying the Belarusian city. The government army then took Brest, where it dealt harshly with the peaceful residents rebelling against the Polish Crown. In Turov all of the residents that failed to escape the city with the Cossacks were killed on the orders of army commander Janusz Radziwiłł. In Chechersk, on his orders 150 imprisoned Cossacks had their right hands cut off, and 50 people were impaled. The residents of Bobruisk, having heard about Radziwiłł's atrocities, opened up the gates of the city without resistance. But this did not save them; 270 people had their hands cut off and 150 were impaled. In the Summer of 1649 the government forces regained control of the southern cities of Belarus, the army of Bogdan Khmelnitskiy returned to Ukraine, and the commander of the Belarusian government army Janusz Radziwiłł returned to the fortress in Slutsk.

But the rebels did not want to acquiesce. To have their revenge in Belarus Bogdan Khmelnitskiy sent a Cossack army of 45,000 men from Ukraine to Belarus. In July 1649 near the city of Loyeva a major battle took place, but the government forces were victorious, even though they were a third of the size of the rebel army. More than 8,000 rebels were killed on the battlefield and 3,000 drowned in the Dnieper as they were retreating. The Polish government's troops settled along the border between Belarus and Ukraine to shut off access to Belarusian territory for the Ukrainian Cossacks. The Polish King Jan Kazimierz took steps to appease the Belarusian population by adopting a new declaration in which he promised amnesty to all of the rebels and guaranteed new privileges for the Belarusian Orthodox clergy and nobility. All of this contributed to the signing of a truce. The year 1650 was a year of respite from hostilities on Belarusian territory. Echos of the Cossack uprising reverberated through small peasant revolts but these were quickly subdued. Fighting resumed in the Summer of 1651 when the 100,000-strong Polish government army went on the offensive towards Kiev. A decisive battle took place again in Loev, and was again won by the government troops who then took Kiev with ease. On 18 September 1651 Bogdan Khmelnitskiy was forced to sign a peace treaty whereby all Cossack detachments would leave Belarus for good and would never again fight against the Polish Crown. By the Winter of 1651 the insurgency had finally been suppressed.

As a result of the war the land in south-eastern Belarus was devastated; Brest, Mozyr and Pinsk were all destroyed. The Polish government, realising that this region had suffered complete economic ruin, was forced to drastically reduce state taxes, and in some places even completely remove them for a period of 5 years.

The Orthodox uprising in Ukraine and Belarus against Polish influence and the Uniate Church did not resolve any problems and did not result in any positive benefits. Religious strife after the bloodshed escalated like never before and it was clear that the peace would not last for long.

———◆———

Some overly nationalist Belarusian historians are inclined to present the Uniate Church as truly Belarusian, neither dependent on Rome or on Moscow. They assert that this new church was conducive to reinforcing the national consciousness of the Belarusian people. Such an interpretation does not correlate with the historical facts. The Uniate Church was of course in no way dependent on Moscow, but the aggressive expansion of Rome and the numerous cases of forced shifts of Belarusian Orthodox followers to the Uniate Church are an indisputable historical fact.

Firstly, the Uniate Church was created by the Jesuits and based on a scenario developed by them. With the complete rejection of Catholicism by the broad masses of the population the Jesuits were willing to maintain Orthodox worship so that the people would not know which church they were walking into and what the difference was in reality.

Secondly, the Uniate Church, especially in its early stages, spread through violence and strict administrative decrees. Orthodox priests were subjected to false denunciations, persecution and exile. Because of this, sometimes entire districts and parishes were left without Orthodox priests.

Thirdly, the Uniates actively helped numerous Catholic orders – Franciscan, Bernadine, Carmelite, Dominican – they all came from Prussia, Poland or Italy and, of course, had no relation to Belarusian spiritual culture and traditions.

Fourthly, the mass popular uprising of 1648-1651, which involved tens of thousands of Belarusians and Ukrainians clearly shows that the people were not accepting of the union with the Catholic church and for many years took up arms to defend their ideals.

All of these circumstances do not give any reason to believe that the Uniate Church was a true Belarusian church or that it contributed to the development of the national consciousness of the Belarusian people. It was no accident that a church created artificially never came to be widespread or long-lived.

Currently, according to 2008 data, the number of Uniate church-goers in Belarus totals about 10,000 across 14 parishes. Outside Belarus there are small parishes in London, Antwerp, Prague and Rome.

CHAPTER 5
Back to War with Moscow
(1654-1667)

Moscow decided to take advantage of the popular uprising by the Belarusian and Ukrainian people and to make Bogdan Khmelnitskiy its ally in the struggle against Poland. The Muscovite tsars never gave up hope of dealing a decisive blow to the Polish-Lithuanian Commonwealth and annexing Belarus and Ukraine. Bogdan Khmelnitskiy proposed that Tsar Aleksey Mikhailovich take Ukraine as an autonomous region of Russia. Moscow started to prepare for war, starting to purchase arms *en masse* from Western Europe and recruit officers and soldiers for its army. On 22 June 1653 Tsar Aleksey Mikhailovich officially notified Bogdan Khmelnitskiy that he had decided to annex Ukraine to his state and to take the nation under his protection. In October the Zemskiy Sobor in Moscow decided to declare war on the Polish-Lithuanian Commonwealth and to welcome "the Commander of the People's Army of Cossacks Bogdan Khmelnitskiy and all of his army from the cities and lands under the control and protection of the Russian Tsar". In this decision the Zemskiy Sobor cited as its grounds for war the persecution of Orthodox believers and Orthodox sacred sites and objects. Bogdan Khmelnitskiy finally achieved what he had fought for many years, a union with Orthodox Moscow. In the Ukrainian city of Pereyaslavl in January 1654 Bogdan Khmelnitskiy summoned the council of commanders and representatives of the Cossack armies to get their consent to the union and to issue a response to the Russian tsar. From

Moscow came a diplomatic mission headed by members of the tsar's council and Orthodox ministers. Those present at the Pereyaslavl council meeting declared their desire to join the Russian kingdom and vowed a mass oath of allegiance to the Russian tsar.

After the Pereyaslavl council meeting a Russian-Polish war was inevitable, and its main victim would again be Belarus, which lay between the two adversaries: Poland and Russia. In Spring 1654, Tsar Aleksey Mikhailovich amassed a 100,000-strong army on the border with Belarus, together with roughly 5,000 cannon. Neither Moscow nor any other country in Europe had ever had such an army. Belarus was completely unprepared to defend itself, and many of its fortresses had been destroyed in the previous war. Hetman Janusz Radziwiłł managed to assemble an army of 12,000, and with such a disproportionately sized army it was hard to envisage any successes.

The authorities in Moscow, as ever, wanted to use the issue of creed in the war and neutralise, or even win over, the Belarusian Orthodox population. With this in mind it sent hundreds of royal messengers to Belarus to read out letters from the tsar, according to which the Russian tsar was starting a war in the name of defending the Holy Orthodox Church and encouraged anyone who wanted to fight back against the Catholics to come over to his side. The abbot of the monastery in Polotsk, Afinagen Kryzhanovskiy, hastened to send a response to Tsar Aleksey Mikhailovich, assuring him that "as soon as the Russian army is on our doorstep, all Belarusians, however many there are, will rise up against the cursed Poles". In an effort to provide support for the Belarusians the tsarist government promised not to rob the nobility, to protect its possessions and even to reward them with money if it came over to the side of the Russian Tsar. The urban population was promised free trading with Russian cities and customs privileges.

In June 1654 the Russian army entered Belarusian territory. Despite the active propaganda and support of the Orthodox church, the Russian tsar did not receive any support from the Belarusian population. The Belarusians quickly came to realise that the promises of the Russian Tsar that he would not steal from them were empty, and documents on the war offer numerous details about the atrocities, looting and violence by soldiers in the Russian army.

In July 1654 the Belarusian noble Konstantin Poklonskiy, who had defected to Moscow and was made a colonel as a result, brought a letter to Mogilev from Tsar Aleksey Mikhailovich. It was read in a public square, and in it the Tsar promised that if the city voluntarily surrendered to the Russian army all of the rights and privileges of the citizens would be upheld, and any form of ownership that the townspeople and gentry had would be "royally approved" in full. The townspeople were divided into two camps: those who wanted to surrender the city and those who did not believe the promises made by the Russians and wanted to fight. They did not rush in making the decision, and in the meantime new information came on the progress of the war. The Russians had captured Mstislavl, after which out of the 33,000 inhabitants of the rich trading city no more than 3,000 had survived. Vitebsk and Dubrovno were now under siege. Mogilev's city council was faced with a choice: defend themselves, and see the city burned to the ground and looted, or open the gates. On 25 August the gates to the city were opened. A few days later any hopes placed in the promises of the Russian Tsar as a "believer in the same faith" that he would not use violence dispersed. The Russians engaged in looting and violence across the city. Soldiers took money and horses, bread and household items. A bitter fate befell the Jews in Mogilev. The occupying authorities announced the expulsion of the Jews from the city and commanded them to gather together their most prized possessions and leave the city. In the fields outside the city the exiled Jews were nearly all slaughtered and had their possessions taken from them. On the site of the massacre, after the end of the war, a memorial burial mound was made where fellow Jews from across the Polish-Lithuanian Commonwealth gathered to mourn the dead.

The Russians triumphantly marched across the Belarusian territory. After a four-month siege Smolensk was taken (15 October) and later Vitebsk (18 November). The Russian army was led by Tsar Aleksey Mikhailovich himself. To assist he called on the support of Bogdan

Khmelnitskiy's Cossack detachments, and Bogdan, an ardent supporter of the Russians, started to willingly destroy and loot Belarusian cities and villages which were only recently (in the 1640s) his allies in the struggle against the Polish government troops. Peasants in the Vitebsk district wrote to Tsar Aleksey Mikhailovich to inform him that his soldiers and the Cossacks "had taken cattle and crops from us, burnt our huts, and we are now roaming through the forests and swamps". When the Russian army occupied Druja the "military and other people in the city were killed and the city, and Polish Roman-Catholic churches and the homes of residents were burned to the ground so that the Poles could not longer take refuge in Druja". All of these calamities of war which devastated the Belarusian peasants and townspeople had an impact on their political position and did not facilitate the mood *vis-à-vis* the alliance with Moscow.

After the first major losses the Belarusian-Polish army of Janusz Radziwiłł launched a counter-offensive and in Winter 1655 recaptured Druja, Orsha, Borisov and Bobruisk. Not having the strength for further military action, the army stopped the offensive and set up a winter encampment.

The Muscovite army, having a huge numerical advantage, took Slutsk, Pinsk, Davydov and Turov in Spring 1655. The residents of these cities had to swear allegiance to the Russian tsar and Catholic and Uniate churches were closed immediately. The Russian troops took the heavily defended Belarusian fortress in Troki which nobody had ever managed to capture before, not even the Crusaders.

In June 1655 near the city of Ashmyany the main forces of the Russian and Polish armies met. On 26 June Janusz Radziwiłł's army was completely defeated and the road to the capital Vilno was open for the taking. On 31 June Vilno was taken by the Russian army, and by Autumn the entire Belarusian territory had been taken by the Russian forces and Bogdan Khmelnitskiy's Cossacks. After this the Russian tsar began to refer to himself as "Tsar and Autocrat of Great, Little and White Rus".

Some of the Belarusian nobility willingly took the oath of allegiance to the Russian tsar. But at the same time an anti-Moscow noble militia began to form in Belarus. The armed groups fought a partisan war, attacking members of the Russian administration and small detachments of Russian soldiers. In Belarus society had split into two groups with opposing political views: those who were for and those who were against the Russian rule. By the end of 1655 a civil war had broken out. Detachments of Cossacks led by Ivan Nechay, who declared himself the "Belarusian general", actively fought against the Muscovites. These troops liberated some small villages, and ravaged and burnt the estates of gentry that had sided with Moscow.

In 1647, Bogdan Khmelnitskiy died and was succeeded by hetman Ivan Vygovskiy, who was not such an ardent supporter of Moscow and therefore suspended the military action of his Cossack armies. In 1658 he even signed an agreement with Poland whereby he sided with the Polish-Lithuanian Commonwealth against Russia. This news caused a great deal of confusion at the royal court in Moscow; the tsar was outraged by the treachery of those who he "had taken under his protection and saved from the cursed Catholic Poles". Moscow's foreign policy started to change dramatically, and the views of the head of the Russian diplomatic service, A. Ordyn-Nashchekin, started to prevail. He believed that the Belarus and Ukraine problem would have to wait for later, as they needed at the time to urgently address the "Baltic issue" and wage war against Sweden for access to the Baltic sea. The Russian army ceased hostilities in Belarus, and this, together with the partisan war led by the Belarusians, saved the Polish army from complete destruction. The Polish troops got a break to regroup and recruit new soldiers.

Hetman Ivan Vygovskiy continued his secret talks with the Polish king and received assurances that if Ukraine were to remain in the Polish-Lithuanian Commonwealth it would be granted autonomy. After this, his interest in Moscow was gone for good, and he began to call on Ukrainian and Belarusian peasants to disobey the Russian administration and to revolt. Across Belarus there was a wave of massacres on the estates of nobles who had defected to the Russians. The Russian high command sent heavily armed detachments out to combat the "Cossackised slaves", and the Belarusian Colonel Ivan Nechay was captured and executed.

In Mogilev in February 1661, after six years of occupation, the uprising began against the Russian garrison. The grounds for the people's mass indignation was the fact that Russian soldiers had robbed a female baker on the market. On 1 February across the city church bells rang out and the rebels, together with captive Belarusian soldiers released from prison, attacked the occupiers. The Polish army, let in by the city's residents, quickly came to the support of the rebels. The seven-thousand strong Russian garrison was slaughtered, and the city liberated. In November, the army of the Polish-Lithuanian Commonwealth recovered Vilno from the Russians, which greatly increased the military and patriotic spirit of the Belarusians. The gentry who had sworn allegiance to Moscow began to side *en masse* with the government army or joined the partisan troops. The war dragged on, but indisputably there was a gradual ousting of the Russian troops from Belarusian territory.

The government of the Polish-Lithuanian Commonwealth sent its diplomatic mission to Moscow to start peace negotiations. It was a long and complex process which was interrupted on numerous occasions. Moscow did not want to resign itself to the fact that the "tidbit" of Belarus would once again be taken straight from under its hands. A peace treaty for 13 years was signed in Andrusovo only in 1667. Belarus remained part of the Polish Kingdom, and Russia received Smolensk, Chernigov, Kiev and the Ukrainian lands on the left bank of the Dnieper. Poland reacted ambiguously towards the Andrusovo treaty. Some barons and nobles welcomed it, but a large group of senators, led by King Jan Sobieski (ruling 1674-1696) categorically opposed the peace treaty and called for continued hostilities with Russia. This was complete and utter utopia, as Poland did not have the strength to continue the war.

In 1686, another peace treaty was once again signed with Russia, this time referred to as "eternal", and reinforced the borders established in 1667.

Thus, the "liberation" campaigns by Moscow were in part successful: half of the Ukrainian territory, together with Kiev, became part of Russia, but the second half of Ukraine and all of Belarus remained with Poland.

The long wars of the 17th century brought bereavement to the Belarusian people. According to some historians, from 1648 to 1661 Belarus lost about 50 per cent of its population, and in its eastern regions, where the fighting was at its strongest, roughly 80 per cent (54). The population of Belarus shrunk from 3 million in 1650 to 1.4 million in 1673. In the Polotsk district more than 60 per cent of homes were vacant because the peasants had fled either to the south of Belarus or to Muscovy. In the Radziwiłł estate prior to the war there were 16 villages with 1,087 homes, whereas in 1664 only 215 homes were left. In Minsk only 156 people were left, and the city itself was in ruins. Trading and crafts were less than 40 per cent of their levels in 1647. In the north of Belarus in the winter of 1655-1656 famine reigned, as half of the land had not been worked. Only by the end of the 18th century did the population of Belarus return to its 1640 levels.

The war with Russian ruined large and small cities across Belarus, their inhabitants were taken away to Russia and then sold into slavery on the markets of the Tatar Crimea. This total regression caused by the war changed everything: the living conditions of Belarusians, the social structure of the population, as well as the language and religious situation. The consequences of the war had a profound impact on many features of Belarus' subsequent history. These events were the source of the crisis suffered in Belarusian culture for a long time. Cities that had been built up gradually were now different cities, and the tradesmen, merchants and nobles all had different faces. Belarusian society had practically been deprived of its elites and aristocracy, and Belarusians became a people without a complete social hierarchy, thereby regressing to a rural people. Thus, Belarus lost the very basis on which a national bourgeoisie could emerge and a national statehood could develop. Belarusian culture and language moved once and for all into the category of a minor "rural" culture and could no longer compete with the "urban" and "masterly" culture of Poland. The basis of Belarus' national consolidation had been catastrophically undermined.

The war cast aside the former religious tolerance, which for many centuries had been a mainstay of Belarusian society, as well as completely changing the conditions of the Orthodox Church's existence. After the Reformation and Counter-Reformation the Orthodox Church was still the greatest concession in mid-17th century Belarus. It worked within the boundaries of legality and tolerance, and was supported by the Constitution. After the war with Moscow, the fearful Polish government and Polish authorities took decisive action to limit the rights of the Orthodox Church. The dangerous pro-Russian outlook of the Orthodox church prompted the Polish authorities to support the Uniate Church – which it would appear had no desire to root itself among the Belarusian people and had no popularity whatsoever. The Belarusian nobility, guilty in the eyes of the Polish Crown for having all too quickly moved over to fly the Muscovite banner, hastened to vindicate itself and went *en masse* to Catholic and Uniate services. The Cossacks, who were fierce supporters of Orthodoxy, had been practically wiped out over the years of war.

The war with Moscow from 1654-1667 completely dispelled the myth among Belarusians regarding the liberatory mission of the Russian Tsar, shattering the illusion of Orthodox brotherhood, even though Russophile sentiments, of course, still remained in Belarusian society.

From a political perspective the peace struck with Moscow in 1667 came to be one of the most important events of the 17th century in Eastern Europe. The balance of power was broken in favour of the forces taking power in the Russian kingdom, which had come out on top in terms of military and economic might and took the political initiative into its own hands. The central authorities of the Polish-Lithuanian Commonwealth had been severely weakened and the war helped to strengthen the role of the barons in the political life of the country. Since 1655 the Polish *sejm* introduced the "liberum veto" – the right of veto – which brought anarchy to the activities this government body. All delegates of the Polish *sejm* – the supreme governing body – had this "right of veto", and so just one person could sabotage any decision or law. King Jan Kazimierz, appointed in 1648, came to recognise this disorder within the government and so in 1668 abdicated and left for France. The Polish-Lithuanian Commonwealth essentially sealed its own fate; from this time onwards a steady decline set in from which it would never recover, and which in the end in 1795 led to its complete annihilation as a state.

CHAPTER 6
The Northern War with Sweden
(1700-1721)

UNFORTUNATELY, BELARUS WAS NOT SPARED THE PERENNIAL Northern War (1700-1721) which raged between Sweden, Russia and the Polish-Lithuanian Commonwealth. The cause of the war was Sweden's aggressive policies, and as a result of several wars of conquest, by the start of the 18th century Sweden was coming to be one of the most powerful states in Europe, ruling over Finland, Estonia, Latvia, as well as all of northern Germany and the duchies of Bremen, Verden and Weismayr.

In 1697 the young Karl XII (1682-1718) came to the Swedish throne. He devoted most of his time to his own amusement and hunting, and the capital's inhabitants readily gossiped about his eccentricities and pastimes. Perhaps the King's merry lifestyle persuaded the leaders of neighbouring states to recognise that it was time to regain lost ground. Denmark, Russia, Saxony and the Polish-Lithuanian Commonwealth entered into a military alliance against Sweden. The allies were well aware that the situation in Europe was convenient for Sweden's isolation. England and Holland were able to support Sweden, but at the time the two nations, together with France and Germany, were preoccupied with other problems, fighting for the Spanish Succession.

Each of the allies had their own interests in the war. King Augustus II of Poland was keen to annex Estonia and Latvia to the Polish-Lithuanian Commonwealth and gain a foothold on the shores of the Gulf of Finland. It was Poland that started the war. In February 1700 the 10,000-strong Polish army arrived in Latvia and marched on the city of Riga. Russia declared war in November 1700 and from this point on the theatre of war centred around the territories of Latvia, parts of Poland and the whole of Belarus.

The experienced, well-armed Swedish army won victory after victory. Karl XII took Warsaw and began to prepare a plot to rid King Augustus II of Poland of his power and to take the throne of his protégé, transforming Poland into an ally against Russia. The Swedish army then moved to Belarus to launch an offensive on Moscow, passing through Smolensk and Vitebsk en route. Over the years 1702-1703 the entire territory of Belarus was under occupation. Again the geographical position of the country between two enemies played a deplorable role in the history of the nation. Overall, the number of wars taking place in the country in the 16-18th centuries was in the dozens. It can be said that Belarus was not only a constant battlefield, but also an inn and tavern for foreign troops who came when they wanted to, enjoyed themselves and plundered, but always forgot to pay for it.

The sympathies of the Belarusian peasants were with the Russians, in spite of the fact that just a couple of decades ago the Russians had killed Belarusians on the same soil. With the approach of the Swedes the Belarusian peasants gathered together all of their food stocks and fled to the forest, and anything that they were unable to take was burned. The Swedish army, expecting to get food on the conquered lands, began to starve.

Peter I sent a 70,000-strong army to Belarus. In February 1705 part of the army approached Polotsk and set up a military encampment near the city. In June, the Tsar himself arrived in Polotsk. From here he issued a decree forbidding the nobles from going to sessions of the *Sejm* and other congresses, and leaving the city in general.

Peter I was not renowned for his piety. Although he did occasionally attend church, removing his wig as an emphatic gesture, with the clergy, even his own Russian clergy, he was not ceremonious. But what more can be expected of Catholics and Uniates. And Tsar Peter I was not reticent in showing his attitude, and not just anywhere, but in St. Sophia's Cathedral, which then belonged to the Uniate church. Once when drunk, Peter, Prince Aleksandr Menshikov and several officers came to St. Sophia's and demanded a tour. There were only several priests at the cathedral at the time, currently engaged in prayer. Vicar Konstantin Zaikovskiy was forced to interrupt his prayer and yield to the demand. At each altar the Tsar would stop and the priest would tell him about the origin of the icons on show. In one of the icons there was a depiction of Iosif Kuntsevich, the Jesuit and a supporter of the Uniate Church, killed by its opponents and later sanctified. Zaikovskiy found the courage to tell Peter about this icon. "Who exactly sent this saint to that world?" the Tsar asked furiously. Zaikovskiy replied firmly: "He was killed by Vitebsk heretics". Peter drew his sword and killed Zaikovskiy. Prince Menshikov and the offices attacked the other priests and all of them were killed. A stream of blood flowed across the floor. The next day the bodies were burned in front of the townspeople in the square and their ashes were scattered over the river so that their graves would not become a place of pilgrimage in future. The savage murder in Polotsk showed Europe that the Russian Emperor had the mind set of an Eastern tyrant, which in fact he did. By Peter's orders St. Sophia's was handed over to the Russian soldiers to plunder. All of the valuables and 3,000 zlotys – all of the cathedral's money – were taken from the temple. They then used the Cathedral to store arms and ammunition, and in the cellar they set up a gunpowder store. On the eve of the Russian army's departure from Polotsk the store was blown up, the explosion destroying half of the cathedral. For many decades the inhabitants of Polotsk had to look upon the blackened ruins of their shrine. It must not be forgotten that during the war with Sweden Russia and Belarus were in fact allies. But during the Northern War Belarus suffered just as much from its Russian allies as it did from the Swedes.

The Swedish army suffered its first defeat since the start of the war in Belarus, near the city of Mogilev. In October 1708 the 16,000-strong Swedish army met with a detachment of 12,000 Russian guards. The battle lasted for three days with the Swedes suffering complete defeat with the loss of 10,000 soldiers. But the end of the war was still a long way off.

The main battle of the Northern War took place near Poltava in what is now Ukraine in June 1709. Numerous generals advised Karl XII to leave Ukraine and Belarus for Poland, as the partisan war in these countries had greatly weakened the Swedish army. But the proud Karl XII did not heed this advice as he believed that his troops were invincible. The Russian army was victorious at Poltava and demonstrated a high level of military skill. Peter and his commanders used new earthwork fortifications and powerful artillery. They blocked all of the possible Swedish routes for retreat and forced them towards the Dnieper. When the remnants of the Swedish army were on the banks of the wide and full-flowing Dnieper, only Karl XII and a small group of officers managed to cross to the other side; the remaining 12,000 soldiers were forced to surrender to the Peter I's minion General Aleksandr Menshikov.

After the victory at Poltava the Russian troops led several successful operations in Belarus and the Baltic states, and the Swedish army withdrew from Belarus. The military operations moved to Sweden and continued to Russia's advantage. Augustus II, a supporter of Tsar Peter I, once again took the throne of the Polish-Lithuanian Commonwealth (1670-1733). Russia was the victor of the Northern War. The Polish-Lithuanian Commonwealth failed to achieve its goals, and Estonia, Latvia and Finland, which it was keen to annex, went over to Russia. And although the Polish-Lithuanian Commonwealth did not lose its territory as a result of the Northern War, and its boundaries remained unchanged, it lost a lot of its political sovereignty and came to be dependent on the interests of the Russian emperor.

Russian had finally overcome its long-standing strategic goal: it had gained access to the Baltic Sea. The victory brought glory to Peter the Great and served as a basis for his later imperial aspirations. Belarus lost 700,000 of its population in the Northern War and its territory was left ruined (55).

CHAPTER 7
The Economic Situation

B ELARUS' ECONOMIC BACKWARDNESS IN THE 18ᵀᴴ CENTURY WAS largely down to the long and protracted wars. It is not difficult to calculate that out of the 70 years of the Polish-Lithuanian Commonwealth's history from 1648 to 1718, 65 of them were spent at war, with the fighting taking place largely on Belarusian territory. Troops, looting and excessive indemnities brought the early developing agrarian nation to the brink of devastation. A typical scene in the early 18ᵗʰ century was one of unworked fields and deserted villages. Approximately sixty to seventy per cent of the workable land was empty.

After the end of the Northern War the Belarusian people started to restore their damaged economy bit by bit. Major landowners, striving to revive the economy – as well as their income – were forced to somewhat lesson their exploitation of peasants and give some short-lived respite. The royal treasury had no funds to restore state agricultural holdings, and so the government started to give peasants significant plots of land and levy only relatively small monetary taxes. The nation had but one goal: for the land to no longer be empty, and no longer overgrown with forest. It was a great incentive for peasants to work more efficiently, and by the mid-1750s the empty land was once again being worked and bringing in harvests.

Private landowners and landed estates went the other way. They did not want to distribute the land among the peasants, since land and ownership of peasants was their only source of income. They strove to restore their own estates, but often did not have enough manpower: the number of serfs decreased significantly following losses in the wars, and landowners could not afford to hire workers. As a result, private ownership among the nobility recovered much more slowly than state ownership, and the conditions of peasants on noble land holdings was far worse.

The lack of labour caused a decline in the quality of land cultivation, and the limited number of domesticated animals restricted the nation's ability to dress the fields. As a result, productivity was low, and by the mid-18th century it did not exceed 2.5 or 3 times the amount. Most agricultural produce was used for personal consumption. On small farms this was due to the small scale of production, giving low yields, and on the larger estates of barons there was a greater demand in order to provide for the farmstead and numerous servants. Only a small portion of each harvest was for sale, but it was only ever sold domestically as the many years of war had paralysed foreign trade.

The timber trade played a significant role in the manor-house economy. Wood and timber went from Belarus to Riga, Warsaw, Berlin and even Paris. Initial wood processing was well established at landed households, especially those on the banks of a river, close to a timber floating site.

From the 17th century onwards many landowners' farms housed small industrial enterprises belonging to feudal lords: iron ore mines, iron production workshops, paper mills, etc. Of particular economic importance was the distillation industry. Feudal lords extensively used their monopoly over the production and sale of vodka and beer. For this they processed the grain from their own crops and set the sale price of the alcoholic beverages that they owned.

Many Belarusian peasants were also artisans. They were still serfs, and so they worked off their statute labour by making crafts for the noble's home. This forced labour was not very effective and the quality of products was low. The petty gentry made use of these very simple pieces of furniture and household items, whereas the rich feudal lords and barons bought it all in Western Europe, which did not help the development of quality local products made by artisans.

According to the law peasants were fully dependent on their owner. They were forbidden to acquire ownership of the land and to abandon the land to which they were assigned. The landowner could deprive his subject of their plot of land, move it to a different location, or even sell it to another landowner. And if a landowner urgently needed money they had no problem with securing the required sum against their serfs for a year or two. And if the debt was not paid on time the peasants would transfer to the ownership of another landowner. These 'mortgages', as well as sales in general, were not without their drastic stories of husbands and wives being separated, or children being left without a father. Serfs were forced to carry out numerous services as required by their owner, the most important being statute labour and tributes. Statute labour was the number of days that the peasant had to work on his owner's land, whereas a tribute was a payment to the landowner in the form of a tax on money and the crops that the peasant had to give away. But aside from this there were roughly 100 various small duties that had to be done for the landowner, such as providing him with poultry, cleaning work around the farmstead, maintaining the distilleries, etc. It was at the expense of the gruelling labour and destitution of the Belarusian peasantry that the state, nobility, army and church came to be fed.

As the rural economy started to recover the landowners repealed the former privileges and increased levies on the peasants. The statute labour, which on many estates was 5-8 days per month, increased to 12-15 days by the mid-18th century, and on some estates landowners required 20 days. Discontent started to reign among the peasantry. In Krichev between 1740-1744 there was a major peasant uprising which, this time, was not political or religious in nature, but was in fact directed against their ruthless exploitation in order to improve their own social status. The village belonged to Prince Hieronim Radziwiłł, and for many years it had been rented to him. The tenants, the noble Volkovitskiy family, were only interested in squeezing out as much profit as possible over the period, cruelly exploiting the peasants, and robbing them where possible. Over just two years they pocketed 100,000 zlotys more in rent from the peasants than the amount payable by law. The peasants wrote letters of complaint to Prince Hieronim Radziwiłł, but he ignored them. Finally, he was forced to react and replaced the tenants. But things got worse still. The new tenants, the Itskevich brothers, were even greedier and ingenious in their unlawful ways to raise money. They not only introduced numerous illegal taxes but rode about the district with armed guards robbing the peasants, demanding "gifts", "treats" and "adornments". If they refused, the peasants were simply killed, and this kept them in a state of permanent fear. But when their patience had run out, they started a peasant revolt. In May 1740 the peasants created their first armed detachment, headed by Vasiliy Vashila. The rebels burned the courthouse together with all of the debt documentation archived there, and then looted the property of the tenants, forcing them to flee. The rebels set up a committee headed by burgomaster Ivan Korpach Mstislavl, and only the committee was then able to decide who should rent Radziwiłł's property. It was split up into parts and rented to noblemen highly respected in the district. Each new tenant signed a tenancy agreement, the first clause of which was that the tenant was aware of the sanction for extortion, namely, confiscation of all of their possessions or heavy fines. Measures were even put in place to combat usury. So as to not fall into full debt bondage, peasants were forbidden to borrow large sums of money or large amounts of grain. Low interest rates were set for small loans, and it was forbidden to increase rates. These actions and decisions by the rebellious peasants were the first acts of a conscious struggle by completely powerless people to improve their economic standing. The unique nature of the uprising is attested to by the fact that for almost four years Krichev and its surrounding district were under the control of the rebel committee.

Prince Hieronim Radziwiłł hesitated for a long time over taking military action against the rebels, hoping that with the help of some minor concessions he might be able to pacify them. But when the committee started to rent out his property in his name and signed more than a dozen agreements, the prince realised that this had never happened before and that he had lost control of the situation. Radziwiłł, one of the biggest barons in the Polish-Lithuanian Commonwealth, was not going to share power with peasants. In January 1744, from his residence in Slutsk, he sent his well armed and well trained cavalry and infantry to Krichev. The uprising leaders' committee learned of this move in advance and decided to give the prince's army a fight. There were approximately two thousand people in the rebel army, but they were armed with guns at best, but mostly with knives and axes. The fight for Krichev ended in total defeat, with hundreds of rebels killed or captured. In February, Radziwiłł himself arrived at the conquered city and ordered the hanging of thirty people and the impalement of another thirty. The indisputable authority of the rebels, burgomaster Ivan Korpach, was executed. The property of all of those who participated in the uprising was confiscated, and they all had their foreheads branded.

But despite this defeat, the uprising was fruitful. Prince Radziwiłł no longer rented out their possessions, he hired more or less honest managers, cut taxes both for peasants and the urban population, and he personally oversaw economic operations to prevent any abuse.

The economic decline in the 18th century was not only agricultural, but also urban in nature. The time of prosperity and wealth across the Belarusian cities of Minsk, Polotsk, Vitebsk and Grodno was in the 16th and early-17th centuries. At the time these cities traded with foreign nations, they employed hundreds of craftsmen, and had the real right to self-governance, or Magdeburg rights. But in the 18th century they fell into destruction and ruin, with the urban population decreasing two to three times over. The process of renovation was extremely slow, as the general economic situation in the crumbling Kingdom of Poland was unable to contribute to the work. Only in 1791 did the population of the cities come close to 1640 levels. Before the collapse of the Polish-Lithuanian Commonwealth Belarus had more than 40 major cities, and roughly 390 smaller ones. 360,000 people lived in cities, accounting for about eleven per cent of the population.

It is worth singling out the Jewish population as a special group of urban residents in this period. In the late 18th century, Jews accounted for fifty per cent of the population of Belarusian cities. Under the rule of Catherine II (the Great), the Jewish Pale of Settlement was demarcated, and Jews were allowed to settle across the majority of Belarusian and Ukrainian cities, but not in Moscow or St. Petersburg. Jewish merchants and artisans played a significant role in the economic life of the cities.

A new feature of the economy in the 1720-30s was the emergence of the first production plants where they started to employ machines and hired labour for the first time. The largest of these was a business in Uruche and Minsk producing glass and glassware. They made tableware, chandeliers and lamps and were known far beyond the borders of Belarus. In Sverzhen there was a porcelain factory, and in Slutsk a silk factory. In the second half of the 18th century the manufacturing sector became huge. In the 1790s there were 53 large factories in Belarus, employing 2,500 people.

The foreign market essentially played no role whatsoever in shaping the Belarusian economy. Relatively inactive trade links were maintained only with Russia and some Baltic countries. Only major barons such as the Radziwiłłs, Ogińskis and Sapiehas had their own ships and exported gain, vegetable oil, flax, honey to Riga and Gdansk, and from these cities brought back luxury goods, textiles, porcelain and arms. In the second half of the 18th century Belarusian cities started to trade actively with the now fully-grown St. Petersburg, the new capital of Russia.

The domestic market was used to sell agricultural and industrial products. In the major cities fairs (called *yarmarki* in Russian, from the Dutch *jaarmarkt*) were held annually, where a variety of goods were sold and contracts were signed. Most feudal lords sold their goods in stores on the land of their estates.

The government authorities, represented by the King and Polish *Sejm*, did little to promote and develop trade. Conflicting laws, the on-going conflicts within the *sejm*, internal customs duties, and the import-export privileges granted to certain barons did not facilitate the development of the internal market or the formation of a national bourgeoisie. Compared with the rapid economic development of European nations in the 17-18th centuries, the Polish-Lithuanian Commonwealth and its agrarian lands in Belarus were essentially in a lethargic daydream-like state.

CHAPTER 8
Political crisis

IN 1733, AUGUSTUS III WAS APPOINTED KING OF THE POLISH-Lithuanian Commonwealth, where he reigned for 30 years. The only distinguishing feature of his rule was the absence of any wars. However, in terms of domestic affairs, the King did not have any real authoritative leverage. Augustus III lived in Dresden, the capital of his principality, and he only visited the Polish-Lithuanian Commonwealth for sessions of the *Sejm* or for hunting. A growing political crisis was starting to emerge in the Polish kingdom. The celebrated Polish liberties granted to the nobility were gradually turning into waves of anarchy and abuse. The Polish-Lithuanian Commonwealth was witnessing a situation whereby aristocratic democracy was leading to a weakening of the central royal powers. In fact, the country came to be nothing but a plaything in the hands of groups of oligarchs. Using the "liberium veto", where a single member could block any decision by the *Sejm*, the supreme authoritative body had essentially been paralysed. This right was first applied in 1652 and over the next 112 years, out of 55 *Sejm* sessions 48 were forced to end due to being unable to reach a final decision (56). Clearly, this figure suggests that the *Sejm* did not really fulfil its role of managing the state and adopting important political decisions.

The absence of any law on succession played a negative role in the political life of Poland. After the death of the last king of the Jagiellonian dynasty, Sigismund II Augustus, in 1572, who left no direct descendants, the Poles were unwise in not selecting any of the numerous noble families to take the throne. Instead they went along the path of electing a king, and worse still, they invited a monarch from abroad to take the Polish throne. This very fact attested to the existence of deep-seated divisions within the leadership of the country. This led to constant struggles by groups of barons and to long periods of "interregnum", or more accurately, anarchy. The election of the monarch in Poland also brought about constant interest on the part of neighbouring nations in the internal affairs of Poland; gradually they started to become drawn into decisions on Polish internal conflicts, sometimes with weapons in hand, while always pursuing their own political agenda.

In was only in 1764 that they finally implemented some restrictions on the use of the "right of veto". Economic decisions now had to be adopted with a majority of votes; but some groups of barons managed to assert the "right of veto" when voting on political decisions.

Small changes to legislation could not significantly improve the situation, and this led, in the second half of the 18th century, to the Polish-Lithuanian Commonwealth finding itself in a state of profound crisis. The old mediaeval forms of the political system and social relations became obsolete and took on monstrous forms. New laws were not developed and were not adopted. A small group of oligarchs had *de facto* authority in the country, but only used it for their own gains. Even the privileged cities with the benefit of Magdeburg Rights and self-government were unable to adopt decisions independently of local barons as the barons had their own armies. Corruption reigned in the courts and they were so helpless that their authority carried no weight. Due to the prolonged wars and poverty among the population as a whole, trade and commerce declined whilst the higher elite, drowning amid of a sea of extraordinary luxury, continued to enjoy their foreign goods.

The weakness of the Polish-Lithuanian Commonwealth was beneficial to its nearest neighbours. For example, there was a diplomatic agreement between Russia and Prussia which had a secret article whereby the allies were obliged to devote all of their forces to retaining the noble democracy, the election of the king, and *"liberum veto"* in the Polish-Lithuanian Commonwealth.

The weakened Polish-Lithuanian Commonwealth had lost its international prominence and at the end of the 18th century came almost to be prey to its powerful neighbours, Russia, Austria and Prussia. After the death of Augustus III the political anarchy in Poland allowed Russia to put the minion and lover of Catherine II, Stanisław Poniatowski (reigning 1764-1795), on the Polish throne, acting as nothing short of a puppet in her hands. It was essentially overt intervention by Russia in Poland's affairs. All of Belarus' previous history had shown that Moscow continually took on the role of "saviour and liberator" of the Belarusian Orthodox people from oppression by the Polish Catholics. Tsar Peter I made the dissident question the main weapon of his political influence in the Polish-Lithuanian Commonwealth, and his interference in the religious problems of Belarus created yet more tension. A tsar and "reformer", who would "open a window to Europe" for his state and wanted to unite it or, at the very least, bring it closer to European civilisation, was not at all desirable for Belarus. On the contrary, fighting with the Uniate and Catholic churches, he "would not allow" Belarusians there, wishing instead to keep them fully within the Orthodox – and therefore Russian – sphere of influence. Empress Catherine II (later referred to as "the Great"), who later came to power in Russia, considered this issue to be very important to Russia's foreign policy, as she understood that a demagogy of "liberating the Orthodox" could bring a large agricultural nation under Russia's control. The question of protecting the Orthodox people right up to the third and final division of the Polish-Lithuanian Commonwealth was a key weapon in Russia's fight against the weakened Kingdom of Poland.

But it should be noted that the internal politics of Poland had changed considerably. The religious tolerance that had characterised the 16th and 17th centuries was gone by the 18th century. After the arrival on the Polish throne of the Saxon dynasty religious fanaticism started to reign. Gentiles, or as they were called at the time "dissidents", which included Orthodox and a small number of Protestants, were stripped of their political rights. They were denied access to public and military service, and they could not be elected as deputies at the *Sejm* or as members of the courts. Dissidents, both Orthodox and Protestant, were forbidden to build new churches. This political and religious inequality was enshrined in religious resolutions handed down by the *Sejm* in 1717, 1733 and 1736.

In the mid-18th century, the population of impoverished Belarusians stepped up the struggle to improve their situation, and as ever this struggle assumed a religious perspective. The Orthodox faith was viewed in the Polish-Lithuanian Commonwealth as being second-rate, and its representatives were in every way ignored and excluded from government. Bishop Georgiy Konisskiy of Mogilev became the leader of the Orthodox church and in 1765 gave a speech in front of the King of Poland in which he convincingly demonstrated the numerous infringements of Orthodox rights in the Polish-Lithuanian Commonwealth. Although the demands of the Belarusians were limited to minor concessions, such as the right to be elected to public office and to be elected as deputies on local *Sejms*, they seemed excessive and outrageous to the fanatically-minded Catholic gentry. The Catholic church immediately launched a powerful anti-Orthodox propaganda campaign, damning the dissidents in their churches. Russia believed itself to have the right to intervene and reminded the nation of its treaty with the Polish-Lithuanian Commonwealth from 1686 whereby Poland pledged to ensure that the rights of Catholics and Orthodox believers would be equal "in perpetuity" after the bloody wars with Moscow. Russian demanded performance of this treaty, and in 1766 the Polish *Sejm* refused arrogantly.

In 1767, with the assistance of Russia, a Confederation was set up in Slutsk, a union of Orthodox, Calvinist and Lutheran gentry. They decided to work together to fight for the equality of believers of different faiths. The Act of Confederation was signed by 248 people, including the Belarusian bishop Georgiy Konisskiy. The Russian Empress Catherine the Great took the Confederation "under her protection" and sent a 20,000-strong army in support. Russia was, of course, concerned about the fate of dissidents in the Polish-Lithuanian Commonwealth, and all of this activity was purely directed at rocking the boat of the Polish authorities, which had already been swaying perilously for some time. The Russian army supporting the confederates again marched through the lands of Belarus to Warsaw, robbing peasants en route. The Russian troops surrounded the *Sejm* building, where a meeting was in progress, and its members started to panic, forcing the *Sejm* to repeal all laws directed against the dissidents and to adopt a resolution granting them equal political rights to the Catholics. The frightened *Sejm* deputies, in their flattering address to Empress Catherine the Great, gave her the powers not only to "continue to defend Orthodox Belarusians, but also not to forsake their kindness or the Polish-Lithuanian Commonwealth itself". The Warsaw Treaty was signed, in which Empress Catherine the Great assumed the role of guarantor of Orthodox rights. It is noteworthy that the Russians did not intervene in the "right of veto" issue as it was advantageous to Russia that it be preserved for as long as possible, and the frightened Poles again did not address this problem, meaning that the "right of veto" remained in force. The Polish-Lithuanian Commonwealth was not really any more able to manage itself and was agonising in a state of anarchy.

In order to restrict Russia's over-excessive political and military interference in Polish affairs, Prussia entered the fray. It provided funds for the creation of a Confederation of Opponents of Russia in Bar, which Belarusian and Ukrainian Catholic gentry began to join *en masse*. An army of five thousand people was amassed. The Confederates requested support and assistance for the troops from France, Austria and Turkey, but they did not receive any aid and were forced to fight alone against the much superior Russian army. After heavy defeats of the Confederates at Slutsk and Nesvizh, the movement began to die down. Having defeated the Confederates, Russia, Austria and Prussia entered into negotiations on the division of the Polish-Lithuanian Commonwealth.

CHAPTER 9
The Division of the Polish-Lithuanian Commonwealth (1772-1795)

I N 1772 THE FIRST DIVISION OF THE POLISH-LITHUANIAN Commonwealth took place between Russia, Prussia and Austria. Russia took the eastern part of Belarus with the cities Polotsk, Vitebsk, Orsha, Gomel and Mogilev. Russian diplomats demanded that the Polish *Sejm* meet in Grodno and recognise the voluntary transfer of these lands to Russia. On the one hand the bribery among the deputies, and on the other hand their utter passivity contributed to the fact that this unprecedented demand was in fact satisfied.

The first division of the Polish-Lithuanian Commonwealth did not bring the Polish barons to their senses, who were in a constant state of competition with one another. But they did allow some policy changes in relation to the Orthodox Church. In 1783 the Polish *Sejm* agreed to open a Belarusian eparchy within the Polish-Lithuanian Commonwealth. Archimandrite Viktor Sadkovskiy was appointed as Orthodox bishop in Poland and he fully supported the Russian authorities and maintained strong pro-Russian sentiments. Russia continually made use of any political complications to interfere in the internal affairs of Poland.

After the first division of Poland three parties formed. One of them, the royal party, sought specific reforms in society, but in cooperation with Russia. By this time, paradoxical as it may sound, there were a large number of officials in Poland's government who received salaries from Russia, including the last king of Poland, Russia's protégé Stanisław Poniatowski. At the head of the second party was hetman Ksaveriy Branitskiy (1731-1819). This party also consisted of members supporting closer cooperation with Russia, but was against the king and his entourage. The third party was markedly anti-Russian and wanted independence for Poland, but it was unable to develop any ideas to save and reform the collapsing nation.

From 1788 to 1792 four *Sejm* sessions took place in Warsaw, at which a substantial majority of deputies were opponents of Russia. They formed a large group of "patriots" led by Tadeusz Kościuszko (1746-1817) and advocated the need for urgent political reform. They had a chance of success as Russia at the time was occupied in a war with Turkey and Sweden, and it was for a time unable to oversee its guardianship of Poland. A large influence on the *Sejm*'s work came from the *Prussian Note*, a statement from the Prussian ambassador that Prussia (which had only just been involved in the first division of Poland and had already broken off a piece of the pie for itself) was prepared to enter into an alliance with Poland against Russia. This inspired many *Sejm* deputies who were opposed to Russia. Despite the opposition and inability to reach a consensus on many issues, on 3 May 1791 the *Sejm* succeeded in adopting a new Constitution which opened the way to move away from the crisis and transition to a bourgeois-democratic developmental path. The new Constitution finally provided for the succession, rather than the election, of the monarch, definitively abolished the "right of veto" and regulated the activities of the state executive. Full executive powers were transferred to the king and the council, made up of five ministers. A great deal of attention was paid by the *Sejm* to the discussion about the bourgeoisie; this was due to pressure from active struggle by this "third class" for their rights. 141 cities in Poland, Belarus and Ukraine sent residents as representatives to the *Sejm*. They were all dressed in black, and their appearance bearing a Petition citing their demands made a lasting impression on the *Sejm*'s delegates. The "Black Procession" had achieved its goal: the new Constitution granted this third class rights that had never been seen until now: occupying secular and ecclesiastical positions and being elected as deputies to the *Sejm*. The Constitution prohibited barons from having their own army and the gentry from forming a Confederation (military alliances to protect their rights and interests). All of the provisions of the new Constitution, of course, hinted that the ideas of the French revolution had reached and spread across the Polish-Lithuanian Commonwealth. There then started a process of consolidating and stirring up the third class, which until now had been entirely isolated from political life.

This in many ways democratic Constitution ran entirely contrary to the interests of Russia, as it enabled Poland to overcome its period of crisis and to follow a new, healthier and more independent developmental path. Unfortunately, the new Constitution was only in force for 14 months and 3 weeks. Catherine the Great, who found this Constitution to be most disagreeable, responded by ordering troops to Poland, and in early 1792, on yet another occasion in recent years, the Russian army marched on Poland. The hopes of the Polish "Patriots" party of Prussia's support never materialised, as the Prussia government entered into negotiations with Russia on the second division of the country. At the time, the Belarusian gentry put up no resistance whatsoever to the army, as they were already mentally prepared for a complete union with Russia. In May, almost without any bloodshed, the Russian army took Vilno and Minsk, took Warsaw in June, and in July King Stanisław Poniatowski of Poland announced the disbandment of the Polish army. It should be noted for comparison that the Polish army at the time of its disbandment totalled sixteen thousand people, whereas Catherine the Great's Russian army had three hundred thousand armed men. To imagine that Poland could continue to fight against this war machine was entirely unthinkable.

Active negotiations were held between Russia, Prussia and Austria regarding the second division of the weakened country. In January 1793, the second division was announced. Russia took the Belarusian territories of the Minsk, Vilno and Grodno provinces, and Prussia received Poznan, Gdansk and Torun. The Constitution of 1791 was repealed. The Polish *Sejm* was called for a second time in Grodno so as to ratify the division of the country. The deputies at this meeting of the *Sejm* were silent for three days, causing this *Sejm* to go down in history as the "Silent *Sejm*". These were tragic days for Poland. At the end of the third day a Russian observer at the *Sejm* declared: "Silence is a sign of consent", and the *Sejm*'s work was done. As a result of the second division of the Polish-Lithuanian Commonwealth's territory, it was split in two and the country was rendered fully dependent on Russia. Russian garrisons were set up in Warsaw and other major cities and the leaders of the "Patriots' Party" were forced to flee abroad, setting up their own headquarters in Dresden in preparation for an uprising. The Patriotic movement in Poland was led by Tadeusz Kościuszko.

The uprising began on 12 March 1794 when General Antoniy Madalinskiy refused to disband his brigade of cavalry, taking them to Krakow. En route to the rebels other parts of the disbanded Polish army joined him. In Krakow on 24 March a Rebels' Act was announced, defining the goals of their struggle: restoring Poland's sovereignty, its borders as of 1772, and the Constitution of 1771. Tadeusz Kościuszko took an oath of allegiance to the Polish people, and was given full civil and military powers in Poland. A Supreme National Council was set up as the highest authoritative body in the country.

On 4 April, under the command of Tadeusz Kościuszko, the rebels defeated the Russian troops at Racławice, and on April 17 liberated Warsaw. On 22 April the uprising began in Vilno. The rebels defeated the Russian garrison and established its own authority in the city, the Supreme Council of Lithuania, which included the leaders of the "Patriots' Party" and representatives from the local population. Under the Council departments for safety, security, the military and finance were all set up. Y. Yasinskiy was appointed commander of the armed forces of Lithuania and Belarus. A criminal court was set up, which ordered the hanging of the Russian army general Count S. Kasakovskiy on 25 April.

There were immediately conflicts which broke out between the rebels in Poland and the Grand Principality of Lithuania. The creation of the Lithuanian Council in Vilno contravened the Krakow Act and Belarusians and Lithuanians were accused of separatism.

Over the period from April to July 1794 the fighting of the insurgents in Belarus was active and successful. An army of volunteers, amassing five thousand soldiers under the command of Yacob Yasinskiy, expelled the Russian garrison from Oshmyan and Grodno, and then rose up in revolt in Brest. Yasinskiy started to form cavalry detachments for military action against the rear of the Russian army. Three hundred cavalry were formed, largely of Belarusian peasants. They were not prepared militarily, were poorly armed, and in spite of this had to fight against the experienced Russian army.

The uprising in Belarus lasted a little over five months. It was not supported by the majority of the Belarusian population, who had peacefully accepted the fact that it would join Russia and had no desire for bloodshed in order to restore the old Polish order.

In September 1794 the ten-thousand-strong army of General Aleksandr Suvorov (1730-1800) arrived on the theatre of war in Belarus and the situation quickly began to change to the disadvantage of the rebels. On 10 October there was a large battle at Maciejowice, the rebels were routed, and Tadeusz Kościuszko was seriously wounded and taken prisoner. Out of the ten thousand soldiers of the insurgents, only two thousand managed to escape to Warsaw. All of the remaining insurgent army were called on to travel urgently to Warsaw in order to make another stand against the Russians. But this did not happen. On 5 November, Warsaw, which had nobody there to defend it, was forced to capitulate. With this the rebellion was finally crushed.

The leader of the uprising Tadeusz Kościuszko was a remarkable man. He was born in Belarus into the family of a nobleman. In 1769 he graduated from the Knight's Academy in Warsaw, Poland's most prestigious military school which trained highly educated officers. The teaching programme included world history and Polish history, philosophy, mathematics, law, economics, Latin, German and French. From his youth Kościuszko surprised his friends with this asceticism, strong will and determination, for which he earned the nickname "the

Swede". He graduated from the Knight's Academy with honours and received a royal scholarship to continue his studies at the Military Academy in Paris. His studies in Paris from 1769 to 1774 and passion for the ideas of Voltaire, Montesquieu and Rousseau completed him as a brilliant officer and a highly erudite individual. In 1775, Kościuszko was sent to America to serve as a colonel in the War of Independence for the North American colonies of Great Britain. Tadeusz Kościuszko successfully dealt with the construction of fortresses to protect Philadelphia, after which he was appointed Chief Military Engineer of the Northern Army. In recognition of his military merits, the US Congress awarded him the rank of General of the US Army on 13 October 1783.

During the Russo-Polish War of 1792 Kościuszko commanded divisions, and after the defeat of the Polish army he emigrated to Paris, where he played an active role in the French Revolution. The French love of freedom infected him and inspired him to organise an uprising in his desecrated homeland of Poland.

After he was captured by the Russians, he was taken to the Peter and Paul Fortress in St. Petersburg, a prison for the most senior of prisoners. But his authority as an officer was so high that he was not locked up in a cell, but as in fact housed in the home of the fortress' commandant as a guest. Within the walls of the Peter and Paul Fortress, which occupied a relatively large area, he enjoyed complete freedom.

After the death of Catherine the Great, Tadeusz Kościuszko was immediately freed upon the orders of Catherine's son and successor, Emperor Paul I, who started his reign by quickly eliminating everything that his mother, whom he hated, had done. Kościuszko agreed to accept his freedom only on the condition that all of the other participants of the Polish uprising would be released from Russian prisons. Paul I agreed to his conditions. In addition, he paid the former honourable prisoner 12,000 roubles, presented him with a carriage, sable coat and hat, fur boots and silverware. Tadeusz Kościuszko went to the US, as Poland, where he was born, was no longer on the world map. In 1798 he once again returned to Europe and settled in Paris. When Napoleon came to power, he repeatedly asked the brilliant Polish general to serve in his army, but Kościuszko refused, as he could not forget freedom of thought and considered Napoleon to be a tyrant. When this hero of the Polish people died in 1817, not a single compatriot was by his bedside.

The process of the Polish-Lithuanian Commonwealth's destruction was irreversible. The defeat of the uprising led by Tadeusz Kościuszko sealed the final elimination of the Polish Kingdom. In October 1795 the Polish, Ukrainian and Belarusian territories were split three ways between Austria, Prussia and Russia. All of Belarus' remaining territory was transferred to Russia, with the exception of a small region near Grodno, which went to Prussia. In the end, after the division of the three regions of the Polish Kingdom, Russia took all of the Belarusian territory, bringing with it a population of over 3 million people.

The Polish-Lithuanian Commonwealth, a multinational federal state, had ceased to exist on the political map of the world.

For the Belarusian people, a new period of history had begun, one where they had to continually strive to defend and preserve the cultural and spiritual achievements. In place of the Polonisation, there was now an era of Russification and assimilation of the Belarusian nation.

Soviet historians invariably called the seizure of the Belarusian territory a "reunion with its fraternal Russian people". The Belarusian people voted for this reunion with their feet: two decades after the division in 1772, forty thousand people left the occupied districts of Polotsk, Vitebsk and Mstislav for Poland. Catherine II called this flight "foolish emigration". The total number of fugitives from Russian territory to Poland over the period between the first and third divisions from 1772 to 1795 amounted to three hundred thousand people. But after the third division there was nowhere else to run.

PART 5

THE CULTURE OF THE ENLIGHTENMENT

CHAPTER I
Sarmatism, the ideology
of the aristocracy

IN THE POLISH-LITHUANIAN COMMONWEALTH OVER THE 17TH TO 18th centuries there was a unique spiritual and cultural phenomenon which came to be known as "Sarmatism". It was manifested in all spheres of life amongst the Polish and Belarusian nobility: in politics, culture, art, family and friendships.

Essentially, the concept of "Sarmatism" was linked to the myth that the Polish nobility had descended from the ancient militant tribe the Sarmatians, as wrote about by ancient authors such as Herodotus and Juvenal. Herodotus wrote that the Sarmatians were descended from Amazons who had married Scythians. Their tribes had settled in Eastern Europe north of the Black Sea from the 4th century BC to the 4th century AD. Mediaeval western European cartographers used the term to refer to the lands east of Germany: Poland, Belarus and Ukraine. For example, the Carpathian mountains were called the Sarmatian Alps, the Baltic Sea the Sarmatian Ocean, and the Belarusian woodlands the Sarmatian swamp. In French and German mediaeval chronicles Slavs were frequently referred to as Sarmatians, even though they often belonged to different tribes.

The Renaissance period developed the notion of Sarmatism and brought sublime and romantic nuances to the concept. This era was characterised by a broad interest in ancient culture and history, and myths and legends. In the 16th century, the Kingdom of Poland and the Grand Principality of Lithuania achieved considerable political power and a high level of cultural development, they occupied vast swathes of territory in Eastern Europe, and from that time onwards they started to call it Sarmatia, using the word as a synonym for "great power". The gentry were proud to use this name, and the Jagiellonian dynasty of Polish kings was declared a dynasty of noble Sarmatians. Polish literature of the Renaissance period featured numerous works describing the courage and honour of the Sarmatian people.

In the classical sense, the term "Sarmatism" was fully developed by the end of the 16th century. It took on a class colouring and started to be used to refer to the lifestyle and way of thinking of the gentry in the Polish-Lithuanian Commonwealth. The term "Sarmatism" entered into the consciousness of the upper echelons of Polish society as an expression of the feeling of their class and social exclusivity. Whilst they would use the words "Pole", "Belarusian" or "Lithuanian" to refer to members of the lower classes, they would use "Sarmatian" only to refer to nobility and barons. The Polish, Lithuanian and Belarusian nobility were all considered part of the Sarmatian people; in other words, they were a united people. The petty bourgeois and peasants were not part of this people, and the nobility referred to them as *bydlo*, or the 'rabble', often viewed as similar or synonymous to the Russian *skotina*, 'beast' or 'cattle'. It was a kind of social racism: the aristocracy were considered descendants of the Sarmatians and the commoners were Lithuanians and Slavs. One of the tenets of Sarmatism was the assertion that a true Sarmatian would prefer to die of hunger than to disgrace themselves through physical labour. Such hypertrophy towards their own kind often took on relatively comic forms.

It should be noted that the idea of Sarmatism, i.e. exclusivity, was particularly attractive to the middle and petty gentry. Barons, often having been educated in Western European universities, were not keen on the Sarmatian myth, as their tastes and customs were rather cosmopolitan in nature. The Lithuanian upper nobility had their own genealogical legend, considering themselves to be descendants of Roman aristocracy. The Belarusian nobility, not forgetting their shared past with the Russians, identified with the descendants of the first

Russian dynasty, the Ruriks. So only ethnic Poles and Belarusians who considered themselves Polish were ardent followers of Sarmatism.

The government of the Polish-Lithuanian Commonwealth used the postulates of Sarmatism depending on the political situation. During the *interregnum* in 1575 the supporters of Fyodor, the son of Tsar Ivan the Terrible, even called for unification of the two Sarmatian peoples – European and Asian – into one state. In the early 17th century the Sarmatian myth was used as an ideological basis for the expansion of Poland to the east, to the lands that had formerly belonged to the Sarmatians in ancient times.

Sarmatism gradually led the Polish gentry to the idea of the messianism of Poland as the main foothold of Christianity. This was helped considerably by the Catholic Church and its successes in expanding its influence. The successes of the Catholic Church, in the eyes of the public, were the wars with Muslim Turkey, with Protestant Sweden, with Orthodox Moscow, and a successful Counter-Reformation in Poland itself. The large Polish nobility (larger than any other country in Europe), making up ten to twelve per cent of the population, saw themselves as God's chosen people, who had created a great state and had won back great freedoms and rights for their people.

In reality, the Polish nobility had many "golden" privileges that the nobility of Western Europe did not. Members of the nobility were all equal in this class, unlike the nobility of Germany and France were there were titles such as prince, baron and count. Nobles considered themselves equal irrespective of wealth, not only towards each other, but also towards the king. The "right of veto" that each nobleman had was unprecedented in European legal systems.

Gradually an ideal Sarmatian image was developed: a patriot of Poland and defender of the interests of his class, a brave knight who upheld the traditions of the ancient order of Sarmatian knights, and an eloquent and verbose speaker at the *Sejm*. Even in everyday life Sarmatians would speak in a pompous and bombastic manner, and would certainly use Latin aphorisms in their speech. The exclusivity of this image brought with it the right to vote held by each Sarmatian nobleman when electing a new king, irrespective of their financial position.

The weakening of the monarchy, the appearance of petty baron states and their struggles with one another led to the decentralisation of the state. The underdeveloped governing apparatus and protracted *Sejm* sessions, which were unable to adopt the right decisions due to the extraordinary talkativeness of the Sarmatians and their right of veto, all required urgent reform. But the Sarmatians took any reform projects as an attack on their "golden freedoms". The political ideal of Sarmatism was a national conservatism based on the principle of "nothing new is better for us" and a complete rejection of absolutism. The best monarch for Poland was one who took care of military affairs and protected the privileges of the nobility; all other state affairs were secondary and occupied a less important position, as Sarmatians' conviction in their political and national exclusivity made them think that society was in a fine state. Such narcissism, which prevailed in the minds of the ruling class, steadily led to the decline of society and the country as a whole.

The successful completion of the Counter-Reformation and the signing of the Union of Brest manifested itself in terms of Sarmatian ideas to reduce tolerance towards other religions. The Polish and Belarusian Sarmatians believed that a true Sarmatian could only be a Catholic. There were frequent xenophobic statements in Sarmatian publications and public rhetoric and they would regularly criticise the manners and customs of non-Christian peoples. Due to this megalomania, the Sarmatians were extremely hostile towards Christian nations: the French were called frivolous, the English sanctimonious, the Dutch simpletons, and the Spanish arrogant. Travel abroad was considered foolish, as they believed that it would only bring back disease and bad habits. In an anonymous Belarusian political pamphlet of the 17th century, *The Story of Ivan Meleshko*, it poignantly and sarcastically describes the behaviour of foreigners: "… and if a German is walking down the street and his wife next to him proudly struts about, they will squeak their boots, rustle their clothes, but they will stink something rotten… and if you invite a German to sit down, he will sit like a sulking devil, fanning himself for some reason with his hat, before starting to itch…" (57). In the same work the author approves of King Sigismund I as he "had no fondness for dogs or Germans".

But whilst the political and social life of Sarmatist ideas had a negative, and at times just complex, influence, they still gave rise to new forms and styles in culture and art. The flourishing of Sarmatism coincided with Baroque dominance, and so the unique features of both of these phenomena crossed over into one another. The arrogance of Sarmatism contributed to the rapid development of baroque architecture: in the 17th century churches were built with luxurious interiors, sculptures and an abundance of gold. In painting, portraits came to be the dominant art form, referred to as the "Sarmatian Portrait" on account of its stylistic features. Since the nobility were very proud of their unique lineage from the ancient Sarmatians, there was a need to have "genealogical" galleries. Sarmatian portraits were characterised by their outward resemblance to paint portraits and at the same time a tendency for primitive painting styles. An inherent part of the portraits were depictions of the weapons and chivalric demeanour of a particular person. Sarmatian portraits always contained baroque elements: accessories, columns and drapes.

In history Sarmatism has come to be synonymous with conservatism, pomposity, and pretentious piety. In modern-day Poland, the word "Sarmatian" is a form of ironic self-identification, and is sometimes used to underline the freedom-loving nature of the Polish.

CHAPTER 2
Education and science

THE SPIRIT OF THE ENLIGHTENMENT, WHICH WAS CONCEIVED IN England and France, swept across virtually the entirety of the European cultural milieu. The heyday of the Enlightenment came in the 18th century. But its origins were in the late Renaissance, when interest in the sciences and atheism grew unusually quickly. Belarus was home to the forerunner of this revolutionary thinking, often compared to that of his spiritual brother Giordano Bruno. This man was the Belarusian noble Kasimir Lyshchinskiy (1634-1689) (58). He graduated from the Jesuit College in Brest and University in Krakow. At the age of 25 he joined the Order of Jesuits, and at 30 became the rector of the Jesuit College. Having an excellent education and being highly erudite, he could have had a glorious career, as the Jesuits were highly appreciative of educated people. But instead Lyshchinskiy chose to leave suddenly, announcing his departure from the Jesuit Order to live at his small family estate near Brest. There he worked as a judge at a local court and opened a school for children at his own expense, where he also taught. But he had another life, hidden from the public. He spent a lot of his time studying books by ancient philosophers and thinkers of the Renaissance, and theological and scientific treatises. In them he was searching for answers to dangerous "sinful" questions. In 1674 Lyshchinskiy started writing a treatise entitled *On the non-existence of God*. In it he wrote that nature existed and developed according to its own laws, without God's involvement or the involvement of any other supernatural forces. He rejected the Christian dogmas and denounced the greed and hypocrisy of his contemporary clergymen who considered themselves carriers of higher truths and morals. But he was unable to keep his work secret. It transpired that the Jesuits did not leave their former associate unattended. It was clear from the materials on the court case that they placed Kasimir Lyshchinskiy under surveillance. The information that they collected spoke of Lyshchinskiy's changing outlook on the world: "... Ignoring the secrecy of our Christian brother, he gave his daughter away to marry a relative, ...made a will in which he ordered that his body be burned after death, ... he does not go to church, and does not donate money for charitable affairs..." (59).

His neighbour and friend Yan Bzhoska, who incidentally owed 100,000 thalers (a type of silver coin) to the secret atheist, assisted the Jesuits in dealing with Lyshchinskiy. He stole fifteen notebooks on the rebellious treatise from Lyshchinskiy and also seized from him his library of books by Calvinist theologians. In 1687, on the basis of the denunciation by Yan Bzhoska, the "criminal" was arrested and imprisoned in Vilno. The nobility in Brest were angry and protested that an nobleman of high society should be judged by the ecclesiastical court, and that the case needed to be brought before the Polish *Sejm*. In Warsaw on 15 February 1689 the *Sejm* started the proceedings against Lyshchinskiy. The case lasted for several weeks. The Pope's nuncio Jeromy Cantelni and other bishops of the Catholic church demanded the death penalty. The majority of deputies voted in favour of him being burned at the stake. The final ruling read: "The 265 pages of the atheist treatise written by Lyshchinskiy shall go up in flames, and he shall hold them in his right hand while standing on the scaffold. The condemned atheist shall be reduced to ashes. His property shall be confiscated and divided between the informer and the state treasury. The house in which the condemned atheist wrote this folly, as a haven of the madman, shall be destroyed". King Jan Sobieski showed mercy on him and ordered that he be beheaded rather than burned at the stake. On 30 March 1689, in the old market square in Warsaw, the sentence was carried out. Newspapers across France, Italy and Sweden all carried stories on the execution of the Belarusian freethinker.

———————◆———————

The main focus of the cultural development of all European nations during the Enlightenment was the resolute secularisation of all spheres of spiritual life. And the Polish-Lithuanian Commonwealth was no exception to this. The Commonwealth was already on the brink of collapse, but it continued to seek salvation through major reforms, including in the field of education.

In Belarus in the mid-18th century there were about thirty secondary schools and seventeen Jesuit colleges. The Jesuits still played a leading role in the educational sphere. They had maintained a good reputation for a long time, they had experienced tutors and educators, and the Jesuit colleges were held up as examples of educational institutions to be used by schools of other orders.

In the 1720s Piarist Schools started to appear in Belarusian cities. Unlike the Jesuits, they did not simply follow to the Catholic teaching orientation, but also offered secular and civil, and even physical, education.

The luminary and scientist Stanislav Kanarskiy (1700-1773) started a process of structural reform across secondary and higher education. Under his leadership new teaching programmes were developed and textbooks were written and published. In the end, the Jesuits could no longer ignore these new developments and so the colleges started to teach geography, physics and foreign languages. So as to not lose their edge to the Piarists, the Jesuits opened a new prestigious college in Vilno where wider educational fields were taught far more than religious subjects. Students were also taught dance and fencing.

After the Pope suppressed the Order of Jesuits in 1773, school educational reform continued at a considerable pace. In 1773 Warsaw set up Europe's first state ministry of education, called the Education

Committee. This committee had authority over all schools and all of the assets of the now defunct Order of Jesuits.

The main objective of the Education Committee was not just educational reform, but the creation of an entirely new system. This system had to be state-run and logical. First of all, it set itself the task of creating secondary education institutions that would provide basic knowledge for further enrolment at a university. The need for the complete secularisation of the education was reflected by its motto: "The youth are not for the church, but for the people". The Education Committee cancelled the teaching of religious education in school curricula. In all new secondary schools they introduced natural sciences, foreign languages, and physical education, with all theological subjects being excluded from the teaching programme. To create new textbooks an Elementary Books Partnership was set up under the Education Committee, guided by experience from French educational reforms. The largest problem for a long time was the lack of secular teachers; schools were still largely run by former Jesuits and monks as there was simply no other choice. They offered their services as guides for the new policies and reforms, but in actual fact often sabotaged the new system and did not follow the instructions of the Education Committee. The nobility, still faithful to the ideas of Sarmatism, and therefore hostile towards any changes affecting the "old order", did not react well to the reforms. Parents often forbade their children from learning using the new textbooks, and their protest frequently found support in the monks working as teachers at schools. There were lingering conflicts in schools. The Education Committee regularly sent its employees to inspect schools, and in the name of the government literally forced schools to adopt the new teaching principles.

The reorganisation of the school system in Belarus was overseen by state chancellor Ioakhim Khraptovich (60) and bishop Ignat Massalskiy. Khraptovich once said: "Education is the training of the heart and the mind. I am not about to explain to the nobility what a pitiable state our country is in at the present time. The citizens make the state how it is. But whatever shape the education of our youth takes, this is what will shape how they are as citizens".

Despite the difficulties, the school reforms were rapid and successful. Belarusian children had already been going to school for generations, and the trend of foreign tutors which was so widespread in Russia had not caught on in Belarus. There were of course a lot of foreign tutors, but as a rule they worked in schools teaching foreign languages or subjects related to their professional training: theatre, music, ballet, medicine and military-based studies. The rapid development of such vocational training was characteristic of the Enlightenment. For example, in Grodno, the efforts of Antoni Tyzenhauz (1733-1785), who for several years was the city elder, brought about the opening of an accounting and medicine school, which the French scientist Jean Gilbert (1741-1814) was invited to head. Over a short period of time he created a rich research library, natural sciences laboratory and anatomical theatre. Gilbert planted the first botanical garden in Belarus in Grodno, bedding more than two thousand plants, including numerous rare and exotic species. He encouraged his students to study the flora and fauna of their native land and to collect and study minerals. In 1781 his research was published in two volumes entitled *The Flora of Lithuania*. Antoni Tyzenhauz financed numerous progressive initiatives and, in the end, unfortunately went bankrupt. But thanks to him, by the end of the 18th century Grodno had come to play a major role as a Belarusian centre for culture and science.

In their homes in Nesvizh, Slutsk and Minsk Belarusian barons started to open music, theatre and ballet schools to train theatre artists. These schools were attended by serf and lower middle class children, and after their education they would move to another, more educated and affluent class. But despite this, the serfs were extremely reluctant to send their children to such schools, largely because they wanted their children to stay at home so that they would have more pairs of hands available for work.

The fashion of owning theatres gripped the Polish and Belarusian aristocracy. The Radziwiłłs, Sapiehas, Ogińskis and Tyzenhaus all had their own theatres. They constructed separate buildings on their estates to house the theatres, and often Italian and German architects and landscape artists would be brought in by the barons for the work.

In 1773 the Education Committee began to reform the only higher education institute in Belarus, the Academy of Sciences in Vilno. After the dissolution of the Jesuit Order the Academy was falling into decay. The Academy was transformed into the Graduate School of the Grand Principality of Lithuania (Schola Princeps Magni Ducatus Lithuania). In addition to the three already existing faculties (theology, philosophy and law), the Graduate School began work on two new (both in terms of name and content) sciences: the faculty of natural sciences and the faculty of moral sciences. At the first they taught mathematics, astronomy, physics, chemistry, mechanics, geography, medicine and education, and at the faculty of moral science they read history, literature, philosophy, rhetoric, theology and jurisprudence. The structure of the new Graduate School cleared showed that the main aim of the reorganisation of the higher education structure was secularisation. The theological sciences that once reigned supreme in the Academy now only occupied a modest position. The rector of the new academy was the scientist and astronomy M. Pochobut-Odlyanitskiy (1728-1810) (61). He was born in Grodno and graduated from a Jesuit college in the city. He then taught in Polotsk, studied at the Academy of Sciences in Vilno, further developed his knowledge of astronomy in Germany, and received the title of correspondent member of the Paris Academy of Sciences. His works on astronomy were well known across Europe. In 1764 he became a professor of the Academy of Sciences in Vilno, where he headed its reformation as rector. In the 20 years of his governance at the Graduate School he formed a strong team of professors made up of a new generation of academics.

Under the leadership of M. Pochobut-Odlyanitskiy an astronomical observatory was built in Vilno, one of the first in Europe. From the observatory they studied sun spots, developed a method to calculate the distance between the Earth and the Sun, and many numerous important scientific discoveries for the time.

The ideas of the Enlightenment could not fail to incite some resistance among former Jesuits, and this was reflected in the numerous scientific works of the professors at the Graduate School. For example, in was only in 1788 that a student of M. Pochobut, A. Stretskiy, decided to openly lecture students in the department on the relevance of the heliocentric system proposed by Copernicus and its scientific credibility. Unable to endure the struggle with supporters of the "ideological purity of the faith", the Italian professor of medicine S. Bizio and the German naturalist and ethnographer of world renown I. Forster were forced to leave the Graduate School. But, leaving Vilno, they left behind not only their opponents, but also hundreds of grateful students who then became teachers themselves.

The Age of Enlightenment changed the relationship between Man and his external reality, and with it there were significant changes in the development of philosophical thought. Gradually it came to be freed from the dictates of theology and scholasticism. One of the first Belarusian philosophers who adhered to the ideas of the Enlightenment was a professor at the Graduate School, K. Narbut (1738-1807).

The library played a key role in the dissemination of Enlightenment ideas. The richest of the libraries was the Radziwiłłs' library in Nesvizh, founded in 1600. It held more than 20,000 books in almost all European languages. There were ancient and rare manuscripts, works by ancient poets and philosophers, treatises from Western European luminaries, and ancient historical chronicles. One of them was the *Radziwiłł Chronicle* of the 13th Century, describing the history of the Vladimir-Suzdal Principality. After the first division of the Polish-Lithuanian Commonwealth in 1772 this library was seized and transferred to St. Petersburg on the orders of the Russian Empress Catherine the Great. It was later transferred to the Academy of Sciences in St. Petersburg, and according to the inventory it had 14,892 books, not including prints, cards and notes.

The second largest library in Belarus was a library in Shchors, in baron Khraptovich's family palace. It held 6,000 books, manuscripts and maps of Lithuania, Poland and Belarus. Among its unique historical rarities were correspondence between Bogdan Khmelnitskiy and the Polish government, a journal of the Polish Embassy in Russia, and a diary of Marina Mnishek, the wife of Tsar False Dmitriy.

From the second half of the 18th century the library started to receive works by European Enlightenment authors: Diderot's encyclopaedia, and books by Voltaire and Rousseau. All students and scholars were able to visit these libraries.

Thus, the second half of the 18th century in Belarus was a time of significant change in the sphere of education, social thought and the sciences. The cultural space of the once habitual Sarmatian ideology had been destroyed and became a thing of the past. The public consciousness quickly came to be penetrated and developed by the ideals of the Enlightenment, and especially the ideas of scientific omnipotence. The prestige of education and learning, to which the Sarmatians for many centuries did not attach any great importance, increased dramatically. Moreover, learning was no longer associated only with the church and monasticism; it came to be characteristic of secular culture.

The third and final division of the Polish-Lithuanian Commonwealth halted all of these processes, or at the very least took them in a different direction. The Education Committee was eliminated, but it still left behind a functioning, progressive education system, thousands of freshly educated specialists and a good reputation for its work.

CHAPTER 3
Literature and theatre

THE GRADUAL SHIFT OF A SIGNIFICANT NUMBER OF BELARUSIAN nobles to Catholicism or the Uniate Church changed the course of development of Belarusian ethnic culture, as it was primarily members of this class which were leading figures in science, education and literature. The increasing Polonisation of Belarusians took place under the auspices of state policies and a well-run religious structure headed by the Pope. In 1696 the *Sejm* of the Polish-Lithuanian Commonwealth removed the status of the Belarusian language as an official language in the Grand Principality of Lithuania which it had enjoyed until then. From then on, all institutional documentation and paperwork had to be written in Polish. The Belarusian language gradually came to be the language spoken in peasant households and city suburbs. The displacement of the Belarusian language from official use had a negative, and arguably even catastrophic, impact on the development of Belarus' spiritual culture. National roots were stripped out of literature, which at the time was in a period of transition from mediaeval traditions to the ideals of the new era, towards Enlightenment literature.

Since the struggle between Orthodoxy and Catholicism had not stopped, but rather took on more and more new forms, it provided a good basis for the development of polemical publicism. The most prominent representative of this genre was Meletiy Smotritskiy (1572–1633). He studied at the Faculty of Philosophy at the Academy of Sciences in Vilno and attended lectures at Württemberg and Leipzig universities. Smotritskiy came to be famous not as a scientist, although he did leave behind a number of scientific papers, but as a talented writer and polemicist. To his contemporaries, the book *Weeping* prompted a heated debate about what religion means to public life. In his work Smotritskiy called on the people, on behalf of his mother church, to remain faithful to the Orthodox faith and not to make any compromises with the Catholic Church. The retreat from the Orthodox Church was seen by him as a direct betrayal of his church, and therefore his homeland Belarus. Despite its categorical nature, the book was written in a bright, excited and persuasive language, and caused widespread controversy in the community. In his work, Smotritskiy proved himself to be a highly educated man, citing or mentioning 140 authors: Orthodox and Catholic father figures, ancient philosophers, as well as Western writers and scholars.

The patriotic appeals of Smotritskiy worried King Sigismund III Vasa of Poland. In 1610 he banned the sale and purchase of the book *Weeping* on threat of punishment. The authorities in Vilno were ordered by the King to close the Orthodox printing house publishing the book, confiscate its property, and burn all of the books in the shop. And they did so.

In 1618 Smotritskiy's main scientific paper was published, *A Slavonic Grammar*, which for almost two centuries was the main textbook for all educational institutions in Eastern Europe. Smotritskiy's *Grammar* formed the basis for a number of subsequent Slavonic grammars published abroad: Heinrich Ludolph (Oxford, 1696), Ilya Kopievich (Amsterdam, 1706), and Stefan Vuyanovskiy (Vienna, 1793).

Meletiy Smotritskiy was not only a writer but a translator too. Through his translations Belarusian readers were able to read the poetry of Petrarch and the works of Erasmus of Rotterdam.

The Enlightenment brought about a revitalisation of social thought, and with it a new genre, the political pamphlet and political satire. Stefan Zizaniy (1550-1634) wrote the pamphlets *The Apocalypse*, *The Little Book on the Roman Church* and *The Protection of Orthodoxy from Papistry* in which he ruthlessly exposed the hypocrisy of the Pope and Catholic bishops. He was also critical of the secular authorities in

Poland, and the Catholic church for their social, religious and national oppression of the Belarusian people. He was an outspoken opponent of the Union of Brest in 1596, and after its adoption decided to stop writing.

Afanasiy of Brest (1595-1648), an Orthodox abbot at the monastery in Brest, wrote a collection of biographical articles entitled *Diariush*. In the form of a diary he wrote about the complex and controversial times in the history of Belarus and offered his views on the Union of Brest and its subsequent implications for the Orthodox Church. Describing the facts and events of his life, Afanasiy of Brest criticised the Polish authorities for their pursuit of luxury and corruption. He described members of the Catholic Church as hypocrites and liars. The author's sympathies were on the side of the lower classes, and he felt that a better future for the Belarusian people lay with a future as part of Orthodox Russia.

After the uprising of Bogdan Khmelnitskiy, whose goal was to reunify Ukraine, Belarus and Russia, Afanasiy of Brest was suspected of having links with the rebels and arrested. In prison, they tried for a long time to force him to abandon Orthodoxy and to adopt the Catholic or Uniate faith, but he categorically refused. The execution was brutal: he was buried alive. In 1984, Afanasiy of Brest was made a Belarusian saint.

Unfortunately, far from all of the authors of the 17th century are known. In Belarusian literature there are hundreds of anonymous works, especially those which harshly critiqued society and the government. These include *A Letter to Obukhovich*. In this narrative the anonymous author creates a fictional literary character, the Belarusian governor Filipp Obukhovich, and writes a damning critique of him. The author highlights the complete lack of the commander's military talent, his greed, corruption, and his indifference to the fate of his homeland Belarus. The author writes not only that Filipp Obukhovich is incompetent, but that his father and grandfather were too, and he argues that the lack of morality and the decline of one family leads to the decline of society.

Poetry evolved relatively slowly in Belarusian literature. All of its various genres were published: epigrams, epics, lyric poetry, and religious verse, but they were not popular. The poem *Crying over the death of the poet Lyavon Karpovich*, whose author is unknown, was reprinted numerous times. It was written in a Baroque style, with colourful epithets and metaphors. In it the poet praises man as the carrier of good moral qualities, and for being courageous and willing to sacrifice himself for the sake of his ideals.

An important role in the development of Belarusian literature was played by Simeon of Polotsk (1629-1680), a spiritual writer, poet, playwright and publisher. He was born in Polotsk into a merchant family and went to study at the Academy of Sciences in Vilno. Polotsk supported the idea of a peaceful alliance between the Catholic and Orthodox churches in the form of the Union, and so he took to following the Uniate faith throughout his life. After his studies, he returned from Vilno to Polotsk where he took up monasticism and started to work as a teacher at the school where he had once studied. At the school he created a theatre, for which he personally wrote interludes and dramas. In 1656 the Russian Tsar Aleksey Mikhailovich visited Polotsk and Simeon of Polotsk had the great of honour of reading his welcoming verses to the tsar. Evidently, the tsar remembered this erudite and talented monk, as he later invited him to Moscow to work in a school at the Kremlin, and later became the tutor for the tsar's own children.

Simeon of Polotsk took advantage of his influential position in the royal court at the Kremlin to try to change the style and content of the Church's sermons, making it less formal, more lively and interesting. In his sermons he started to talk about the meaning of human life, the dignity of simple labour, the little joys of everyday life and values. At the time this was unthinkable in both Orthodox and Protestant sermons. The Orthodox Church was highly suspicious of the erudite Belarusian monk. Simeon of Polotsk felt the same way towards the church: the official Orthodox line with its conservatism and lack of recognition for the sciences was entirely alien to him. He was oppressed with severe orders from Moscow. All the time he had to keep in mind the fact that if, in his homeland of Belarus, the religious struggle took place in the form of theological polemics and disputes, then the dissidents in Moscow would simply have their tongues cut out.

But in the dangerous and stifling atmosphere of Moscow Simeon of Polotsk continued to serve the ideals of the Enlightenment. He opened his own printing house, free from the censorship of the Patriarch, and drafted plans for a higher education institute which would later be used when creating Moscow University, Russia's first university. He wrote and published odes, eulogies, elegies, hymns, and epitaphs; in short, he found success in all genres of poetry. His collection of poems entitled *Multicoloured Vetrograd* was a shining example of the literary Baroque. In fact, the Belarusian poet Simeon of Polotsk was actually the founder of Russian poetry.

In the field of theology, he also left a great legacy: more than 200 of Simeon of Polotsk's sermons were published after his death in the years 1681-1683 in two collections: *Dinner for the Soul* and *Supper for the Soul*.

As a playwright Simeon was famous for two plays: *The Comedy of the Prodigal Son* and *The Tragedy of King Nebuchadnezzar*. The language of these plays was lively and ironic.

The socio-political ideals of the poet and writer were focused on a strong state led by an enlightened monarch. He believed that all of the evil that was going on in society was down to ignorance and was convinced that the development of the sciences and education among the general population would some day lead to harmony and peace in the population. In his lyric poems he often wrote about his Belarusian hometown, Polotsk.

———————◆———————

In the 18th century Belarus entered a period of decline. The endless wars that were being fought on its territory, albeit not for its own interests, were ravaging Belarus. Cities were destroyed, hundreds of villages ceased to exist, and fields were left empty. At the same time, Belarus was going through a deep-rooted social crisis. The political system of the Polish-Lithuanian Commonwealth was a huge obstacle to the progressive development of the country. Outwardly, everything looked good, and even Voltaire and Rousseau, looking from afar, considered the "gentry republic" an example for other nations. But internally, anarchy reigned in the country.

In his memoirs, S. Moravskiy curiously wrote that Rousseau was even considering moving to live in Belarus. The Grodno baron A. Tyzenhaus promised to build him an idyllic home and to protect the great French philosopher from all of life's worries. However, his plan was thwarted by another Belarusian, a certain Vyazhevich. He tracked down which road Rousseau loved to walk down, sat down and started to cry loudly, lamenting his fate and poverty. The sentimental philosopher was deeply moved and took Vyazhevich into his home to work as his secretary and instructed him to bring in visitors to see him. Many of the visitors came with gifts for Rousseau, which Vyazhevich then kept for himself. Learning of this, Rousseau turned out his dishonest secretary and stopped thinking about his idyllic cottage in Belarus, thinking that everyone in Belarus must be liars and cheats like Vyazhevich.

———◆———

The 18th century was a frontier between the Old and the New eras. Mediaeval relapses gradually gave way to the Enlightenment. From the mid-18th century Belarus started to recover, implementing reforms in education, and changing civil ideals. Jesuits started to become the target for criticism and ridicule. Traditional Sarmatians – fanatical and uneducated – gradually started to disappear from the historical scene. In their place, these narrow-minded and conservative men hostile to all that was new came to be replaced by men of understanding and reason. Education, rationalism and humanism became the new social values of the time. Works by the French philosophers Voltaire and Rousseau started to be published in Belarus. The priest Stanislav Shantyr from Slutsk (62) begrudgingly wrote: "The countless books of Voltaire and Rousseau have found themselves in Belarus where they have been read with enthusiasm in their original form or in translation by passionate followers of French philosophy; the works are passed from one person to another, capturing minds, particularly among the youthful, but even among the ladies. Everyone wants to follow this new-fangled sophism which is distorting and destroying our faith".

In the last decade of the 18th century, the fashion of speaking in French quickly spread among the upper echelons of Belarusian society. In the wake of the Enlightenment, together with the penetration of leading Western philosophical ideas, blind worship and imitation of all that was Western European gained strength. The gentry was literally split into two camps. The "Cosmopolitan" gentry started to feel ashamed of their own language, their traditional dress and their table customs. The "Patriots" were strong critics of the "Cosmopolitans" and strictly stuck to their old traditions. "The people in caftans and fur shapkas and the people in evening-dress and top hats were almost like two separate nations which do not resemble each other in the least", wrote one memoir (63).

All literature in Belarus in the 18th century was multilingual. Books were published in Polish, Belarusian, French, German, Russian and Yiddish. In spite of all the impediments, Belarusian literature was still preserved, and oral folklore – stories, songs, epics – even took on new forms. The tales began to reflect social issues where the rich and the poor were radically opposed to one another, and there were a lot of tales with anti-Catholic content, where the Pope was portrayed as a villain. A new genre of epic came into being, taking the form of a long historical song about events which were still recent and alive in the memories of the people, such as the popular Cossack uprisings, the adventures of False Dmitriy, or the battles with the Swedes. These developments interested people more than, say, ancient epics about the Kievan Rus era.

From the 16th century Belarus had already had Batleika, or puppet theatre. The puppet shows were presented in a small specially-built miniature two-story house with a mezzanine. On the top floor they staged scenes from the Bible and Gospels, scenes about Adam and Eve, or even scenes about the birth of Jesus. On the middle floor they would depict scenes of King Herod's evil deeds or the suffering of saints. And on the bottom floor they would show scenes from everyday life. The hero of the interludes was often a simple Belarusian peasant, a simple-minded, simple, sympathy-evoking and compassionate individual. All Batleika performances were accompanied by music and singing. Special musical or vocal pieces would be performed before each show and during breaks.

In the early 17th century the first theatres started to appear. At first they were set up at educational institutions, schools and colleges. The appearance of theatres brought with it the creation of numerous rules and regulations wrote by local officials, for example: "At the theatre it is forbidden to eat and drink, it is forbidden to stamp your feet, it is forbidden to show anything that would be unacceptable for the actors themselves to play and for the audience to watch…". According to the regulations shows could not last more than three hours. Initially, female characters were generally not permitted in plays, and later they were only allowed to be performed by men.

In the second half of the 18th century, serf theatre came to be an important development in the cultural life of Belarus. Major Belarusian land owners such as the Radziwiłłs, Ogińskis, Tyshkevichs and Sapiehas vied with each other to see which of them would have the most luxurious theatre and the best theatre actors. Sometimes as many as two hundred people would work at the theatres: actors, dancers, ballerinas, musicians, painters, decorators, prop craftsmen, dressmakers, etc. By way of example, Michał Ogiński's theatre had 106 musicians, and for several years the great Austrian composer F. Haydn directed the orchestra. Ogiński's theatre stage was so large that it was even capable of staging battles on horseback or lighting up fountains with sparklers. Even more magnificent was the theatre of the Radziwiłłs in

Nesvizh. Winter performances were played at a specially constructed luxury palace, and in the summer they took place at the "green theatre", situated on the natural slopes of a hill and able to accommodate up to one thousand spectators. The theatre owners themselves would often catch the creative fever and act for themselves on their own stages. The Radziwiłł family was a prime example. Many even wrote plays or composed music. To this very day the *Ogiński Polonaise*, written for the serf theatre and formerly called *Farewell to the Motherland*, is still popular. Theatres staged plays by Molière and Voltaire, and in 1778 the first Belarusian multi-act play with the simple name *Comedy* was written by K. Morashevskiy. Many theatres had their own ballet and music schools where they taught peasant children, as acting was still for a long time viewed as a lowly occupation, unbecoming for the gentry and aristocracy. These schools trained dancers and musicians not only for further work in their own theatres, but also sent their graduates to perform in theatres in Warsaw, Berlin and St. Petersburg, and often made a wonderful career for themselves there.

The ability to play musical instruments was an integral part of education for noble children. The widow of Mikhail Radziwiłł lived in his palace in Nesvizh with twenty courtiers, and they all gave concerts and wrote music. Young nobles would play the piano, harp and guitar. Various different types of musical instrument were common in villages among the rural population. Violins, pipes and cymbals were all played at restaurants, festivals and social gatherings.

In terms of secular music of the time, the most popular form was the canticle, which was a type of polyphonic secular song. Music from Western Europe was also popular: divertissements, serenades, arias from operas and symphonies. In the second half of the 16th century a print house in Nesvizh started to publish sheet music collections and books on choral singing and vocals. And it was in Nesvizh that the first musical instrument production workshop was set up in Belarus.

CHAPTER 4
Social portraits of the 18th century

B ARONS. IN THE POLISH-LITHUANIAN COMMONWEALTH, A FEUDAL
state, all of the power, both political and economic, lay with the
gentry. In contrast with the gentry of Western Europe, the Polish,
Ukrainian and Belarusian gentry were larger in number. In the late 18th
century, during the division of the Polish-Lithuanian Commonwealth,
the gentry made up about ten per cent of the country's inhabitants
(the gentry accounted for about two per cent of the Western European
population).

In terms of property, the gentry was extremely varied. At the one
extreme were the barons, owners of vast latifundia, towns and villages,
and at the other there was the petty gentry, whose estate was often just
a small house and a plot of land. This petty gentry filled various posts
for the barons, ranging from clerks to grooms. At the time, a popular
proverb said: "A poor gentleman will have a boot on one foot and the
other in a bast sandal". But between these two extremes there was the
middle gentry, those who owned perhaps one or two villages.

But still, despite the huge inequality in wealth, the gentry was
still all one class with common rights and privileges. Firstly, they had
the right to own land and serfs (the petty bourgeoisie did not have
this right). Only the gentry could hold public office and be elected as
delegates to the *Sejm*, both in its local and national form. The gentry
were in charge of all local affairs through the local *Sejms* (they were
called *Sejmiks*), where even the least powerful gentry had the same
voting rights as barons. Members of the gentry had to take part in all

wars waged by the Polish Crown. However, the gentry was prohibited by law from taking up a trade. If someone were to ignore this law then it was assumed that "he had humiliated his class with an unworthy business and should therefore be deprived of the title of noble, thereby moving into the class of petty bourgeoisie".

The Polish-Lithuanian Commonwealth did not have any noble titles: prince, earl, baron, marquis, etc. Formally, all of the gentry were equals and addressed one another as "brother". But in reality, the barons and petty gentry were divided by a social chasm.

The barons owned tens of thousands of hectares of land, towns, villages and thousands of serfs. Their palaces were filled with enormous riches. This is what was written in a memoir on the treasures found in the Radziwiłłs' palace in Nesvizh: "The collection occupied three huge halls. They were filled with paintings and tapestries, weapons, hats with precious jewels, clocks, marshal staffs, shields and swords in gold sheaths. There were twelve wooden horses with luxurious seats and golden harnesses, Egyptian mummies and ancient Indian ornaments. Many hours could be spent in these halls looking at these rarities".

Hundreds of people served in the court and palace of a baron. The service was honorary or paid. Nobles occupied the paid roles of secretaries, messengers, guards, valets and officials. There was even such a service as coming to the palace in the morning and waiting for further instructions. This honour could also only be awarded to nobles. All other services fell to the serfs.

Each baron had their own army. Geronim Radziwiłł had an army of six thousand men, made up of cavalry and infantry. In addition, he could also quickly raise another six thousand Cossacks and soldiers bearing firearms, known as *streltsy* (literally, 'shooters').

Owing to the tremendous wealth and property of barons' armies, they considered themselves superior to all, even the King himself, who was none other than the protégé that they themselves elected to the throne at the *Sejm*, a decision which could be reversed at any time.

The arrogance of the barons knew no bounds. They only considered those who were *"bene natus et posessionaltus et catholicus"* (Latin for 'noble landowner and Catholic') to be fully-fledged human beings. The barons genuinely believed that the lower middle class and peasants, both physically and mentally, were other creatures because they were not derived from the Biblical noble Japheth, but from the lowly Ham. The Polish and Belarusian languages still retain the word "ham" as a synonym for a vile and rude person.

The 18th century saw a distinct physical and moral degeneration of the barons. A century before it was considered a great honour and joy to have many children, and yet now brothers Geronim and Karol Radziwiłł died childless, with their many wives also having many lovers. Mental disorders, sadism and debauchery started to become commonplace. In the 16th and 17th centuries barons often had to fight, and the ideals of military prowess were very high. But in the 18th century the elite preferred to spend their time holding endless balls and hunting (64).

Among the numerous Belarusian baron families, the leading position, in terms of wealth, and in terms of the public offices held, of course lay with the Radziwiłłs. Their family legends spoke of their ancestry descending from the Roman emperors, but in reality the first mention of their family in the chronicles was in 1401. The power of the Radziwiłłs began in 1547 when King Sigismund Augustus of Poland married Barbara Radziwiłł. Her brothers Mikołaj "the Red" and Mikołaj "the Black" immediately took up high-ranking positions, and from that time the political influence of the Radziwiłłs in the court only grew. Mikołaj "the Black" became the leader of the Reformation in Belarus and spent a lot of money opening print houses and Protestant churches. His son Mikołaj "the Orphan" decided to "atone for the sins of his father", as a hater of Protestantism, and closed all of the print houses, mercilessly seeking out all of the books published in them, burning them in their thousands.

All of the Radziwiłłs clearly had their own fair share of literary talent. Starting with Mikołaj "the Orphan" Radziwiłł, they all left behind literary works, often in the form of diaries or memoirs. The book *Journey* by Mikołaj "the Orphan", in which he described his pilgrimage to Jerusalem, was translated into many languages. Michał Radziwiłł Rybenko kept a diary every day for thirty years, resulting in a work of ten thousand pages. Memoirs were written by the wife of Martin Radziwiłł, Marta Trembitskaya. All of these works offer a wealth of material about the lifestyle, customs and beliefs of the Radziwiłł family and their surroundings. A short description of some of these accounts is given below.

Maciej Radziwiłł was remarkable for his progressive views, expressing his strong support for the new constitution of 3 May 1791 and taking part in the uprising of Tadeusz Kościuszko after the first division of Poland. He did not come empty-handed to serve the rebels; he brought his army with him. All of the serfs who voluntarily came to serve as soldiers were freed from the serfdom. After the defeat of the uprising, he returned to live in his palace, and the Tsarina, Catherine the Great, did not dare punish him. In his old age Maciej Radziwiłł wrote literary works, and in particular he wrote the libretto for the opera *Agatha* in which he wrote that "the serfs feed us all" and therefore also have the right to a life of dignity and respect. When the opera was staged in Warsaw, the libretto was heavily censored.

Ulrik Radziwiłł had a very likeable personality. He had a keen interest in mechanics and astronomy, wrote poetry, and translated German authors into Polish and Belarusian. His contemporaries considered him eccentric and original. He commissioned a local artist to paint a portrait of a beautiful lady, and he spent many days playing hymns on the piano to this portrait as his fictional ideal. He married at the age of fifty to a young poor neighbour, which caused anger and resentment in the whole family. Even at his old age Ulrik Radziwiłł wrote an entirely frivolous *Guide to the cost of love*, in which he used his own experience of love, but also borrowed from French authors, who, in this genre, could not be beaten.

His cousin Martin Radziwiłł was rather peculiar. In his youth he took an interest in the natural sciences, especially chemistry. Gradually, his interest grew into a fanatical belief in mysticism and alchemy, and he started looking for a "philosopher's stone" to turn base metals into gold. His madness manifested itself in his sexual promiscuity and violent reprisals against the people. In his court he created a harem of young peasant serfs whom he starved. They lived in the basement, slept on straw and wore nothing but rags. Obviously, expecting Jesus not to forgive him of his sins, in his old age he turned to Judaism. Every Friday at his home he would gather together Jews for secret rituals. Terrible rumours circulated about these events. In the end, the madman's conduct exasperated his relatives and his powers were transferred from Chernivtsi to Slutsk and he was placed under the guardianship of his cousin Geronim Radziwiłł. The situation was so absurd that it later transpired that Geronim was also a maniac and a sadist.

Memoir literature provides extensive material about the life of this baron and his exceptional cruelty. Having received a huge inheritance in his youth, he spent several years in Germany. After returning to his palace in Slutsk he established German order there. He was constantly at loggerheads with the local gentry. Geronim once saw through the window that a court gentleman was walking back and forth along the fence. "Why do you keep walking here all the time?" Geronim asked. The courtier ingratiatingly replied: "I want to be seen so that I can serve you at all times". This angered Geronim, and he ordered that the man be hanged directly on the gate. The order was carried out immediately. "Now you will be seen for a long time," Geronim said to the hapless victim before his death, and for several days the corpse hung on the gate. Considering himself to be a great figure, Geronim Radziwiłł built his own equestrian monuments in his park. He married three times, but left no offspring after his death.

Of course, it cannot be said that the barons in the 18th century were not beneficial to society. There were active, educated, creative individuals among them and it did not suit these people to spend their lives hunting and holding balls. Antoni Tyzenhaus founded work houses and opened a medical school in Grodno, Anna Radziwiłł modernised the agriculture in her estate and the peasants led prosperous lives there, and Michał Oginski wrote music. But in general, the psychological portrait of the barons is suggestive of the degeneration of this class.

MIDDLE AND PETTY GENTRY. The social psychology of the middle and petty gentry was extremely complicated, with highly opposite and conflicting origins. On the one hand, the gentry was proud of their class unity with the barons and their right to participate in public decision-making. On the other hand, they had to serve the barons, were financially dependent on them and often experienced all sorts of humiliation. Formal equality was in fact fictional. The gentry could sit at a table with a baron and drink with him, but the gentry would have to sit in the right place, designated by the baron.

The land owned by barons amounted to tens of thousands of hectares, whereas the petty gentry had only small plots, which was the subject of a popular joke at the time: "If a dog settles down comfortably for a sleep on one plot of land then its tail is bound to be on someone else's land".

The most numerous group among this class were the court gentry which performed various functions in the baron's court. Their payment for their services just about allowed them to make ends meet. The other group was the tenant gentry. They would receive a plot of land from a baron and the payment for the plot would largely depend on the will of the owner. Therefore, the gentry were constantly at loggerheads with one another to better serve their master and to get a tastier piece of the pie at their master's table for a lower price. But even with the land they had, the gentry were not able to and could not manage the economy in good faith. The Sarmatian arrogance did not allow them to carry out day-to-day duties, as it was far more important to show off to one another on the back of a horse with an expensive harness and wearing a hat with an artificial diamond.

The gentry's homes were untidy and dirty, but there always had to be a couple of portraits of ancestors and sabres in gold sheaths hanging from the walls. The poorest of the gentry envied the middle gentry and tried as best they could to live the way of the Polish landowners, and the middle gentry envied the barons and imitated them at least by wearing expensive clothes and fake jewels.

Economic dependence gave rise to political dependence. The barons always got the votes of the local gentry which were reliant on the barons for their living. The gentry voted at the *Sejm* not according to their own convictions on a particular matter, but according to the wishes of their local baron. Rebellious gentry were easy to punish: they could be deprived of their land, dismissed from their services, have their home destroyed by the baron's soldiers, and even given a thrashing. And as a general rule, such acts by barons would often go unpunished.

Above all, the gentry were afraid of somebody questioning their noble origins. In the 17th and 18th centuries false genealogies started to be produced *en masse*. The children of gentry had to learn their own "family tree" by heart from early childhood. The Belarusian and Lithuanian gentry believed that they were descended from Roman emperors, and were very proud of it, compared to the Polish gentry, which allegedly came from the Sarmatians, who were but simple nomads. As a specialist department of heraldry did not exist, and nobody was responsible for checking the genealogy of a family, it was easy to "attach oneself" to a particular noble family.

TOWNSFOLK. In the first half of the 18th century, after many years of war, the Belarusian cities experienced a decline. Their population decreased by almost half. Only from the 1770s onwards did the cities start to grow in line with the economic recovery. After Belarus' annexation by Russia the demographic situation was this: Belarus had 40 major cities and 390 towns with a population of 360,000 people, representing about 10% of the population.

The largest cities were Vilno, Vitebsk, Minsk, Grodno and Mogilev. These were on the banks of large rivers which also served as important trade routes. The cities developed a wide range of crafts and opened more and more new workhouses. Artisans made up about 30-40% of the population in the larger cities and only 15-20% in the smaller cities.

Judging by contemporary descriptions, the most beautiful city was Vilno. In the 18th century there were a lot of stone houses, 40 churches and monasteries and the population totalled more than twenty thousand.

Memoirs from the 18th century give us only a general idea of the lifestyle of the townsfolk, from artisans to merchants and workhouse workers. When these people do appear in literary works it is only in connection with the gentry and related events. These ordinary people, as individuals and personalities, did not attract the attention of writers at the time as they were of no interest to them.

According to literary sources, cities at the time were very unattractive. Rubbish was not cleared away on the streets and the roads were not cobbled. Only a few main streets were paved with cobblestones, and on the rest dust simply swirled around in the summer, and in the spring and autumn the mud made them impassable. Streets had no official names and at night the cities were not lit, so people would have to carry their own lanterns. Homes were largely single-storey and wooden. The palaces of the barons were often neighbouring poor people's homes with thatch roofs. Many townsfolk kept cows, goats and sheep, and so next to many residential buildings there were often stables. The regular, planned development of cities in Belarus did not begin until the early 19th century, after it came to be part of Russia.

As in all other times, the cities were cultural centres, but in the second half of the 18th century there was a change in their cultural significance. Polotsk lost its former prominence, and in 1780 its population was only just over one thousand. By the late 18th century the focal point of European culture came to be the city of Grodno, occupying the leading position in cultural and economic respects.

The most prosperous city residents were the merchants, despite the many rules and laws that restricted trading. For example, the profit margin was determined according to the origins of the merchant. Jews had the right to make only a 3% profit, non-residents 5%, and local residents 7%. Merchants were far more prosperous than other townsfolk and were richer than many petty gentry. This aroused envy among the gentry, and since it was the gentry that made the laws, and no other class, sometimes their laws and decrees were quite simply ridiculous. For example, merchants were forbidden to wear silk clothes, expensive furs, or to build houses with more than one storey. The gentry strove to adopt such measures as if to emphasise their superiority over the merchant class.

In the cities there were plenty of restaurants, and in many it was possible to engage the services of prostitutes. Prostitution was banned and punished extremely severely, and in the memoirs of A. Zhavusskiy we read that the baron Obukhovich ordered that the ears, nose and lips be cut off an old noble women who opened a restaurant in Navahrudak where "amorous meetings were organised".

A special group of townsfolk were the Jews. In 1579 King Stephen Báthory issued a decree giving the Jews the right to engage in trade and craft. In 1679 King Jan Sobieski expanded the rights of the Jews such that they could now buy or rent plots of land to build their own home. Judicial authorities were banned from summoning Jews to court on Saturdays and Jewish holidays, and the city authorities were obliged to provide Jews with protection in the event of any attack. Throughout the 17th century the Jewish population of the cities grew rapidly in Belarus. This was due to continuous migration from Ukraine, where the Jews were regularly subjected to pogroms by the Cossacks, especially during the uprising of Bogdan Khmelnitskiy. The Jews engaged in crafts and trading, and restaurants and inns were popular among Jews. Inns were not just seen as drinking establishments but also like a sort of club. They housed meetings of artisans and were a focal point for news from all around. Nomads would come and tell their stories: pilgrims, elders, monks, and beggars. The Jewish owners knew everything and were necessary both to the gentry and the poor. There were often fights in the inns, and they were often directed against the owners. Drunken guests began trying to persuade the Jews to convert to Christianity and would even throw them out of the home, with the innkeeper sometimes spending all night on the street. But the next day all was forgotten: the townsfolk would again go to the inn to borrow money, make deals and meet friends.

The governing bodies of the cities were the *Rada* and an elected burgomaster, and numerous officials worked on the city council and at other administrative services. They were all from the petty gentry, as the middle classes could not take up even the lowest of government positions. Officials took bribes on everything up for discussion, and it was not just money that they got. It could be clocks, sabres, a beautiful beaded belt, bags of flour, or a barrel of honey. The memoir writer G. Dobrynin describes the daily work of officials at the chancellery of Mogilev as follows: "A few of them sat in the office behind their papers, most just wandered back and forth. Sometimes officials would send out a whole party to a trading area, kick up a fuss, laugh and brush up against passers-by. Then they would return to the chancellery where their favourite thing was to play cards" (65).

PEASANTS. In the Polish-Lithuanian Commonwealth in the 18th century everyone complained of having a hard life: the gentry, the bourgeoisie, officials, merchants and tenants. Even the powerful Radziwiłłs found cause for complaint, arguing that they did not have enough power. But, of course, the lives of the other classes paled into comparison with the life of the peasants. The peasants did not have any rights and were entirely economically dependent on land owners. And in the Polish-Lithuanian Commonwealth there were three main land owners: the gentry, the church and the King of Poland.

The main levies on the serfs were taxes in kind or monetary taxes and statute labour on an owner's land, which was sometimes up to 5 days a week. Economic dependence was combined with full personal dependence. A landowner owned both the body and the soul of peasants: he could marry them at his discretion, sell, exchange, pledge them, separate them from their families, send them off to become recruits, and even subject them to physical punishment. Men cost about 200 roubles and women and girls about 100. By way of comparison, the price of a good horse was 500 roubles.

The Russian General S. Tuchkov in his memoirs described his journey through villages in the Vitebsk district: "The local peasants seem to be the most miserable people on earth. Extreme poverty and total illiteracy reign here. The landowners are remarkable for their excessive pride and tyrannical attitude towards peasants." The author also adds: "If we were to draw up a list of all the barons and landowners together with their numerous servants, monks and nuns, Jews, military and civilian officials, the old and the young and everyone else that does not work the land, it would appear that one peasant has to feed 30 people, if not more".

A serf's property depended on many factors. The first was who the peasant belonged to. Peasants who were owned by a monastery, as a rule, lived in the best conditions and were not subjected to the cruel treatment that many tyrannical landowners handed out. Still, the difference was small: an ordinary peasant at the time would live in a small, dark hut with a clay floor, wear ragged clothes, eat from earthenware crockery and sleep on a straw mattress. Since peasants and their wives had to work their statute labour from dusk until dawn 4-5 days a week, they did not have any chance to establish and maintain their own household. They only had the bare essentials to sustain life: one cow and one horse.

The gentry were convinced that peasants were created solely for physical labour and were not entirely human, often being compared to wild beasts. "It is safer to unleash a hungry tiger or a hyena than to remove a peasant's bridle of full obedience", landowners would say. Only at the end of the 18th century, under the influence of the Enlightenment, do we start to see a new outlook on peasants in literature as a person equal to the other classes. Influenced by the ideas of the French Enlightenment, and especially Rousseau, some landlords started to put these ideas into practice. The writer and educator F. Karpinskiy described in detail in his book *Memoirs* how he, as an owner of several estates in Grodno, went out to work with the peasants in the field, taught the peasant children to read, and never used corporal punishment. But this was a rarity. The great Russian writer Count Lev

Tolstoy did the same in the late 19th century to prove his equality with
the commoners: he worked in the field, taught the peasant children, etc.
But such ideas on equality barely gained any currency on Slavic soil.

The spiritual culture of the peasants, far from education, was centred
primarily around traditions and customs. A peasant would exhibit his
character, his sense of *joie de vivre*, through folk customs and holidays.
The beautiful and poetic rituals that accompanied the life of a peasant
would be passed from generation to generation. Popular culture in the
18th century still retained many Pagan rituals and holidays. Despite
centuries of Christian dominance, both Orthodox and Catholic, in
Belarus both in the 18th century and to this day there are still remnants
of ancient Pagan rituals such as *Maslenitsa* (now frequently known as
Pancake Week), *Kupala* Night, *Dziady* and Christmas carols.

A distinctive feature of Belarusian culture was a celebration of the
summer solstice, the celebration known as *Kupala* Night. It followed
the same pattern for centuries. On 7 July at sunset in a field near each
village large fires would be built, around which young people would
gather, dance and sing. In the evening, women would gather as many
bouquets of flowers as possible. Bouquets would be stuffed in all the
cracks and holes around the house, they would be put in tables and
benches, attached to clothing belts, woven into wreaths and used to
decorate their hair. It was believed that the flowers protected people
from evil spirits. At night the wreaths of flowers would be put in
water, and the most courageous young men and women would go
into the forest in search of fern blossom, which was supposed to bring
happiness.

Christmas Carols (or *Kolyada* in Russian) were celebrated in the
winter. In ancient times it was a celebration of the winter solstice,
and with the adoption of Christianity it was timed to coincide with
Christmas. The holiday started on 25 December and lasted until 6
January. During these days groups of children and youths dressed in
animal costumes would walk up and down the streets with big bags
in hand for gifts. In front of every house they sang songs and staged
performances. The houses went out and generously gave gifts to the

children: biscuits baked in the shape of animal heads, toys, and money. Youngers arranged dances and competitions and burned bonfires and wheels which they sent rolling down hills alight. In the squares they gave puppet theatre performances. At night the girls would guess who they might marry. Christmas Carols was a cheerful and joyful celebration. With regard to the etymology of the word *Kolyada*, there are two theories: either *Kolyada* comes from the Belarusian word *kola*, which means 'wheel', or *Kolyada* was the ancient Pagan God of merriment. On 6 January they would lay hay and money on the table so that they would always have one or the other in future, and would sit down to dinner when the first stars came out. But they would always dine modestly, without music or dancing. The next day, 7 January, was Orthodox Christmas day.

The word *dedy* ('forefathers') refers to the "souls of deceased ancestors". The same word is used to refer to days of remembrance for the dead. *Dedy* was held once a year in Autumn on the first Saturday of November and is a family holiday celebrated at home. People did not go to cemeteries to visit the souls of the deceased, but rather invited them into their own homes. This day was associated with cleanliness and everyone would go to wash at the bath house where they would leave behind a bucket of clean water and a new broom for the souls of the dead. Women prepared a modest dinner; treating people to delicacies in abundance on this day was not accepted. The number of dishes on the table had to be odd. A dish that had to be on the memorial table was *kutya* – wheat porridge with honey – a dish known to all Eastern Slavic peoples. The solemn memorial dinner lasted for a long time, and conversation at the table was only about dead ancestors, remembering them for their best moments, their wise guidance and their good deeds. This happened every year, an information would gradually be passed on to children and grandchildren.

Pagan principles can be clearly detected in all descriptions of folk holidays and festivals. Oddly enough, Belarusian villages still celebrate them to this day, but they are not celebrated in such a consistent and traditional form, as in the past. At *Kupala*, for example, they light bonfires and put a lot of bouquets of flowers around the home, on *Kolyada* they give gifts to children and organise all sorts of games and competitions, and nobody forgets the day for remembering the deceased (*Dedy*) when everyone goes to the graves of their loved ones to honour their memory.

Family was always the basis of a peasant's life. The man played the most important role as the father, master and the main worker. The woman was both a hostess and housewife. The wedding ceremony was the most important holiday in a peasant's life and there were many strict rules for the ceremonies. Wedding times were not arbitrary, but were in fact strictly restricted. Weddings were forbidden during Lent. The best time was considered early Autumn, as the main agricultural activities had been completed and the crops had been harvested.

A child's baptism was one of the happiest occasions in a peasant's life. After a baptism at a church this joyous occasion was celebrated by the entire village and pagan traditions remained at its roots. For example, the new-born was immediately initiated into the land, the family and society: it was placed on the floor (land), taken to an oven (family), and was symbolically beaten (society). The house in which the baby was born had to be visited by all of the villagers and gifts were brought, mainly consisting of food. The baptism, by a poor peasant's standards, was celebrated in quite a rich manner: the peasant would slaughter a pig and buy a barrel of beer.

Thus, for centuries folk spiritual culture remained unchanged, with the original, beautiful and poetic rituals that accompanied a Belarusian peasant throughout his life being passed from generation to generation for many centuries.

CHAPTER 5
Icons and architecture

Paintings in Belarus in the 16th to 18th centuries were an entirely peculiar phenomenon in European art. While in Western Europe, since the Renaissance, there had been rapid development of secular painting, Belarus was still painting only icons. The small-scale influx of genres of secular painting such as the portrait from the 17th century did not receive much popularity and their development continued to be a feeble imitation of European specimens, simply executed at a less professional and more primitive and naïve level.

Belarusian, as well as Russian Orthodox icons were created on the basis of a strict canon borrowed from the Byzantine culture. The unique style of Belarusian icons had formed by the 16th century as a result of the synthesis of the Russian schools and local traditions and unique features. The Belarusian icon was unique for its strict adherence to the canon, symbolic visual language, and widespread use of ethnographic and decorative elements. In the earliest icons of the 16th century, such as *Virgin Hodegetria* from Slutsk and *Virgin of Jerusalem* from Brest, show clear visible signs combining elements of mediaeval art with Renaissance features. From the Middle Ages there was still severity and restraint. During the 16th century, the Renaissance style gradually came to dominate and the icons changed: the colours became lighter, the image became less austere and more of a lyrical human figure, more proportionate and realistic. Volume and perspective started to appear.

In the 16th century, which we have repeatedly referred to as the heyday of Belarusian Culture, there were several well-known icon painters working in Belarusian cities: in Mogilev there were Makar Akulinich, Makar Malyar, and Dmitriy Ivanovich, in Grodno there was Afansiy Antonovich, and in Minsk there was Ieronim. Archival materials indicate that painters from the Balkans were keenly invited to work in Belarus, especially Serbs and Greeks. In every city, the monastery or Orthodox brotherhood ran art workshops. The largest of these workshops for almost two centuries in a row was in Mogliev, which was conducive to the rapid formation of the Mogilev school of icon painting.

In the 17th century Belarusian art from Western Europe took on a Baroque style and its development over two centuries was based on the European style in continuous union with the Byzantine and Russian tradition. This resulted in substantial changes not only to the style of painting, but also to the design and decoration of the icon. Silver or gold icon settings started to appear, the creation of which required a great deal of mastery in jewellery. The top of icons were decorated with a wreath, and along the edges with a moulded ornament. All icon painters at the time started to use household motifs, landscapes, still lifes and architecture in their icons. These innovations penetrated into the Belarusian icon through prints from Western European books. For Baroque style icons, the pathetic element and folky, cheerful colouring started to become a characteristic feature. Out of the icons from the 17th century which were signed, we only know of the works of Petr Evseevich from Golynets which clearly demonstrate all of the features of the Baroque style. One of them is *The Birth of the Virgin* (1649) (66) in which the artist not only restricts the icon to the faces of the saints, as before, but also showed us the architectural landscape and many everyday ethnographic details: a ceramic vessel, a pitcher with a bouquet of flowers, and pillows embroidered with Belarusian designs – all of which are clear Baroque features.

In the late 17th century, hundreds of artists and icon painters were employed in Belarus. It should be stressed that the painters always worked anonymously, never signing their works (with only a few exceptions). This was allowed, but not encouraged, only when the icon was not for the church but for an individual; but even in this case, artists and monks did not give their name. All painters had to be monks, as secular men were not allowed to create icons. Therefore, despite the fact that numerous documentary sources provide many artists' names, for art historians these names exist apart from their works.

In relation to the consolidation of the Russian State in the 17th century, in Moscow there was a drastic increase in the construction of temples and palaces. In this regard, the need for artists, wood carvers and blacksmiths increased considerably. The Armoury came to be a major artistic centre in Moscow (referred to as the royal treasury at the Kremlin). Belarusian craftsmen were renowned for their talents and were invited to work there. 138 Belarusian painters, wood carvers and jewellers worked together with Russian craftsmen at the Armoury, including Simon Lisitskiy, Ivan Mirovskiy and Stanislav Laputskiy. They certainly enriched the palette of the Russian icon, which in the 17th century did not have the stylistic originality and artistic diversity of the Belarusian icon.

In the 18th century, several icon painting schools were founded in Belarus in Mogilev, Polotsk, Polessk and Grodno. These schools differed from one another in terms of their stylistic and iconographic traits. The Mogilev school, for example, was characterised by restraint, and even a muted palette, while Polessk icons were unique for their bright colours. As for the Grodno school, one cannot ignore the influence of the late Mannerist movement which distinguished the Polish manner of depicting saints and influenced the style of icons in the Grodno region. But for all the variety of icons in the 18th century, their unifying feature was increased decorativeness and greater expression of figures with Baroque influences.

Having studied the evolution of Belarusian icon painting, one can assert with confidence that the icon of the 16th and 17th centuries had considerable originality and artistic expression. During this period, there was an active effort to form and develop a national art school. Unfortunately, in the 18th century artists simply repeated the achievements of their predecessors, and in the 19th century the Belarusian icon gradually lost its identity and stylistic features and ceased to exist as an independent art school, eventually merging entirely with the Russian style of iconography.

───────◆───────

From the 16th century, the main artistic focus inside an Orthodox church was the iconostasis, a solid partition from the northern to the southern wall of the temple, consisting of several rows of icons in a certain order. The function of the iconostasis was to separate the altar of the church from the church's nave. The iconostasis had three doors, with the centre door referred to as the Royal Gate. Those who were not members of the priesthood were prohibited from entering these doors.

Iconostases have not always been present in the Orthodox church, replacing the low altar barrier in the 15th century. Icons have to be situated on the iconostasis according to a strict order and hierarchy. The largest icons are usually found on the bottom row. To the right of the Royal Gate is a large icon of Christ the Saviour, and to their left the Mother of God holding a baby. On the far right is a "temple icon" showing which festival or saint the church had been erected in honour of. In the same position but on the left is the "local icon" from which one can ascertain precisely which is the most revered saint in the region. The Royal Gate is often adorned with icons from the Annunciation, the Last Supper and images of the four evangelists. Thus, the bottom row is dedicated to fundamental aspects of the Christian doctrine and local features of the church. The second row adheres to an even stricter canon: in the centre, over the Royal Gate, there is a depiction of Christ Pantocrator seated on a throne with a book in his hand, representing Christ as a stern and omnipotent judge of all heavenly and earthly affairs. To the right of this icon there is John the Baptist, and to the left, the Mother of God, both depicted to scale. Next, on either side there are archangels, prophets and saints. As a rule, the third row contains relatively large icons dedicated to the most important events in the life of Christ, as described in the Gospels, starting with the Nativity of the Mother of God and ending with the Assumption. This row is called the "festivals" or "feasts" row as the subjects of the icons coincide with the main Christian feasts: Christmas, the Resurrection, Pentecost, etc. If all of the icons on the third "feast" row are illustrations from the New Testament, then the fourth row returns to the Old Testament: here there are iconographic depictions of biblical prophets announcing that the Messiah is coming soon. Often at the centre of this row there is a depiction of the Mother of God with her hands raised up in the *orans* position and with a child, not in her hands, but on her bosom. The fifth row consisted of icons of ancestors from Adam to Moses, and in the centre, an image of the Holy Trinity.

The canon described can be observed on the iconostasis in all churches. The only aspect that may change – depending on the size and wealth of the church – is the number of rows. The most common form in Belarus in the 18th century was the three-tier iconostasis, which ended with the "feasts" row.

The richest collection of Belarusian icons from the 16th to 18th centuries is held by the Belarusian National Art Museum and the Museum of Ancient Belarusian Culture of the Academy of Sciences of Belarus. But they are not remarkable for the size in their collections. The many wars and destruction, but above all the Communist regime when churches and icons were destroyed *en masse*, inflicted irreparable damage on this unique Eastern Slavic art form.

Unfortunately, the same has to be said of surviving architectural monuments. Compared with other Western European countries there are very few remaining in Belarus in the 21st century. Prior to the Baroque period stone architecture was not widespread; it was mostly wooden, which is not conducive to longevity. Stone temples, palaces and castles, created during the Golden Age of Belarusian culture (16th to early 17th centuries), were largely destroyed in the period that followed with the many wars with Russia and popular uprisings.

But those that have survived to this day are fine examples of original Belarusian architecture integrating features of the Latin West and the Orthodox East.

———————————◆———————————

The Castle in the village of Mir, Grodno Province.

Mir Castle was built between 1506 and 1510. Two brick factories were specially built prior to its construction, to which stones from all around were brought, hewed and sorted by size. The construction work was carried out by peasants. Built in the form of a quadrangle, with towers in each corner, the castle housed a palace which was rebuilt on several occasions.

After the castle had been built, up to 1568 it belonged to the Ilinich family, before coming into the ownership of the Radziwiłłs, the richest barons in Belarus. The Radziwiłłs made numerous changes to the castle, surrounding it with an earthen wall 10 metres tall and surrounding the ramparts with a moat. Under the Radziwiłłs' ownership the palace incorporated Renaissance and later Baroque elements in appearance. From the 17th to the 18th centuries Mir Castle was a luxury palace-cum-castle complex where features of military fortifications were surprisingly combined to great success with the splendour and comfort of a palace. From the late 18th century, after numerous family happenings within the Radziwiłł line, the castle came to be owned by the Wittgenstein family, and from the late 19th century up to 1939 (prior to joining the USSR) it belonged to Svyatopolk-Mirskiy princes.

The military history of the castle is also replete with interest. During the Russo-Polish War of 1654-1667 the castle was partially destroyed but quickly restored. In the Great Northern War of 1705 it was stormed and ransacked by the Swedes. In 1785, at the invitation of the Radziwiłłs, King Stanisław Poniatowski of Poland, a minion of Catherine the Great, was invited to the Castle, who was struck by the interior and riches of the palace. In 1794, when all of Belarus was seized by the anti-Russian uprising of Tadeusz Kościuszko, Mir Castle was stormed by Russian troops, and in its dungeons a prison was set up for the rebels. During Napoleon's invasion in July 1812, there was a major battle between the Russian army of General Bagration and the French army of Marshal Davout just outside the walls of the castle. During this battle the exterior fortifications were destroyed. The palace and its rich collections of paintings and weapons fell victim to looting by the French soldiers.

The last owner of the castle in 1891 was the Belarusian prince Nikolai Svyatopolk-Mirskiy. By this time, the castle had fallen into disrepair, and Mirskiy, and later his son, carried out a large-scale renovation and restoration of the castle. After the Grodno Province had jointed the Soviet Union in 1939, the castle was nationalised, and within this remarkable architectural complex an industrial workshop was set up to produce metal products, which was typical of the Soviet government and its relationship with cultural monuments. During the Second World War and the German Occupation, the Nazis set up a Jewish ghetto in the castle grounds. After the liberation of Belarus in 1944, the castle fell into complete disrepair, and some of the rooms were used as communal apartments for workers and some were even turned into warehouses, resulting in the near-total loss of the interiors. Only during the period of perestroika was the castle brought to the government's attention when it was transferred to the National Art Museum and work began to restore and refurbish the castle. In 2000 Mir Castle was included on the list of UNESCO World Heritage Sites.

Nesvizh Castle.

The city of Nesvizh, which was written about in chronicles from the 13th century, was the family seat and main residence of the Radziwiłłs. Mikołaj "the Orphan" Radziwiłł travelled extensively throughout Europe, spending two years in Italy and evidently appreciating the achievements of the Italian military and palatial architecture. In 1583 he ordered the demolition of the old wooden castle and the construction of a new stone castle. He entrusted this task to the Italian architect Giovanni Gernardoni (67).

The castle was built on a peninsula of the river Ushi, on which a dam was built, which aided the creation of two lakes. Surrounded by a wide moat, whose water level was regulated, the castle was actually an island. To access the castle there was only a long wooden bridge, which could easily be dismantled in danger.

The Castle was rectangular and covered an area of 170 by 150 metres, and was surrounded by an earthen wall 20 metres high and a water ring. For ultimate defence, the wall was reinforced with stones, inside the wall there were stone stables, secret passages went around the castle, and at the corners there were four defensive towers.

For two centuries this castle was not only a military fort, but also a fashionable palace and rich cultural centre, a hub for mediaeval and Renaissance art. 12 rooms housed an art gallery, gathering together more than one thousand paintings, a library with twenty thousand works, and a collection of Arabic, Japanese and Chinese weapons. There were also entirely unique, life-size sculptures of the 12 apostles made out of gold and silver. Each of the rooms had its own name: Royal, Gold, Knights', Marble, and Hunters'.

During the war with Russia, Nesvizh was twice, in 1654 and 1659, taken by storm and had its fortifications destroyed. Both the King of Poland and the Radziwiłłs were well aware of the strategic importance of Nesvizh to the centre of Belarus, and in 1669 the fortifications were built afresh right from the very foundations. But the Great Northern War once again brought destruction in 1706 when the Swedes destroyed the palace. In 1726 it was fully restored in the prevailing Baroque style of the time, and this form has been preserved to this day.

In 1812, the castle's owner Dominik Radziwiłł sided with Napoleon's French army, after which he was forced to flee to France. In 1860, the Radziwiłłs started to expand the castle and palace complex, creating a Castle Garden, English Garden, Japanese Garden, and new buildings incorporating features of various styles: Renaissance and Classicism, Baroque and Rococo, and Neo-Gothic and Modernism. In 1939, during the accession of the region to the USSR, the Nesvizh Castle and Palace Complex was situated on land occupying 90 hectares. Right up to the dissolution of the USSR the castle buildings housed a KGB sanatorium.

All of the collections once kept at the palace and castle were, over time, lost, looted or removed by the Germans during the occupation, or destroyed. Currently, a process is under way to gather together a collection from cities in Belarus, Russia and Europe. The restoration of the castle is still on-going, but most of it is now open to tourists. In 2005, the castle was declared a UNESCO World Heritage Site.

Paskevich Palace in Gomel.

This beautiful palace is the main attraction in Gomel and is part of a palace and park architectural complex which, aside from the palace, includes a city park, the Sts. Peter and Paul Church and a mausoleum and chapel.

In 1772 during the first division of the Polish-Lithuanian Commonwealth, when Gomel, like all of Eastern Belarus, was annexed to Russia, Catherine the Great gave this city as a gift to her minion General Petr Rumyantsev "for his amusement". In 1777-1794 Rumyantsev commissioned the building of a palace, a two-storey building on a high base with a perfectly cubic belvedere with a large dome. The exterior decoration of the palace was entirely Classical, and the main decoration on the palace façade were Corinthian style porticos. His architect, Ivan Starov, was famous for the construction of the Tauride Palace and the Kazan Cathedral in St. Petersburg.

In 1834 the palace was bought by General Ivan Paskevich. During his ownership a magnificent park was built around the palace. Ivan Paskevich was well known as a philanthropist and owner of a vast collection of antiques and works of art, most of which were placed in the palace in Gomel. The Paskevichs owned the palace right up to the Bolshevik coup in October 1917, after which the palace was nationalised and its collections confiscated. Fortunately, unlike many other palaces, the Bolsheviks turned it, not into a warehouse or factory, but into a museum, the basis for which was the collection confiscated from the Paskevich family.

Tyzenhaus Palace in Postavy

Count Antoni Tyzenhaus was a highly educated man for his time. He corresponded with the philosopher Jean-Jacques Rousseau and was a friend of the last King of Poland, Stanisław Poniatowski. This man contributed to the development of the two Belarusian cities Postavy and Grodno like no other.

In the 18th century Postavy was a very small town located in a very scenic area, and before the arrival of Count Antoni Tyzenhaus there was not a single stone building. The Count invited the Italian architect Giuseppe Sacco to the city and built a beautiful palace in 1770 in the Classical style. This one-storey stone building was built in a U-shape and fitted with high ceilings and attics. The building was decorated with a round belvedere with open apertures, a dome and a sculpture of the Goddess Ceres over the main entrance. Later, to the left of the palace a room was built for a theatre, and the French professor Jean Geliber built a botanical garden with illuminated fountains and ponds covering an area of 15 hectares, which, in terms of its diversity, rarity and the exotic nature of the plants, was one of the best gardens in Europe.

Antoni Tyzenhaus' grandson Konstantin was an avid fan of ornithology, and an ornithological museum was set up at the palace at Postavy, which was unique throughout Eastern Europe. Konstantin Tyzenhaus gathered together a rich collection of paintings, which, according to 1840 data, numbered 600 paintings, including works by Dürer, Brueghel and Rubens.

During the First World War the art collection was looted and no traces of it have been found since. But during the Communist period nobody was looking for it, as the Communists were concerned with other things, and not culture. Attempts to find traces of the brilliant painters' paintings were made only after perestroika, but, unfortunately, to no avail. Now, a hospital is based at Tyzenhaus Palace.

A HISTORY OF BELARUS

PART 6

ONE WITH RUSSIA

(1795-1917)

CHAPTER I
Domestic policies
of the Russian government in Belarus

AS A RESULT OF THE THREE DIVISIONS OF POLAND, THE BELARUSIAN lands, inhabited by approximately 3 million people, came to be part of the Russian Empire. Belarus had started a new period in its history. What changes took place first of all in this country together with the change in its political affiliation?

Back in 1762, when Catherine the Great took the throne, in Moscow, on the day of this solemn festival, the Orthodox Bishop Georgiy Kanisskiy arrived, among other guests (68). During an official audience with the Empress, the Bishop urged the tsarina to protect the Orthodox religion within the Polish-Lithuanian Commonwealth. Catherine, who had barely started to occupy herself with public affairs, cautiously asked of the benefit of this policy. The response was quite frank: by making use of rhetoric on the protection of Orthodoxy, Russia could take from Poland an entire country with 600 versts of fertile land, and even thousands of peasants who would work the land (69). After the collapse of the Polish-Lithuanian Commonwealth, this is precisely what happened.

The Russian government immediately implemented an array of measures to consolidate its influence over the new land. Firstly, within one month of a decree being issued on the annexation of Belarus to Russia, the entire Belarusian population was to take an oath of allegiance to the Russian Empress. Those who did not agree to take the oath were granted three months to leave Russian territory having sold their property, following threats that after three months it would be appropriated by the state. The overwhelming majority of barons and gentry agreed to the oath.

In 1796, the first year of the accession, sweeping administrative reforms were carried out. Like Russia, provinces were established in Belarus: the Belarusian Province with its provincial capital of Vitebsk and a population of 1.5 million, the Minsk Province with its provincial capital of Minsk and a population of approximately 800,000, and the Lithuanian Province with its provincial capital of Vilno and a population of 1.6 million. The executive power in the provinces was held by governors who were appointed by the Empress.

Catherine the Great did everything she could to immediately curb the rights of the Belarusian nobility who, according to her understanding, were accustomed to excessive liberties and freedoms. The barons lost the right to keep their own armies, lost the right to private ownership of a city, and they were no longer allowed to build their own castles. The nobility was banned from uniting in a confederation (military alliances to defend certain political interests).

In relation to the Catholic Church, Catherine the Great initially conducted a very cautious policy. The property of Roman-Catholic Churches and monasteries remained intact, and no restrictions on Catholic rites followed. The Empress even issued a *Instruction to the Churches* which allowed them to create a Belarusian Catholic Eparchy, which was clearly in the interests of the Catholic clergy and created an administrative basis for the existence and management of the Catholic Church. Through this act, Catherine showed not only a concern for the Catholic Church, but anticipated and prevented the Catholic Church from being controlled entirely from abroad, from Rome, which would therefore be subject to fewer controls from Moscow. The only thing that Catholic priests were categorically prohibited from doing was baptising Orthodox believers as Catholics, whereas Catholics were allowed to convert to Orthodoxy. There is no doubt that the pressure to which the Orthodox Church was subjected in the Polish-Lithuanian

Commonwealth was not felt by Catholics in the first few decades as part of Russia.

Generally, Catherine's policies towards the annexed territories of Belarus were relatively flexible and peaceful, but there was one undeniable feature: she immediately sought to assert the fact that she looked upon this territory as another Russian territory. This was how Catherine herself saw the matter, and this was understood by the governors that she appointed (70).

All Belarusian cities had to change their system of governance to tie in with the Russian regime. New regulations and principles were declared by Catherine the Great in her *Instruction to the Cities*. All cities which had previously been privately owned by barons were transferred to state ownership and the barons' courts were liquidated. Governance of city life was taken over by a City Duma, a representative body elected from all of the urban classes. The executive and administrative apparatus overseen by the governor was strictly subjugated to the central authorities. The *Instruction to the Cities* clearly shows that the laws enshrined in the document were decisively eradicating the remnants of the mediaeval rules which Belarus took with it into Russia and served the interests of a new social class, the bourgeoisie.

Special laws were adopted by the Russian government in relation to the Jewish population. In a Decree dated 23 June 1794 a "pale of settlement" was demarcated on the new Belarusian territories by the governors. They established cities and towns where the Jews were allowed to live and engage in craft and trade, and, correspondingly, other cities were off limits to them, such as Moscow and St. Petersburg. This law remained in existence until the February Revolution of 1917, and even the term "pale of settlement" became synonymous with anti-Semitic policies. Such a long-standing application of this law, which was strictly enforced, led to the places where Jews were allowed to settle becoming very crowded. For example, in Bobruisk the Jewish population in the mid-19th century was approximately 50% of all residents. Jews were forbidden from leaving their homes, and the only exceptions were top guild merchants (of which there were very few) and students. They were also forbidden from acquiring land. For a considerable payment Jews were allowed to enlist in the merchant or lower middle classes, but with the proviso that in future they would have to pay state taxes twice as high as the Christian population.

An inspection carried out by the Russian government and a census of the Belarusian lands showed that land was abandoned, huge areas were simply not cultivated, and out of necessity serfs were forced to continuously work their statute labour (on the land of their owner) and were not able to have their own plot, making them inefficient and forcing them to live in a state of extreme poverty. While the basis of the economic system was the same (feudal land ownership), in Russia the level of development of economic relations was higher than in Belarus, which experienced many years of devastating wars. With the plight of the economy in mind, for two years the Russian government exempted the Belarusian population from payment of all state taxes, and for the next 10 years taxes were levied at half the rate of Russian taxpayers.

While in Western Europe in the 16th to 17th centuries there was active development of the capitalist system, in the Polish-Lithuanian Commonwealth there was only the end of the process of the mass enslavement of peasants and the feudal system was at its apogee. In Russia, the development of trade and monetary relations among the bourgeoisie was much faster than in Belarus and Poland, such that it now had to "drag" these regions up to its level. In the first few decades after accession, the economic development of Belarus was much faster. Demand for agricultural products increased dramatically, and this contributed to an increase in cultivated land. Trade ties expanded, new manufacturing establishments were created, and previous production volumes increased several times.

New administrative authorities carried out regular audits on the material conditions of peasants by polling the peasants themselves. To set up the Russian government as the saviour of the Belarusian people from the heterodox Polish oppressors and to better control the work of new local officials, there were senator inspections and visits

by ministers of members of the Empress' family. In 1780 Belarus was
visited by Catherine the Great. During the visit she made a speech
in front of the people, made a large donation to the Orthodox church,
and ordered the creation of reserve food warehouses, which were to be
a form of insurance fund in the event of a bad harvest.

The caution, and even generosity in many domestic political issues
in relation to Belarus which was characteristic of Catherine the Great's
policies was, of course, dictated by strategic objectives. The Empress
paid great attention to every class and religion and thereby gently
washed away the oppositional mind set, thus creating the basis for
easier integration and subsequent gradual assimilation. In one of her
letters Catherine wrote: "So that they may be Russified and conducive
to assimilation, we need to send not ardent Russians there for local
governance, but calm and respected people, whose actions will result in
mutual respect". The majority of nobles, who had been placed entirely
on the same footing as the Russian nobility in terms of their rights,
were happy with their new position and even sent a message to the
Russian Empress which read: "Not living in Poland, we feel like we
are in Poland and perhaps somewhere better than Poland is now…".

However, the Russian authorities were decisive in their position
on land ownership. It was clear that the government wanted Russian
estates to be expanded as widely as possible to the annexed territories
at the expense of the state. Vast amounts of land in Belarus, which had
previously been owned by the Polish Crown, were now transferred to
state ownership by Russia. In addition, the Russian state fund increased
significantly from the land of barons which had been acquired from
them or appropriated. This land, together with resident serfs, started
to be generously placed in private ownership by Catherine the Great
exclusively with Russian nobles and government officials. From 1772
to 1796, out of the 750,000 male serfs living on the annexed Belarusian
territory, 208,000 were transferred to Russian landowners. From
1796 to 1801 Catherine's son, Pavel I, gave Russian landowners land
from the state fund with a population of 28,000 male serfs. Virtually
all state land became the property of Russian landowners, whereas

ownership by the Polish and Belarusian nobility did not even increase by a single square metre. Catherine gave her loved and long-standing minion Grigoriy Potemkin land with 15,000 serfs, and another lover Count Petr Rumyantsev grounds near Gomel with 11,000 peasants. As a result of such policies the Belarusian lands were settled *en masse* by new Russian masters, and not just by the petty nobility, but by influential members of the ruling class. The distribution of the land solely in favour of Russians caused tension in Belarus, both from the nobles and from the peasants. Small-scale peasant revolts broke out, incited by discontented nobles. Pavel I was forced to issue a decree in 1797 limiting serfdom to three days a week. But it did not remove the discontent, and in 1801, the new tsar on the throne, Emperor Aleksandr I issued a decree prohibiting the small amount of remaining state-owned land from being transferred into private ownership. But significant demographic changes had already taken place: according to data from the mid-19th century, property owned by "new Russian" landowners accounted for approximately 25% of Belarusian land.

Another effective way to limit the power of the Belarusian nobility and to undermine its economic position was the confiscation of land. For this it was enough to simply apply a relatively vague wording which was widely used in Russia: "for anti-governmental activities". In the Polish-Lithuanian Commonwealth punishment for political opposition, in the form of confiscation of land and expulsion from the country, was also permitted, but it happened only rarely and was only enforced against major leaders and inciters of rebellions, and not against ordinary participants. Often if the guilty leader repented he would then receive a pardon. After the death of Peter I in 1725 several decades passed in Russia guided by endless palace coups. Each replacement on the throne was accompanied by violent confiscation of the property of former supports of the king and the distribution of the land to new minions. For example, the participants in the Orlov brothers' conspiracy, who brought Catherine the Great to the throne in 1762, received huge land holdings and 18,000 serfs. Such confiscations among the Belarusian and Polish noble opposition started to occur immediately after the first division of Poland. The Russian government did not require special evidence of opposition; suspicion was enough. Mass confiscation was also enforced against all of the participants of the uprising instigated by Tadeusz Kościuszko, and later against those who did not take the oath of allegiance to the Russian government. According to 1800 data, in the two small Belarusian districts of Nevel and Sebezh 30 estates were confiscated, together with 39,000 peasants.

———————◆———————

The implications of Belarus' accession to Russia should not be oversimplified. A change of nationality is a huge change in the life of any nation. Such events cannot be examined from one perspective alone, as they can be seen in both positive and negative lights. By way of positives, clearly it stabilised the domestic political situation, ended the anarchy of the feudal system and the endless wars, and kick-started the economy. But this did not fully remove the tension from Belarusian society; there were numerous opponents of Russia who disagreed with the union. And so, the Russian government's ignorance of Belarusian culture, identity and language, and the expansion of the Catholic church, were all negatives for Belarus.

CHAPTER 2
The Napoleonic War
(1812)

THE SITUATION BEFORE THE WAR WITH FRANCE WAS AS FOLLOWS. The main protagonists on the European political scene at the time were Britain, France and Russia. The initiative was with France, which with Napoleon coming to power seized and established control over all territories. In the years 1806-1807 the anti-French coalition (Britain, Prussia, Russia and Sweden) was broken, and Napoleon's troops stood on the border with Russia. After convincing victories over the coalition Napoleon began to talk about the need to restore the borders of the Polish-Lithuanian Commonwealth as they were in 1772. This strangely inspired the Poles. On Polish territory, which had been handed to Prussia with the division of Poland, and had now been conquered by the French, the Principality of Warsaw was established as the first step of this plan. But these actions and the political rhetoric of Napoleon was purely propagandistic in nature, and in fact, Napoleon had no plans to restore the Commonwealth. The propaganda and flirtation with the Poles was aimed at winning over the Polish nobility for the forthcoming war with Russia. To the same end, the Russian Government declared its readiness to grant the Polish-Lithuanian Commonwealth and the Grand Principality of Lithuania full autonomy under its protectorate. But this idea from Moscow was not attractive to the Poles or the Belarusians. In both Polish and Belarusian noble circles there had long been sympathies for France, which was also a long-standing political ally of the Polish-Lithuanian Commonwealth. France offered shelter to thousands of immigrants from Poland after its division, and now they had voluntarily enlisted in the French army, viewing Russia as their main enemy.

On 24 June 1812 Napoleon's 600,000 strong army, of which 120,000 were Poles, crossed the Russian border in the region of the Belarusian cities of Kovno (now Kaunas) and Grodno and began to advance quickly without resistance. A significant part of the Belarusian nobility did not support the defensive measures of the Russian administration, and even sabotaged them, in particular by keeping back food stores before the arrival of the French army. At his own expense Prince Dominik Radziwiłł formed a cavalry regiment that fought on the side of Napoleon. Regiments were also formed by the Minsk landowner Ignatiy Monyushko and Prince Rudolf Tyzenhaus (71). The nobility who had not long ago sworn their allegiance to Russia almost everywhere greeted the French as liberators from the Russian invaders. Both the Belarusian and Polish nobility believed that this was the main reason for Napoleon starting the war with Russia: the restoration of the Polish-Lithuanian Commonwealth to its previous borders.

On 28 June the French took Vilno without a fight. Napoleon wanted to consolidate support for him among the nobility and announced the establishment of a provisional government of the Grand Principality of Lithuania in Vilno. But the only thing that Napoleon asked of this new puppet government was that it furnish the French army with recruits and food. On 25 July the provisional government issued an order to amass 10,000 recruits and to create cavalry regiments with full provisions at the expense of the people. Out of the noble volunteers 1,000 people were ordered to create a guards regiment. But all of this was a very slow process; the peasants had no desire to join the army, preferring instead to flee to the woods and create partisan detachments. But the nobility showed sufficient enthusiasm, with students from Vilno University quick to sign up as recruits, and the guards regiment was still formed.

Napoleon's sizeable army confronted three Russian armies: the 1st army of General Barclay de Tolly (120,000 men and 580 guns), the 2nd army of General P. Bagration (50,000 men and 180 guns), and the 3rd army of General A. Tarmasov (44,000 men and 168 guns). In the first few weeks of the war the Russians retreated, not wanting to make a big stand, as they understood that their enemy was considerably superior to them in terms of numbers.

From 16 July to 1 August Napoleon, advancing at speed, was in Vitebsk. For these two weeks he halted the advance of his army as almost the entire territory of Belarus had been occupied, and the commander was deciding what to do next. His aim was to defeat the Russian army on Belarusian territory and to sign a peace treaty that would be advantageous to him, but this was not achieved. The Russian army retreated, forcing Napoleon to advance further into the depths of Russia, which he had not originally planned to do.

During his two week stay in Vitebsk two Russian armies had formed near Smolensk, 100 kilometres from Vitebsk. Taking over command of the two armies was General Mikhail Kutuzov. It was finally here, near Smolensk, that the first major battle took place with the French, resulting in defeat for the Russians. The losses were enormous: 30,000 dead on both sides. Smolensk was handed over to the French. With this Napoleon decided to stop his military campaign. The imprisoned Russian General P. Tuchkov was told by Napoleon to contact Aleksandr II regarding his desire to start peace talks, stating: "We have already burnt rather a lot of gunpowder and shed rather a lot of blood, but it has to stop some day, you know!" (72). But Aleksandr I gave no response to the peace request.

The Russian army retreated towards Moscow, preparing for a decisive battle. It happened on 26 August near the village of Borodino, 100 kilometres from Moscow. The battle lasted for 12 hours, but which side was victorious is still a cause for dispute among historians. Russian historiography has always maintained that it was a Russian victory, although the facts and figures tell a different story. In any case, it was still the bloodiest battle of the 19th century. Based on conservative estimates, losses on each side were about 100,000 people. The Russian army of Mikhail Kutuzov, despite its claim to victory, again gave a surprising order to retreat and to surrender Moscow to the French. On 2 September the French army entered the empty city which had been almost entirely abandoned by its inhabitants. Out of a population of 300,000, there were only a few thousand that had remained in the city.

Immediately after the entry of the French army into Moscow, fires were started around the city, and historians have not stated whether it was the Russians themselves who burned the city, or whether it was done by drunken French soldiers. But such a reception for Napoleon was not witnessed in any other of the European capitals that he occupied. The empty city burned, and the discouraged Napoleon repeated: "What kind of people are they! They have gone and handed over all of their property! Why do such a thing, and what does it mean? Bizarre, senseless Scythians!"

It would seem that Moscow's capture was supposed to be Napoleon's triumph and his final victory. But it all happened so very differently. The occupation of the almost empty Moscow lasted only just over a month. The city was ransacked in the first few weeks, entire districts of Moscow were destroyed by fires, the food supplies from the city had been taken away by the Russians before they left, the French soldiers spent their time drunk and looting, and every day Napoleon sent messengers to Emperor Aleksandr I proposing to start peace talks. But Aleksandr maintained his silence. Keeping the huge army in the devastated and plundered city became impossible, and in October the puzzled Napoleon, not expecting any negotiations now, ordered a retreat from Moscow. He wanted to retreat through the rich southern provinces that had not been ransacked, but the Russian army had blocked this route, and he was forced to retreat to Europe over territory already passed over by the French army. It was almost impossible to get provisions anywhere else, and partisan groups, which were numerous in the forests in Belarus, carried out frequent unexpected raids on the French. In addition, the snow and ice came early that year. It was then that the Russian army, which had until then shirked any confrontation, went on the offensive. During October and November Vitebsk, Polotsk, Brest and Minsk were all liberated from the French. Napoleon's armies were separated by Russian wedge armies. Food shortages, disease and the cold led to large-scale deaths among the French troops. Here is just one eye-witness account from a man named Wilson: "Today I saw a horror that is rarely seen in modern wars: 2,000 people half-undressed, sometimes almost naked, dead or dying. Along the road several thousand dead horses, most of which must have fallen from hunger. Hundreds of unfortunate wounded wandering along the forest roads…" (73).

The final defeat of Napoleon's army came in Belarus when crossing the Berezina River on 14-16 November 1812. The retreating French army were surrounded by the Russian troops, and during the fighting at the crossing the French lost more than 40,000 soldiers and officers. An expression came to exist in French, which still exists to this day, which was: "C'est la Berezina!", meaning a terrible and irreparable failure. From the encirclement a few remnants of the "great army" managed to escape to the west: in October Napoleon led 102,000 soldiers out of Moscow, but by the end of December only about 50,000 were left of the "great French army", which was driven out of Belarus. Napoleon, disguised as a Polish officer, cast off the rest of his troops to fend for themselves and fled to Paris.

Belarus again, as it had been many times in the past, was a war zone with many towns and villages destroyed. An example was Minsk, which in 1811 had a population of 11,200 people; by the end of 1812 there were only 3,480 (74). The losses amounted to 52 million roubles, while the total value of yearly tax dues paid across Belarus to the Russian budget was 1 million roubles.

The heavy impact of the war on the people was compounded by the tsar's policies. Peasants were deceived in their hopes that after the victory over Napoleon serfdom would be abolished and reform would take place. The exploitation of the peasantry, on the contrary, took on a more stringent form and some of the tax benefits previously in place in Belarus were forgotten: Russia was healing its economic ills at the expense of the poorest class, the peasants. And as for the Polish and Belarusian aristocracy, which had served the French government *en masse*, the Tsarist government showed loyalty and caution so as to not incite even greater anti-Russian sentiments. In December 1812 Emperor Aleksandr I issued a decree in which he declared: "…the most gracious public and private pardon and the committing of all that happened to total silence" (75), which meant full amnesty for collaborators, admittedly, upon their prompt withdrawal from the French army and return home. But this amnesty was not taken up by many. Napoleon was not yet defeated. His fight with the armies of the anti-French coalition continued for another 16 months after his withdrawal from Russia and ended only after the arrival of the allied armies in Paris on 31 March 1814. Many nobles in the Belarusian provinces still primarily lay their hopes for political change in Belarus and Poland with him. One figure is worth mentioning: out of the 103 nobles in the Minsk province which left with Napoleon's army, after the amnesty was announced only 10 people returned (76).

CHAPTER 3
Secret societies

AT THE START OF THE 19ᵀᴴ CENTURY THE POLITICAL CLIMATE IN Belarus was influenced by revolutions in Western Europe, in particular the French Revolution, and Polish national liberation ideas. The French Revolution contributed to the spread of democratic mentalities and set in motion radical movements in many European countries. But it also scared all of the governments that had started to seek consolidation with one another to more effectively deal with the "revolutionary contagion". In this fight Russia very quickly gained the reputation of leader and was nicknamed the "gendarme of Europe".

For a large part of Belarusian society the main cause of dissatisfaction was the country's annexation to Russia and a longing for the defunct Polish-Lithuanian Commonwealth. At the same time, in the most radical circles considerable thought was being given to issues such as class inequality and the need for democratic reforms in social and political life, and primarily, the emancipation of the peasants from serfdom.

In Russia, where the tsar's power was absolute, the only legal place where it was possible to discuss political aspirations were local parliamentary assemblies, which were somewhat reminiscent of the local Polish *Sejms* at which nobles were once able to give vent to their opposition sentiments. But the tsarist government quickly decided to eliminate this defective body and adopted a decree banning discussion of all issues except economic matters at local and provincial assemblies.

After the issuing of this decree secret societies and groups started to emerge.

The first secret organisation appeared in Vilno in 1796, immediately after the third division of the Polish-Lithuanian Commonwealth. The main aim of the "Vilno Association" was to restore the Polish-Lithuanian Commonwealth on the basis of the Constitution of 1791. The secret society adopted the "Vilno Uprising Act" in which the methods were set out in detail to achieve their goals. Divisions of the "Vilno Association" were set up in many cities: Minsk, Brest, Kobryn, Ashmyany, and Grodno. But this secret society, firstly, had absolutely no experience in such activities and, secondly, underestimated its ability to conduct political espionage in Russia, and within two years was uncovered. Of its members, nobles were deprived of their noble titles and church representatives were defrocked, and all of them were deported to Siberia.

Russia's victory over France in the war of 1812 and its political consequences did not satisfy the desires of the Belarusian and Polish nobility who were hoping for a French victory and the restoration of the lost Polish-Lithuanian Commonwealth with its backing. In the years 1812-1815 an active national liberation movement was formed in Poland and Belarus and numerous secret groups came into being, for the most part at universities. At Vilno University in 1817, on the initiative of the student Adam Mickiewicz, the "Philomath Association" was formed (from the Greek *philomathes*, 'lovers of knowledge'). The association quickly transformed into a mass organisation with branches in other cities. The members of the association paid particular attention to the idea of a person's moral perfection, seeing it as a basis for civic consciousness. The Philomaths considered it necessary to establish a system of mandatory universal public education, and they themselves taught Belarusian culture, peasant life and folklore, made ethnographic descriptions of various territories, and used the Belarusian language in their dealings, which at the time had no official status. Their political ideas, aimed at changing the existing system were: the unconditional abolition of serfdom, the adoption of a Constitution placing checks and balances on the absolute monarchy, and the equality of all people before the law. Their credo was borrowed from French revolutionary slogans: "Freedom is the birth right of every man and every people". At their meetings the Philomaths read reports on the revolutionary struggle in Greece, Spain and Italy and applauded the fight.

In 1820, at the same university, another secret organisation "Radiant" was created, quickly growing to have 200 members. In Polotsk at the Higher Theological Seminary a "Philoret Association" was set up (from the Greek *philoretos*, 'lovers of virtue'). This organisation adopted a clear political angle, using the motto: "One Poland and Catholic faith".

All of these societies were promoting ideas of liberty and equality, and they were not only joined by students, but also by rich nobles, officials and clergy. Both the Philomaths and the Philorets did not exist for long, only a few years, and in Spring 1823 these organisations were exposed and eliminated. In Vilno more than 100 people were arrested, the leaders of the secret organisations were sentenced to imprisonment with subsequent deportation, and ordinary members were deprived of their noble titles and sent to Siberia or conscripted as soldiers for 25 years. Vilno University and the Polotsk Theological Seminary had their teaching staff purged and professors and rectors were dismissed.

At the beginning of 1825, the "Military Friends Association" was set up at the Lithuanian Special Military Corps in Grodno, which included not only the officers, but soldiers too. This organisation had a strict structure and worked actively among the various strata of the population.

The Russian "Decembrist" movement – the name given to members of all the secret revolutionary groups in Russia which revolted in December 1825 – found some support in Belarus. The "Decembrists" attentively watched the development of the Polish national liberation movement and forged ties with the Polish "Patriotic Association", a branch of which was based in Belarus. The Russian Decembrists (many, but not all) supported the Polish patriots and shared their desire for the return of the Polish-Lithuanian Commonwealth as they did not like to see Russia as an invader and oppressor of other nations. In 1823, Russian and Polish underground revolutionaries elaborated plans for an uprising in the Belarusian city of Bobruisk and the arrest of Emperor Aleksandr I, who was due to visit the city to examine military detachments. But the uprising took place earlier than planned in St. Petersburg, taking advantage of the sudden death of Aleksandr I and the day of swearing their allegiance to the new Emperor Nikolai I. The rebels gathered on 14 December 1825 in Senate Square in front of the residence of the Russian emperors, the Winter Palace, and refused to take the oath to the new emperor until their demands were considered and fulfilled: the adoption of a Constitution, the abolition of serfdom and the implementation of a series of democratic and liberal reforms. The insurgent officers did not take any action that day; they stood on the square and waited too long for support from the troops gathered in St. Petersburg to take the oath. But the troops did not support them. On the orders of Nikolai I, just before nightfall, Senate Square was surrounded by a 3,000 strong cavalry regiment which opened fire on the insurgents. Senate Square was littered with corpses which were ordered to be removed cruelly that night by being dumped into a hole in the ice in the nearby River Neva. The dozens of wounded, unable to put up any resistance, were also taken to the river.

On 25 December, 10 days after the tragic attempt at an uprising in St. Petersburg, the "Military Friends Association" in Grodno attempted an uprising at the Lithuanian Special Corps, but their intentions were found out by the police. The uprising did not go ahead, and dozens of members of the association, headed by Captain K. Ingelstrom, were arrested and sentenced to death or exile in Siberia.

In response to all of these events the tsarist government started to pursue a policy of repression in Belarus. The first day of the new Russian Emperor Nikolai I's regime started with the execution of the "Decembrist" rebels on Senate Square in St. Petersburg, dashing even a hint at any liberal aspirations. All officials at state bodies and academics had to sign statements of political loyalty declaring that they were not members of any secret political societies. Academics had to write regular reports on political attitudes among students. Young people in Belarus and Lithuania were forbidden from studying at foreign universities and censorship intensified for foreign books and local periodicals.

CHAPTER 4
Anti-Russian uprising
(1830-1831)

Affer the division of the Polish-Lithuanian Commonwealth the vast majority of Polish society was constantly seeking to restore their statehood. In Russia, this came to be known as the "Polish question".

The repressive policies of the Russian tsar could not stop the spread of liberation ideas and opposition sentiments, and in Warsaw in 1828 the "Officers Association" was set up to gather together all of the dispersed remnants of former secret organisations. The officers did not engage in propaganda, but were in fact planning to murder Nikolai I during his coronation in Warsaw in May 1829. But on the eve of the assassination the organisation's leaders were exposed and arrested.

Immediate impetus for the onset of mass protests in Belarus and Poland came from the 1830 revolution which started in France and Belgium. An uprising began in Warsaw on 28 November 1830. Cadets at the military school seized the arsenal and started distributing weapons to citizens. Polish military detachments immediately joined the revolt, and all of the inhabitants of Warsaw went out to build barricades. The Russian government was very concerned by the scale of the action, and Nikolai I's governor in Poland, his brother Prince Konstantin, fled and ordered the Russian garrisons to withdraw from Warsaw.

Two uprising factions immediately formed: a conservative-aristocratic faction and a democratic faction. The first sought to restore the Polish-Lithuanian Commonwealth to its 1772 boundaries, or at least to achieve broad autonomy and self-government within the Russian Empire. Matters of socio-economic transformation were not of concern to the conservatives. The leaders of this movement held high-ranking positions in the Polish army and the government apparatus.

The democrats – members of the middle and petty nobility, students, and the bourgeoisie – preached ideas of equality and freedom, economic transformation and restrictions on absolutism. Among them there was no unity or consolidation, and their influence was not strong within the army. The democrats saw their main support as coming from the people, wishing to join the rebels *en masse*. They continually stressed the need not to fight the Russian people, but only Russian absolutism, the main enemy of the Poles, the Belarusians and the Russians themselves. The democrats proposed a slogan which was subsequently adopted by a variety of revolutionary movements in various countries and at various times: "For our freedom and yours!"

Warsaw was entirely in the rebels' hands. The *Sejm* was convened and its first decision was a statement to the effect that the Russian Romanov dynasty, and in particular Emperor Nikolai I, had forever been deprived of the Polish Crown.

The tsarist government tried every possible way to prevent the spread of the uprising to Belarusian territory. All troops were withdrawn from Poland to Belarus and martial law was declared. Belarus was turned into a military bridgehead. A total purge of the state apparatus was started: all officials of Polish or Belarusian descent were replaced with Russians. Belarusian revolutionary landowners fled to Warsaw to join the rebels. In response, Nikolai I ordered the immediate confiscation of the estates of the fleeing landowners.

In early 1831 emissaries arrived from Warsaw in Vilno to start preparations for an uprising in the city. A Revolutionary Committee was set up which set about gathering funds and weaponry.

The uprising in Vilno began in Spring 1831 spontaneously, as no overall leadership structure was in place. The rebels seized settlements where there were no Russian troops and set up their own control authorities immediately. They instituted conscription and the rebel army grew rapidly. In the Vitebsk Province, for example, an armed detachment was formed which was led by Countess E. Plyatter (77), formerly renowned as a collector of Belarusian folklore and a poet. Catholic monasteries willingly became rebel strongholds, always eager to agree to any action against the Russian dominance. The peasantry were not actively involved in the uprising as nobody had promised them anything in the fight, and they were indifferent to the slogans on restoring the independence of the Polish-Lithuanian Commonwealth. Peasants were forcibly recruited into the army by rebels, and the tsarist government immediately announced that any peasants who deserted the uprising would receive forgiveness "and the love of the tsar". Many peasants did flee the rebel groups *en masse* and it was precisely their indifference towards the on-going fight which was the reason for the fact that the uprising did not receive widespread support in Belarus. Russian troops gradually retook all of the captured settlements. The rebels from Poland put up the most resilient fight as they were well organised and armed and consisted purely of Poles who were prepared to fight to the end for their dream of a new independent Poland. These detachments captured Kovno (now Kaunas) and Panevėžys. The Russians advanced an army of 40,000 men. The opposing forces were not balanced and the Poles retreated, leading their troops into Prussia. The commander of the Russian army General P. Tolstoy took the advice of the nearby governor of Mogilev M. Muravev who knew the local region well. His advice on how to strengthen the local hinterland was invaluable to the Russian general. The Belarusian districts were divided into small regions and placed under the supervision of local landowners who, threatened with the confiscation of their property, were required to not tolerate any concentration of rebels and to immediately report any suspicious activity to the Russian garrisons.

During the Summer of 1831 there were some individual battles between the rebels and the Russian army, but by the end of the Summer all of the revolutionary hubs had been wiped out. Nothing on Belarusian soil stood in the Russian army's way, and so it marched on Warsaw, capturing the city on 8 August.

All participants in the uprising as well as those who were at least suspected of involvement were repressed. In every city a investigative committee was set up which was accountable only to the Russian government. The tsarist authorities directed their wrath against representatives of the petty gentry as it was this group that was the driving force behind the uprising. The main punishments included confiscation of their estates, demotion to rank and file soldiers and exile to Siberia.

The events of 1830-1831 were a clear indication to the Russian emperor of how dangerous and harmful the Polish influence and presence of the Catholic Church were to him in Belarus. The Russian government could not find any social or political support, even among those nobles and middle class that were not Polonised and still felt like they were of Belarusian nationality and Orthodox faith and, therefore, should, one would have thought, have had political sympathies for Russia. Therefore, immediately after the uprising, the government started to implement drastic measures to Russify Belarus.

A decisive political step in this direction was the so-called "inspection of the gentry". Russian government officials held an extremely negative opinion of the Belarusian nobility. Governor M. Muravev, for example, described them as "a class of parasites, for the most part even nomadic, accustomed to vagrancy and rebellion" (78). In accordance with the Decree of 1831, all those who could not provide documentary evidence of their noble origin were stripped of their noble titles and were shifted into the category of lower middle class or peasants. Such a fate befell more than 10,000 noble families. Even the word *shlyakhta* ('gentry') was banned and replaced with the Russian words *dvoryanstvo* ('nobility') and *dvoryanin* ('noble'). Thus, any petty nobility who were unable to prove their noble origins were removed *en masse* from the landowning class. This led to significant demographic changes. Belarus still had a large petty landowner class; they were often of relatively modest means, sometimes having a plot of land not much larger than a peasant's, but they belonged to the noble class and, therefore, had more rights, and this was always a source of opposition sentiments. Following the "inspection of the gentry" Belarus was purged of this class. Now nobles were only major landowners, the vast majority of which of Russian descent, who had received their land and estates as a gift from the tsar.

In 1832, on the orders of Nikolai I, all state bodies and officials were given Russian names and it was a requirement that only these names be used. In the same year, a Special Committee for the Western Provinces was set up under the Russian Government. This name, the Western Provinces, increasingly came to be the name used for Belarus in all government documents. This, of course, stressed the fact that there was no one single ethnic or cultural entity called Belarus, but there were just Russian provinces situated to the west of Russia. The Special Committee dealt with all matters of public life and controlled the education system, the working of the courts, and culture. In a speech to members of the Special Committee Nikolai I said: "The Committee should promote the resettlement in Belarus of peasants and lower middle class folk from central Russian provinces who will take with them to this region, which so strongly shuns Russia, our Russian language, our customs and allegiance to the Russian throne". The governor of Mogilev M. Muravev worked actively for the Special Committee. He saw only Poles in Belarusians, denied the existence of a separate Belarusian culture and deemed it necessary to fully eradicate the "Polish spirit" in these provinces and to replace it with the "Russian spirit". There was no place for a "Belarusian spirit".

In 1832, the university was closed in Vilno, as the main hub for dissidents, and almost the entire teaching staff chose to emigrate to Germany and France, which caused significant detriment to the future of Belarusian scholarship.

As noted above, in the first few years after the annexation of Belarus to Russia the government for a long time sought not to assign any preference to one religious denomination over another. But in the 1830s the tsarist government no longer wanted to put up with the

Polish influence in Belarusian lands, much of which was exercised not only through the Catholic Church, but also the Uniate Church. In 1839, at Moscow's initiative and after long ideological preparations in Polotsk, an Orthodox Church council was established. The council abolished the Union of Brest of 1596 and adopted an act to unite the Uniate and Orthodox churches. The Uniate Church went from answering to the Pope in Rome to falling under the Synod of the Russian Orthodox Church. Attached to this council act were written undertakings from 1,600 Uniate priests and monks to comply in full with all decisions adopted by the council. Under the adopted act, for the first time in more than two centuries it was not the Pope's name that was commemorated during the ceremonial liturgy, but that of all the Orthodox patriarchs. The promulgation of this decision throughout Belarusian towns and villages went on for several months and was accompanied by speeches by senior members of the Orthodox Church, bell ringing and solemn church services. The unification of the Uniates with the Orthodox was entirely peaceful and was organised in full "from the top down" without any opposition "from the bottom up". It was an indisputable victory for Russian politics as at the time Uniates accounted for 70% of the Belarusian population (Catholics made up about 17%, Orthodox 6%, Jews 7%, and Protestants and others 2%). The Orthodox Church welcomed 1,607 Uniate parishes and roughly 1.5 million believers. With that, the Uniate Church ceased to exist in Belarus. All of these changes which took place once again in the religious sphere led to Belarusian peasants frequently viewing religion as a formality, or even entirely indifferently.

Of considerable importance was legislation passed on local laws. Belarus was still governed by the Lithuanian Statutes of 1588 and it should be noted that the majority of the legislative provisions of this unique collection of Belarusian laws was not obsolete, and actually continued to be relevant and relatively well suited to all aspects of public life. A decree enacted by the Russian emperor in 1840 eliminated local laws in Belarus, bringing with it a single set of Russian legislation.

All paperwork and teaching in universities now had to be conducted in Russian only.

Despite all of these measures adopted by the Russian government, the idea of a national and social struggle continued to live on in Belarusian society. In the 1830s and 1840s this struggle centred around Vilno where, despite the closure of the university, a lot of members of the educated classes lived and worked. In 1836, when the reprisals against those involved in the 1830 uprising were still in full force, a "Democratic Association" was set up in Vilno at the Medical and Surgical Academy. The organisation's charter proclaimed ideals of social justice and demanded the emancipation of the serfs (79). Members of the association had radically democratic views: they fully repudiated the monarchy and preached in favour only of a republican government. This association first suggested ideas of possible physical violence against reactionary members of the hated autocratic powers, i.e. terrorist ideas. After two or three decades these ideas fully captured the minds of the Russian revolutionaries and led to the emergence of "bombers" and mass terror.

Polish émigrés, especially their radical elements, did not lose hope of a new uprising in "Russian Poland", their name for Belarus, and specific acts were taken to this end. In 1833 a group of Polish émigrés with false passports crossed the border with Belarus and in the Navahrudak region gathered an armed detachment of local peasants. But the secret police uncovered the plot before the detachment was able to act and its leader, Officer M. Volovich, was sentenced to be hanged.

In 1846-1849 there was a secret revolutionary organisation called the "Union of Free Brothers" which had branches in Minsk, Ashmyany, Grodno, Vilno and Lida and consisted of a few hundred members. Near Minsk they even set up an underground factory to produce weapons. The main aim of this organisation was to overthrow the autocracy through an armed insurrection and to implement democratic reforms in Russia and Poland. But the tsarist powers, which had set up a strong political police apparatus after the 1831 uprising, were relatively quick to hunt down and destroy revolutionary organisations, and they all lasted for no more than 3-4 years.

Revolutions in Europe between in 1848-1849 exacerbated the situation in Belarus. Illegal printed and handwritten pamphlets appeared calling on people to share the ideas of the revolutionary nations and to prepare themselves for an uprising. In 1848, a group of officers in a garrison in Minsk led by Captain A. Gusev refused to lead the regiment to Hungary to suppress rebels there. A. Gusev and a further 6 officers were sentenced to death by a military court for refusing to comply with the order and were shot.

At the start of Aleksandr II's reign (1855-1881) Russian policy towards the Belarusian and Polish provinces started to become more liberal. All political prisoners were fully pardoned and returned from exile. The law whereby only those with 10 years' experience in the relevant field and no previous reprimands for political views were able to take up public office was also repealed. Polish was allowed to be used at educational institutions. The Catholic Church was once again allowed to build new churches, which it had been forbidden to do for several years.

All of these liberal changes in Russian policy did not have the desired effect: they did not appease the Polish and Belarusian nobility, but rather gave rise to even greater demands and open opposition. Nobles in Vitebsk Province, for example, sent a letter to the Russian emperor demanding an increase in the number of Catholic churches and the opening of a Polish University in Polotsk. In Vilno brochures with revolutionary content were openly sold and meetings of nobility were held where they called for immediate separation from Russia. Catholic priests turned the numerous sobriety fraternities, which were very popular at the time among the urban population, into centres for anti-Russian propaganda. In 1859, when the Ministry of Interior Affairs began to restrict the activities of these fraternities, a propaganda campaign was launched accusing the government of being interested only in making drunkards of the Belarusian people. Anti-Russian sentiments were widespread in all institutions and educational establishments, and even the gendarme service, which consisted mainly of Belarusians, as Russians considered them to be more loyal than Poles, happily cooperated with the opposition nobility. In peasant circles rumours circulated that if the serfs helped their landowners during the forthcoming uprising against the Russians they would receive free land. Among young people it became fashionable simply to show one's opposition to the Russian authorities. It even reached the point that the Noble Union of the Mogilev Province sent Aleksandr II a petition, which was rather more like a demand. It asked the emperor to restore to the nobility all of the privileges that they had enjoyed under the Polish Crown in the Polish-Lithuanian Commonwealth, to recognise the Polish language as an official language on Polish and Belarusian territory, and to open the university in Vilno. The emperor realised that his liberalism had been interpreted by the Belarusians and Poles as weakness and that his influence over these lands could easily fall from his grasp.

CHAPTER 5
The Abolition of serfdom
(1861)

FROM THE 1840S THE PROCESS OF THE OUT-DATED FEUDAL SYSTEM'S disintegration turned into an economic crisis. The old economic system and complete disinterest among the peasantry in the fruits of their labour hindered the development of bourgeois relations. With this the government launched a series of reforms, but they were all inconsistent and piecemeal, as the government wanted at all costs to preserve the aristocratic monopoly over the land and the cruel exploitation of rightless peasants.

The reforms of the 1840s primarily concerned state peasants, numbering about 465,000 in Belarus. Statute labour was abolished for them, and in its place a single tax was introduced. This gave peasants the opportunity to work much more efficiently on their land, to take an interest in the outcome of their work, and to sell their produce on the market. There was a change in the legal status of state peasants too: after the reforms they could enter into marriage of their own free will, they could receive inheritance, they could engage in trade or crafts, and they could even become lower middle class if they had enough money to pay the fee to obtain this status. To a large degree these rights were only declarative and often not implemented in practice, but it was still a major step forward compared to the outright slavery of the past.

The measures to reform state villages evoked deep resentment among landowners as they considered them to be too radical. But maintaining the mediaeval forms of economic management was impossible, and

Emperor Aleksandr II quite carefully decided on certain progressive measures. In 1855 a law was passed to establish inventory committees to inspect the landownership both of the landowners and of the peasants, and thereafter to establish a single mandatory quota for all: a peasant had to have for use at least 5 *desyatinas* (approximately 13.5 acres) for each adult family member, and had to work statute labour on the landowner's land for no more than three days a week. Clearly, these measures rather improved the miserable situation of peasants, but did not detract from the very nature of feudal land tenure and dependency on serfdom.

The question of the complete abolition of serfdom occupied a central position in the ideological debates of the 1850s. At the time Russia was on the verge of revolutionary upheaval as the reforms of the 1840s had failed to yield any positive results. The government finally realised that the time had come to abolish slavery and that it was better to do it "from the top down" rather than let it happen "from the bottom up". But the government, with Aleksandr II at its head, wanted the initiative for the abolition of serfdom to come not only from the authorities, but from the landowners themselves. Tsar Aleksandr II did not dare to take the official initiative in such a complex issue affecting the ownership rights of the landowning class, the main seat of social support for autocracy. Since the landowners were also in no hurry to propose reform, this initiative had to be organised and stimulated. Preparations for the reform commenced in secret, unbeknownst to the general public. In 1857, the government set up a Secret Committee on the Land Question, which was to gather information from landowners on their ideas and suggestions for reform. In this endeavour, the tsar received considerable support from the Belarusian governor of the Grodno and Vilno provinces V. Nazimov. He persuaded Aleksandr II that all landowners in his provinces were keen supporters of the abolition of serfdom and offered him numerous ideas on possible options for the reform. And these proposals were heeded. Landowners in the Belarusian provinces were much more powerful than landowners in other regions of Russia, they were involved in trade and monetary dealings, their land was worked using modern techniques, and they understood the extent to which serfdom hindered economic progress. As such, they were the first to actively respond to the secret government proposal to develop and propose drafts for the new reform.

This continued for approximately 5 years. The final version of the reform was signed by Aleksandr II in February 1861, after which the *Manifesto on the Abolition of Serfdom* was released and promulgated. In the *General provisions of the Manifesto* it clearly stated that landowners were to remain the sole owners of all of the land that belonged to them prior to the reform, but that peasants would receive plots for their permanent use without any ownership right. Moreover, peasants had to buy their plots from the landowner at a price to compensate the landowner for the loss of ownership over the peasant. When buying the land the peasant had to pay 20% of the purchase price, and the landowner would receive the remaining 80% from the government in the form of securities. The peasant could pay his 20% and the rent for the land over 49 years; in other words, peasants, and their children, would remain indebted for half a century. During this time, the peasant would pay about 300% of the amount borrowed, which is about 3-4 times higher than the market value of the land taken. In addition, for the first 9 years a Temporary Regulation was introduced for peasants: during this period they could not leave their land, they had to work their statute labour and they had to carry out all of their other pre-reform duties. The only aspect of the reform about which peasants could truly be happy was the abolition of their personal dependence on the landowner and the fact that they now had civil liberties. Now peasants finally had the right to leave their landowner to engage in other activities, to acquire movable and immovable property and to inherit it, to enrol at educational establishments and to take up public office. But it transpired that peasants did not receive their personal freedom as a gift from the government, but rather that they had to buy it from their landowner for a very high price.

The peasants were still unhappy with this "freedom". In the first few months after the publication of the *Manifesto* there was a wave of peasant revolts across Belarus and Russia. In Belarus 370 were recorded, 125 of which were suppressed by the army and police. Peasants refused to work their statute labour and to move to land plots allocated to them, and would not obey the orders of the local authorities. In 1863 the peasant resistance to the conditions of the reform coincided with the national liberation uprising of Kastuś Kalinowski in Poland. This immediately caused the authorities concern and prompted them to adopt a number of concessions for the Belarusian peasants. They first repealed the nine-year Temporary Regulation and all of the restrictions associated with it were removed. In April 1863 a Committee which verified the size of peasants' land plots was set up and many plots were actually increased in size. In addition, the authorities, fearing mass demonstrations, were forced to reduce the purchase payments by 15-20% in Belarus.

Thus, the abolition of serfdom had its own unique features in Belarus. The concessions made by the authorities improved the situation of the peasants in the Belarusian provinces compared with other regions of Russia. The size of peasants' land plots were significantly larger and the amount paid for them was lower. After the land became a saleable object, the stratification of the peasantry quickly went, a labour market was formed and agricultural produce was more actively traded, primarily due to Belarus' proximity to the Western European market. All of this created advantageous conditions for the rapid development of bourgeois relations. The reform of 1861 undoubtedly gave a strong impetus to the development of capitalism in Russia. These changes, which took centuries in some Western European nations, occurred only over a matter of decades in Belarus. Nonetheless, Russia retained may feudal remnants which came to be a hallmark of Russian capitalism and remained a powder keg underneath Russian society.

CHAPTER 6
The Kastus Kalinowski uprising
(1863-1864)

A FTER THE DEFEAT OF THE ANTI-RUSSIAN UPRISING OF 1830, A section of the Polish and Belarusian nobility continued to maintain some hope of a return of the Polish-Lithuanian Commonwealth to its 1772 borders. Conditions conducive to mass protests started to materialise at the beginning of the 1860s when Russia was experiencing an economic crisis and was on the verge of revolutionary upheaval. In addition, Emperor Aleksandr II was renowned for his liberal views, and this only reinforced their hope for potential changes. But there was no unity among the supporters of Poland's independence like there had been 30 years previously. By the 1860s a new political force had come into being: the revolutionary democrats who reflected the interests of the peasants, city workers and petty bourgeoisie and set themselves specific goals such as abolishing serfdom, allocating land to peasants, overthrowing autocracy and establishing democratic freedoms. In Belarus, a new generation of revolutionaries was largely formed from low-ranking officials, the clergy, the lower middle class and students, but the unique feature of the political situation in Belarus was the fact that the social revolutionary ideas had close ties to the Polish liberation movement, and especially with the left wing.

On the eve of the uprising two discontented camps formed: the whites and the reds. The whites represented the interests of the upper bourgeoisie and major landowners. They hoped to restore Poland's independence through pressure on the tsarist government from

Western European nations, as well as through peaceful but mass messages and demands addressed to the Russian tsar. This was the conservative arm of the rebels; they were unwilling to take any active military measures and were more concerned with democratic demands. They saw the uprising as a purely noble matter, and rather feared that the uprising would be joined by peasants with their continuing demands for economic transformation, or in other words, land and money.

The reds consisted of members of the petty bourgeoisie, small landowners, intellectuals, students and a portion of the peasantry. Their main aim was to restore the Polish-Lithuanian Commonwealth, but they were later accepting of the self-determination of the Belarusian and Ukrainian peoples and a fundamental transformation of the forms of land ownership in favour of the peasantry. Achieving these goals, according to the reds, was only possible through a universal national armed uprising. The reds saw the key to success as an alliance with revolutionary forces in Russia itself, which should support them and weaken the resistance from the Russian Government from within.

To oversee the preparation of the uprising the reds created the Central National Committee in Spring 1862. The committee was headed by Kastuś Kalinowski, who came from a petty Belarusian noble family and graduated from the Faculty of Law at St. Petersburg University. In Vilno he started publishing the *Peasants' Truth* newspaper, a clear form of agitational publication calling on farmers to take up arms for their economic and civil rights. The periodical was a kind of propaganda in the sense that the current and complex social issues that it covered were presented concisely, clearly and understandably, using colloquial language. The newspaper persuaded peasants that the Russian tsar and the reforms implemented by him in 1861 on the abolition of serfdom, as well as his entire set of political policies, only sought to protect the interests of landowners, and only through armed struggle would peasants be able to rid themselves of this exploitation and attain their civil liberties.

The Catholic clergy played a major role in the preparation of the uprising. In their sermons priests talked constantly about the need to restore the former power of the Catholic Polish-Lithuanian Commonwealth, and in churches services were regularly held for the deceased of the 1830 uprising. Many Belarusians and Poles started to wear clothes adorned with a depiction of a broken Catholic cross, a symbol of their persecuted faith (the Catholic cross has four points, whereas the Orthodox cross has eight).

The uprising began in January 1863 in Warsaw. The Central National Committee issued the *Manifesto of the Provisional Government of Poland* which proclaimed the equality of all citizens, ownership of the land worked by peasants by peasants, and the abolition of all feudal duties. The *Manifesto* called on all peasants to participate in the uprising, but it said nothing about the right of Belarus and Lithuania to self-determination; they were considered part of the future Polish-Lithuanian Commonwealth. This programme and the aims of the uprising did not incite great enthusiasm among the Belarusian people as the peasantry were entirely disinterested in the question of restoring Poland to its 1772 borders. In Russia, even among the democratically-inclined public, the slogans of the uprising evoked not only outrage but a wave of chauvinism. No support for the uprising came from the Russian democrats, and under such circumstances it was doomed to defeat.

Armed detachments from Poland started military operations on Belarusian soil, some of which were initially relatively successful, but only in isolation. Local armed groups were only able to be formed in the Grodno Province, where 6 detachments fought, numbering approximately 2,000 people. But in April and May 1863 they were defeated by the Russian army which was superior in number and also had artillery on its side.

In May 1863, the suppression of the uprising was led by General M. Muravev, who had proven himself highly successful in organising similar actions during the 1831 uprising. He was granted extraordinary powers by Emperor Aleksandr II. He threw 138 infantry units, 66 cavalry squadrons and 120 guns against the rebels (80). But the wise general not only set about taking decisive military action, but also paid considerable attention to organising civil government in the towns and villages. He decided to coax and neutralise the social strata on which the Russian government could rely. A thorough but rapid check of the implementation of the land reforms was carried out, and peasants received numerous benefits: land purchase payments reduced by 15-20%, all feudal duties were abolished, and plots of land which had been taken away from them during the reform process were returned. Land was taken away from landowners who had participated in the uprising and was transferred to the peasants, significantly increasing their holdings; moreover, this transfer was done free of charge, quickly and publicly. Showing his confidence in the peasants M. Muravev ordered the formation of local guard services made up of local peasants who were required to inform the authorities of any insurgents appearing in their region. All of these measures proved more effective than administrative punishments and penalties. But this did not mean that the uprising was suppressed merely through such soft measures as these. 6,000 rebels were killed in the fighting (81), the number of convicts totalled 4,500, and 128 of these were sentenced to death with the remainder exiled to Siberia (82). Around 13,000 people were removed to remote Russian provinces by the authorities. The victims of the repression were mostly the reds, the left wing of the uprising, as the whites had fled *en masse* into exile. Kalinowski was handed over to the Russians by his own comrades and was sentenced by a court martial to be shot, but General M. Muravev personally ordered that he be hanged instead. K. Kalinowski's execution was held in public, which had not been practiced in Russia for some time, on the Market Square in Vilno on 10 March 1864.

The policies of the Russian authorities towards Belarus after the suppression of the uprising were aimed at changing the socio-political situation as a whole. The authorities started to implement a range of both open and secretive measures to prevent any future anti-Russian statements. To develop these measures the government set up a Western Committee which operated from 1862 to 1865. The holdings of landowners who had some connection with the uprising were confiscated and transferred to the state treasury and were then sold at a reduced price to Russian landowners, mostly retired military figures. The only higher education institution in Belarus, the Gorki Agricultural Institute, was closed, and at other educational institutions police and church control was implemented over the teaching. One particularly far-sighted measure was the staff rotation policy: Belarusian teachers, doctors and civil servants were transferred to positions in the depths of Russia's expanses and their places were occupied by workers from Russian provinces. They were drawn to Belarus with the offer of higher wages and the prospects of faster career progression. In 1864 the law on the inspection of Belarusian nobles was updated, again requiring documentary evidence of nobles' aristocratic roots, resulting in thousands of impoverished nobles being transferred to the lower middle classes. The liberal policy towards the Catholic clergy which had been consistently maintained by the Russian Government since Catherine the Great was replaced with a policy of repression. Catholic churches and monasteries were closed *en masse* or transferred to the Orthodox church.

CHAPTER 7
Social thought in the second half of the 19th century

TSAR NIKOLAI I (WHO RULED 1825-1855) WAS REFERRED TO AS THE "hangman" and "oppressor of freedoms" in Russia because he began his reign with the execution of those involved in the December uprising. This was followed by numerous executions over the next few decades and the creation of a vast apparatus of secret police and strict censorship. But Nikolai I sat on the Russian throne for thirty years and died of old age in the company of his family and loved ones. Tsar Aleksandr II was referred to as a "soft liberal" in social circles and the people referred to him as a "Tsar Liberator", as his name was associated with the abolition of centuries of serfdom which had kept all peasants in slavery. But Aleksandr II was assassinated by revolutionary terrorists in March 1881.

After the murder of the Emperor Russia implemented some drastic changes in its domestic policies. Liberalism was done away with and the government was vanquished by conservative forces. The 1880s and 1890s went down in history as a period of counter-reform and reaction.

In 1882 full police control was established over the publications of newspapers and journals. At the request of the Minister of Interior Affairs all editions had to cite the name of the authors, who had formerly published under pseudonyms. In Belarusian publishing houses practically no political literature was published; they chose instead to print mainly religious and theological books, dictionaries, encyclopaedias and geographical accounts. All works put forward for publication were censored. The slightest deviation from the official political line or any ideas about democratic principles were cut out by censors. For a long time in Belarus there were no independent periodicals; all newspapers and journals were state owned. Major newspapers included the *Provincial Gazette* and the *Diocesan Gazette*. These publications did not discuss the actions of the government or local authorities and did not publish any critical or polemical material. Vilno saw publication of the *Western Russia Bulletin*, which from the name alone shows that Belarus was seen merely as a Western geographical part of the Russian Empire. The ideological orientation of the journal was fully consistent with public policy with articles extolling the virtues of the Russian laws and the Orthodox church.

In the 1880s a number of laws and decrees were adopted which imposed restrictions on the education system. For example, the Regulations on Parish Schools of 1884 underlined the religious foundations of primary education, which, clearly, could only be based on Orthodox Christianity. To consolidate its control over the student population in secondary schools in 1887 the Ministry of Education issued a decree prohibiting *gymnasia* from accepting children from the lower urban classes: servants, small-scale shopkeepers and labourers. This decree was popularly called the *Decree on Cooks' Children*. Higher education was also placed under strict control from the tsarist authorities: the Regulations on Universities dated 1884 virtually eliminated the autonomy of university management structures, and the fee for one year of education increased from 10 to 50 roubles. To enrol at university a student would have to provide a police certificate of their "loyalty". After the closure of the Vilno University and the Gorki Agricultural Institute, there was not a single higher education institution open in Belarus.

In the 1880s there was a drastic change to the government's relationship to the Protestant Church. And even though by this time it had relatively few followers, the tsarist government took every possible step to restrict its activities. Measures included bans on the construction of new places of worship and attempts to introduce the

Russian language to its services, despite the fact that the Lutheran Churches had traditionally conducted their services in Polish or German since the 16th century (83).

In 1892 the New Regulations on Urban Governance were adopted which dramatically increased the property qualification for elections to the municipal government. Under the new rules the right to participate in City Duma elections was lost not only by the urban poor, but also members of the bourgeoisie if they were not rich enough. This led to a sharp reduction in voting numbers. For example, in Minsk at the City Duma elections in 1893 there was a turnout of only 1% of the population (in 1870 it was 14%). Thus, city governing bodies were populated exclusively by members of the industrial and financial bourgeoisie (who were, as a rule, Russian), and others from poor backgrounds (Belarusians) played no role. Therefore, it can be argued that the implementation of the New Regulations on Urban Governance took on a form of ethnic discrimination.

The situation in Belarus was further complicated by numerous restrictions on Poles or, more precisely, all Catholics, whether Belarusian, Ukrainian or Polish. The policy of Russifying the Belarusian population was pursued with considerable vigour after the 1863 uprising. An array of decrees prohibited Catholics from acquiring land; they could only inherit what they already had. Catholic landowners and merchants could not receive preferential loans from the main bank in Russia, the Nobles Bank, and Catholic peasants could not have a plot of land more than 60 *desyatinas* in size per family. The Jewish population was subjected to overt discrimination. Immediately after Belarus' accession to Russia Catherine the Great adopted the law on the Jewish Pale of Settlement. Under this law, Jews did not have the right to move at will to Russian cities, and had to remain in the Belarusian cities and towns that they had inhabited for the past centuries. This led to some Belarusian cities, especially smaller ones, having a Jewish population of over 50%. Decrees from 1882 once again declared that Jews were to remain in their own places of residence, and beyond this they were forbidden to purchase or lease land. Jews were not employed in government institutions, by the police, the army or on the railways. There was an interest charge for Jews to enrol in secondary and higher education institutions. The main goal that the tsarist government had set itself, by introducing these educational restrictions, was to consolidate the position of its main social base, the class of Russian landowners, and to lessen the influence on the social life of all other classes and strata. The authorities could not see or did not want to see any other support for their regime.

The changes in economic development after the abolition of serfdom led to changes in the social class structure of society. In the late 19th century the population of Belarus consisted of major landowners, the bourgeoisie and high-ranking officials (2.3%), middle bourgeoisie (10.4%), peasantry (30.8%), and labourers and servants (56.5%). Ethically, the Belarusian population for the most part fell into the peasant stratum (85%) and only 15% into the urban classes. According to the 1897 census, Belarusians (based on language) in the Mogilev Province made up 82.4% of the population, in Minsk Province 76%, in Vilno Province 56%, in Vitebsk Province 52% and in Grodno Province 44% of the total population. Poles and Lithuanians lived mainly in the western parts of the Grodno and Vilno Provinces, Russians lived throughout Belarus, and Jews (making up 14% of the total population of Belarus) lived in towns and cities within the Pale of Settlement. Huge changes towards the end of the 19th century occurred in the denomination of many Belarusians: now, after many years of the Russian Government's and Orthodox Church's efforts, 80% of Belarusians were Orthodox and 20% Catholics.

———————◆———————

The suppression of the 1863 uprising and the ensuing repression slowed the development of the Belarusian national movement, but in the 1880s it became more animated thanks to the ideas of a new revolutionary movement, the populist Narodnik movement (*Narodnichestvo* in Russian). From the 1870s to the end of the 19th century the Narodnik movement came to be the main focus of opposition civil thought. The Narodniks replaced the revolutionary nobles, were made up of numerous intellectuals of various descents and adhered to highly controversial revolutionary theories. The Narodniks believed in a special developmental path for Russia; they did not like capitalism, which was accompanied by the cruel exploitation of labourers, and they believed that Russia could bypass this developmental stage and move directly on to socialism. They saw the peasant society as the basis for socialist relations, and it was this "agrarian socialism" which lay at the foundation of all of the other theories and plans of the Narodniks.

From the very outset of the Narodnik movement there were two different directions: revolutionary (seeing the need for a peasant uprising across the entire country) and reformist. The first group considered a peasant revolt to be the main way to achieve their goals and so did everything possible to encourage peasants to fight actively for a transformation of society. Thousands of Narodniks – students, teachers, low-ranking civil servants – went to live in villages to engage in educational and propaganda-related work among the peasants. This movement was referred to as "going to the people" and lasted for almost twenty years, but it saw no successes over this time. The revolutionary ideas and socialist theories fell on deaf ears among the peasant community, and moreover, they frequently handed over the most active propagandists to the police.

In the 1880s Narodnik organisations were present in almost all Belarusian cities. In Minsk an underground printing house called *Black Redistribution* was set up for the Narodnik organisation across Russia which produced underground newspapers and leaflets.

After the hopes pinned on "going to the people" had failed to materialise, the underground Narodnik organisations came to rely on systematic individual acts of terror against members of the authorities. The Narodniks believed that terror against the most hated statesmen would generate support among all strata of society and would initiate a general uprising against the autocracy. The signal for the uprising was to be the assassination of the tsar. On 1 March 1881, after five unsuccessful attempts, Tsar Aleksandr II was finally assassinated. A bomb was thrown at the tsar's carriage by the Belarusian revolutionary Ivan Grinevitskiy. But the murder of the tsar evoked an entirely different reaction in society to that which the terrorists had hoped for. No uprising occurred, the press published angry articles and indignant letters to all members of society, and at churches where memorial services were being held for the slain tsar thousands of sympathisers gathered. The police carried out a wave of arrests and repression against the revolutionary terrorists which wiped out most of the Narodniks' organisations.

The Narodniks in Belarus attempted to unite into one organisation and to centralise their operations. To this end, the organisation "People's Will" (*Narodnaya Volya*) was created in Vilno in 1882. At the same time in St. Petersburg students from Belarus created several revolutionary groups before merging into the Belarusian socio-democratic group "Noise" (*Shum*). They published journalistic pamphlets entitled *To the Belarusian youth, Letters about Belarus, To the Belarusian Intelligentsia*, and *Epistle to fellow Belarusians*. All of these publications asserted the existence of an independent Belarusian nation as a separate branch of the Eastern Slavs and provided the scientific rationale for this. The revolutionary authors protested against the discrimination of Belarusians and stressed the reactionary nature of the assertions that Belarusians did not exist as a people and that there was only a "Western Russian" people. The brochure *Epistle to fellow Belarusians* described numerous examples of how Belarusians' rights had been infringed by the Russian authorities out of ignorance for their cultural and spiritual needs. The authors of the appeal *To the Belarusian intelligentsia* characterised the Belarusian people as a nation of slaves whose intelligentsia served either the Russian or Polish culture, but not Belarus' own culture. In this regard, they set a task for the intelligentsia: "… to rouse, to stir up the potential of our people, to give them the opportunity to show their national genius deeply hidden within from the predatory aspirations of the Poles and Great Russian chauvinism". The brochure strongly criticised the "Western

Rusism" that the Russian official sciences had started to formulate from the beginning of the 19th century which set forth Russia's right to ownership of all Belarusian lands. The historical school of "Western Rusism" was headed by the Professor of the St. Petersburg Theological Academy M. Koyalovich (84). Where did Belarus' historical path lie – to the east or to the west? With whom should it associate its destiny – with Russia or Poland? Why and for whose sake should Belarus move towards the Slavic Orthodox centre of Russia, and not the Catholic centre of Poland? Attitudes towards these questions formed two camps in Belarusian society. One of them, adhering to Belarusian roots, linked Belarus' historical development to Polish culture. The second group saw Belarus' future as part of an Eastern Slavic people headed by Russia and therefore announced a struggle against Polish influence. However, from the 1860s, when Belarus came to consolidate its position as a national identity, they declared themselves a group of local intellectuals which, although linking the nation's future with new-born Poland, nationally and ethnographically distanced themselves from everything Polish, seeing them as a separate original people.

Questions of its historical past were prominent in debates over the national development of Belarus. The official Russian school of history saw the period of the Grand Principality of Lithuania from the viewpoint of all-Russian unity. The main idea was the leading role of the Western Rus lands in the creation and development of the Grand Principality of Lithuania up to the 15th century. After the series of Unions with Poland, advocates of this school considered that the "Russian" lands fell under foreign Catholic influence and oppression, and that their subsequent history was marked by a constant desire to reunite with Orthodox Russia. The leitmotif of the advocates of "Western Rusism" were these words from the works of M. Koyalovich: "With the East Belarus has common blood and the enemy of the Belarusians is he who opposes this unity. From the East the Belarusians have brought such benefits as the divisions of Poland and the eradication of serfdom. But what has come from the West? Jews, Jesuits, church union, the death of the people's intelligentsia, the system of peonage and serfdom. For any honest individual with an understanding of the situation and the needs of his homeland of the Belarusian youth, there cannot be any hesitation as to where to go – to the East or to the West" (85).

Similar theoretical positions to "Western Rusism" were cultivated in Russia and Belarus in the 19th and early 20th centuries, and after the 1917 Bolshevik Revolution gradually Soviet historical sciences came to the fore, where they remained dominant.

In 1892, St. Petersburg saw the establishment of the underground international "Polish, Lithuanian and Belarusian Youth Circle" led by the Belarusian poet Adam Gurinovich (86). Members of the group were linked to the founding in Geneva of the Marxist group "Emancipation of Labour" and obtained from this group illegal literature including works by Marx, Engels and Plekhanov. They were active in the dissemination of revolutionary propaganda not only among students and intellectuals, but also among workers in plants and factories.

In the 1890s the ideology of the Narodnik movement gradually gave way to Marxism. The objective and subjective conditions at the time were favourable to the dissemination of Marxism and the emergence of social democratic parties in Belarus. The peasant socialism of the Narodniks became out-dated without yielding any results. The working class in formation increasingly started to declare their economic and political interests different to those of other social groups. Groups of workers started to form where they studied the works of Marx and his followers.

In 1895 Minsk saw the formation of the first social democratic underground group. Its members trained propagandists and sent them to factories to educate the workers. As a result, all businesses in Minsk saw a wave of strikes and walkouts demanding higher wages and improved working conditions. These walkouts were relatively successful: a number of laws were implemented, including one limiting working hours to 11.5 hours per day, another banning work for women and under-17s at night, and another which guaranteed all workers 66 weekends and public holidays per year.

The Belarusian labour movement had its own unique features which differentiate it from other labour movements in Russia. Polish and Jewish social democrats sought to create Marxist organisations on a national scale, and the Jews were particularly active in this regard. In September 1897 a congress of representatives of Jewish organisations from across Belarus gathered in Vilno to announce the formation of a General Jewish Workers' Union (Bund). Bund published its own paper *Arbaeiter Stimme* ('voice of the worker') in Yiddish (87). Bund leaders were convinced that only national workers' organisations could consistently defend their interests. Bund became a left-wing socialist nationalist party and followed Marxist ideas.

In March 1898 a prominent event occurred in Minsk which played a huge role in the future not only of Belarus and Russia, but also Europe as a whole. At the congress of Marxist representatives from Russia, Belarus and Ukraine, as well as the Jewish Bund Union, a Russian Social Democratic Labour Party was created. This party and its programme became the basis for the future Bolshevik Communist Party which carried out the Bolshevik Revolution in October 1917 and would later come to rule one sixth of the globe under the banner of the Soviet Union until 1991.

CHAPTER 8
The question of national self-determination

THE FORMATION OF THE BELARUSIAN NATION, WHICH WAS actively in progress throughout the 19th century, had almost been entirely completed by the start of the 20th century. All of the signs of a nation were present: a common economic life, a permanent territory of habitation, and a national language. Due to the poor development of the professional arts the main sphere of Belarusian spiritual culture were folk forms of work, folklore, rituals and customs, literature and lyric poetry. The features of the Belarusian ethnicity were reflected in a form of folk fine and decorative art. Broadly this included artistic weaving, embroidery, knitting, and wickerwork to make household items from vine. The consolidation of the Belarusian people as a nation was accompanied by the growth of a national consciousness. From the late 19th century the name Belarus and the Belarusians as a people finally started to take root. The formation of national consciousness was facilitated by the publication of a series of fundamental scientific works devoted to the ethnography and history of Belarusians, shedding an objective light on the existence of an independent Belarusian people.

The growing bourgeoisie in Belarus, like the bourgeoisie in other outlying districts of Russia, tried to stand at the head of the nation, but was met with opposition from the tsarist authorities through a policy of Great Power chauvinism. Under these difficult conditions, the bourgeoisie sought to unite the Belarusian people around the idea of national independence.

At the start of the 20th century the political leader at the forefront of the fight for national self-determination was the Belarusian Socialist Assembly party. According to some reports there were approximately 3,000 members in this organisation. The BSA actively engaged in the promulgation of illegal propaganda publications, and its influence was particularly strong in rural areas due to the low number of Belarusians among the urban population. The political platform of the party was based on demands for national and social equality and granting the people of Belarus the right to use their own language, to have their own official seal and their own literature. The Belarusian Socialist Assembly advocated the autonomy of Belarus with its own *Sejm* in Vilno. This party saw Belarus' future as a subject of a Russian Federation. In its proclamations the assembly lucidly and clearly expressed its position on some of the most pressing issues of the time: the adoption of a constitution granting the people the right to self-determination, the right to elect members to authoritative bodies through universal, equal and secret suffrage, and the right to freedom of the press, freedom of speech and freedom of assembly. The first slogan of the BSA was "Down with the Tsar and his government!" Its legal print body was the newspaper *Our share* (*Nasha dolya*) which was published in the Belarusian language, for Orthodox Belarusians in the Cyrillic alphabet and for Catholic Belarusians in the Latin alphabet. In these articles the newspaper writers forever stressed the idea that only the workers and peasants could achieve revolutionary change in society and that their interests were one and the same and did not contradict one another. The newspaper *Our Share* was not published for long as a court in Vilno handed down a ruling on its closure. The management of the BSA set up the publication of another newspaper, *Our Field* (*Nasha Niva*), the very first statement of which was that it would "serve all wronged and oppressed Belarusian people". The political line of the newspaper was significantly different and it occupied a restrained position on all questions, and in particular did not make any calls for revolution, but on the contrary pinned its hopes on the government itself starting to implement progressive reforms. The newspapers' materials often contained accusations against both Russians and Polish chauvinists who saw Belarusians as part of their nation, speaking in a dialect of either Polish or Russian.

Much of the credit for the development of the Belarusian national movement lies with the publishing house The Sun is Peeping through our Window (*Zaglyanet solntse v nashe okontse*). Founded in St. Petersburg, it published books in Belarusian, postcards with landscapes of Belarus, portraits of writers, and ethnographic and educational literature.

The Russian government and right-wring parties started to pit the Great Power chauvinism against the growing national movement. Between 1907 and 1910 it practically became public policy. Representation quotas were reduced at the State Duma for Polish and Ukrainian provinces. In Belarus, this policy had its own unique features. To oppose the Belarusian Orthodox peasants to the Polish landowners the government retained a much higher peasant representation than in central Russia: 30%. The quota for landowners among the electorate was on the contrary understated. In the Vilno, Grodno and Vitebsk Provinces the administrative bodies were split into Polish and Russian departments according to their national characteristics. With this, the Russian departments were assigned to cover Orthodox Belarusians, and the Polish departments took care of the Catholic Belarusians. Such a policy was entirely ignorant of the existence of Belarusians as a distinct people.

Along with this, propaganda against the Belarusian national movement and its consolidated ideological centre, the newspaper *Our Field*, was stepped up. However, the authorities did not make any exceptions for the Polish, Ukrainian and Jewish movements. The organisation "Black Hundred" showed particular zeal for this. Its members called themselves "true Russian patriots and royalists", and its ideological convictions were ultra-right wing and anti-Semitist. Their ideological credo was the slogan "Russia for Russians, and Russians to govern it". So they fought actively against all political forces standing for the self-determination of nations and their autonomy.

They rejected the existence of a Belarusian people, and considered Belarus "native Russian land". They owned the newspapers *Borderlands of Russia* (*Okrainy Rossii*), *Minskoe Slovo* (*The Minsk Word*), *The Vilno Bulletin* (*Vilenskiy Vestnik*) and the journal *Peasant* (*Krestyanin*). The Black Hundred's print media declared the Belarusian separatists even more dangerous enemies than those supporting the replacement of capitalism with socialism.

The Russian Government's ignorance of the Belarusian people's national interests was particularly evident in education. According to a law from 1906 all primary schools had to teach children in their native language. However, for Belarusians they made an exception. Their teaching was conducted in Russian as the existence of a Belarusian language was denied. This led many people of Belarusian nationality to register themselves as Poles. The reactionary character of the authorities was especially marked through their ban on certain professions subscribing to and reading the newspaper *Our Field*, which extended to teachers, priests, postal workers, police officers and military officials.

The Belarusian national movement was met with resistance not only from the Russian authorities, but also from Polish clerical and landowning circles. In essence, the policies of the Russian government, aimed at categorising the Belarusian nation by religion into Russians and Poles, was beneficial. In Vilno in 1906, 10 Polish newspapers and journals were published, in 1910 there were 18, and in 1914 there were 28 periodical publications. The majority were anti-Belarusian chauvinistic publications. Like the Russian state press, they denied the existence of a Belarusian nation and declared that the stirring up of its national struggle was a forced phenomenon and that it was simply a form of action and provocation against Moscow with a view to "Russifying Poles" who were ostensibly Belarusians. False ethnographic maps were published which were supposed to prove that the western part of Belarus was Polish soil and that it had long been occupied only by Poles.

The organisation of left-wing democratic parties as a result of the onset of these reactions was significantly weakened. The Belarusian Socialist Association reigned in their underground organisations and temporarily ceased to exist. All of the attention of its loyal members was devoted to legal journalism in the newspaper *Our Field*. This newspaper came to be the political and ideological centre of the national movement. But the newspaper could not legally promote the radical democratic programme as *Our Field* saw its main task as the cultural renaissance of the people, and it considered a national language as the foundation of culture. "First we need to revive our Belarusian language. Only after we have revived the language can our movement stand on a sound footing", wrote the newspaper. *Our Field* included pieces by Belarusian writers and poets including Yanka Kupala (1882-1942), Maksim Bogdanovich (1891-1917), Frantishek Bogushevich (1840-1900), and Yakub Kolas (1882-1956).

In the first few decades of the 20th century Belarusian culture made some significant achievements in the field of literature. The works of prose writers and poets reflected the life of the people, their oppressed condition, their hopes for a better future and their yearning for freedom and a decent life. The start of works by the poets Yanka Kupala and Yakub Kolas were directly linked to the events of the 1905 revolution. In their works, written to a very high artistic standard, they broached some of the most pressing social and humanitarian problems of their time. In his poetry from 1905-1914 Yanka Kupala incited the peasantry to revolution and criticised the social order and Russian aristocracy. Over these years he published his poetry collections *Guslyar*, *On life's road*, and *Fife*. In his poem *Who goes there?* Yanka Kupala raised the issue of Belarusian statehood through its poetic form.

The democrat and humanist Yakub Kolas was another classic Belarusian writer. His first poems were published in 1906 in the newspaper *Our Field*. Later came his collections *Songs of grief*, *Native forms*, and *Stories*. In his prose and poetry Yakub Kolas gave a truly realistic depiction of everyday life and the life of the poor, and it is easy to detect civil motifs and the rejection of exploitation.

With a clear democratic stance in his works, one citizen who lived for his people was the Belarusian writer Maksim Bogdanovich. He sharply criticised the autocratic powers and despotism in a romantic style, describing people's dreams of freedom. Maksim Bogdanovich even translated poetry into Belarusian from Ukrainian, Serbian, French, German and the Finnish languages.

CHAPTER 9
World War I

THE FIRST WORLD WAR OF 1914-1918, WHICH INVOLVED 38 countries from around the world, was a war fought for the redistribution of the colonies, spheres of influence and positions on the global market. All of the landowning classes in Russia supported the military policies of the authorities. The political forces in Belarus took up different positions. State-owned newspapers of all political stances called on the people to defend "the Tsar and the Motherland". Liberal and conservative parties called for class reconciliation within the country and agreement between the various political movements in the name of the success of the war against an external enemy. The Jewish Bund party did not adopt a unified approach to the war: some of its members were in favour of moderate pacifism, others sided with the Russian chauvinists, and the final faction were in support of a German victory. The Bolsheviks, led by Vladimir Lenin, came forward with their own peculiar concepts. They began to call for the transformation of the war from an imperialist war into a civil war, a war between the exploited and the exploiters. To do this, in their eyes, soldiers had to strive for the defeat of their armies in battles with the external enemy, which would accelerate the downfall of the tsarist government and pave the way for revolution. In Belarus, these Bolshevik ideas were actively disseminated by the newspaper *Our Field*.

On 18 July, just a few days after the declaration of war, all Belarusian provinces were placed under martial law. All meetings and demonstrations were strictly forbidden and the publication and sale of any print media other than state-owned publications were banned. The authorities were particularly concerned about strikes on the Belarusian railway, and so they created a Special Committee for the Further Protection of Transport. During the war, even by the end of 1914, the revolutionary and strike movement had ended.

It was on Belarusian territory that a considerable amount of the Western Russian Front was focused. The Supreme Command headquarters were also based in Belarus: first in Baranovichy, and later in Mogilev.

In July 1925 the German troops took Warsaw, using gas for the first time in these attacks, killing 6,000 Russian soldiers (76), before moving further east. Belarus became the theatre of war. There were 2.5 million soldiers of the Russian army on its territory. And as the Germans advanced approximately 1.5 million refugees streamed to Belarus. Thousands of homeless, starving people lined the Belarusian roads from Brest to Smolensk, dying from the typhus epidemic. The Russian Government was unable to cope with this situation. By Autumn 1915 the refugees filled the entirety of eastern Belarus, turning into a mass of poor people entirely deprived of all means of existence.

By early 1916 one quarter of Belarus' territory, with a population of more than 2 million, was occupied by German troops (89). The German authorities immediately imposed its system of taxes and fines, forced labour, and confiscated property. Material and cultural valuables, as well as the working population, were all taken to Germany. The German authorities planned to colonise and Germanise the occupied Slavic territories through mass migration of Germans to the region.

A considerable proportion of the Belarusian intelligentsia, including the Belarusian Socialist Association, supported the occupation by the German authorities and began to urge the Belarusian population to support the victory of the German army. Through its paper *Noise*, members of the BSA spoke out in favour of the revival of the Grand Principality of Lithuania under the protectorate of Germany. Amid harsh war conditions, poor supplies, and ideological confusion, the soldiers did not understand what they were fighting for, and revolutionary sentiments soon started to rise among their ranks. The troops on the Western Front started to actively run various Belarusian revolutionary organisations, including the increasingly popular Bolshevik party. In Autumn 1916 entire detachments of soldiers refused to go into battle, desertion intensified, and 12,000 soldiers left the Western Front. In October 1916, 4,000 soldiers rebelled in Gomel, destroying the punitive team, ransacking the guardhouse and releasing 600 prisoners. The authorities unleashed a brutal crackdown on rebels: nine people were sentenced to death, hundreds were sent to prisoner squadrons or penal servitude (90). But it was no longer possible to halt the process of the army's unrest and disintegration.

From 23 to 27 February 1917, 60,000 soldiers from the military garrison joined mass protests among workers in Petrograd (one month after the start of the war in August 1914 the city of St. Petersburg was renamed Petrograd so that there would be no resemblance to the detested German pronunciation of the word). Workers and soldiers united in unified military detachments, and on 27 February they seized the Main Arsenal, weapons, telegraph offices and railway stations. The revolution in Petrograd, which went down in history by the name of the February Revolution, was a success. On 2 March Tsar Nikolai II abdicated from the throne. The Romanov dynasty which had ruled the Russian Empire since 1613 had finally been overturned.

On 27 February the Soviet (council) of Workers' and Soldiers' Deputies was set up in Petrograd as an alternative governing body alongside the State Duma. On 2 March members of the Duma created a Provisional Government, electing Prince Georgiy Lvov as its chairman. Thus, the country had established a diarchy: on the one hand there were the Soviets, and on the other there was the Provisional Government.

In Belarus the situation was even more confused. On 6 March, in honour of the victory of the revolution in Petrograd, Minsk held a citywide demonstration, flying red flags and chanting the slogan "Long live the democratic republic!". It was attended by almost the entire population of the city. Speakers called for peace in society and the support of the Provisional Government. Throughout March, in cities across Belarus, Soviets of Workers' and Soldiers' Deputies were set up, taking over the functions of the government, but also recognising their subordination to the Petrograd Soviet and Provisional Government whose orders they continued to carry out.

In the countryside at this time there was a wave of peasant uprisings which, following the appeals of the Bolshevik party, began to plunder landowners' estates and divide the loot amongst themselves.

In March Minsk saw the creation of the Belarusian National Committee. It set about organising a congress of all the revolutionary parties. The Congress was held on 25-27 March and was attended by representatives of the revived Belarusian Socialist Association, the Catholic Democratic Party, the People's Democratic Party, and the Jewish Bund Party. The Congress instructed the Belarusian National Committee to begin drafting a new constitution and preparing for elections to a Belarusian parliament. This congress approved the creation of the Provisional Government in Petrograd and called on everyone to obey its orders. The Congress saw the future of revolutionary Russia as a democratic state in the form of a federation, granting all peoples a mandatory right to self-determination. In the eyes of those participating in the Congress, Belarus had to be an autonomous part of the new Russia. The Congress delegates made an attempt to enter into negotiations with the Provisional Government in Petrograd regarding the recognition of the Belarusian National Committee as the provisional supreme authority in Belarus. However, the Belarusian delegation at the Winter Palace, where the Provisional Government was based, was defiantly turned away. The Provisional Government had far too many other problems to deal with the separatist attempts of the Belarusians.

The political aspirations of the various parties differed from one another, from one day to the next. The Constitutional Democrats (Cadets) were the largest party in the first few months of the revolution. Their main concerns were the adoption of a constitution, agrarian reform, the establishment of an 8-hour working day, and the continuation of the war in line with Russia's alliance obligations. Later, after democratic changes, the Cadets recognised the right to cultural and national self-determination as autonomous peoples, but they did not view the Belarusians as a separate people out of their continued support for the "Western Rusism" theory.

The Socialist-Revolutionary Party (SRs) held a strong position. This party was particularly appealing to peasants, thanks to its slogans regarding equal land use for all peasants. The Jewish Bund Union was also one of the most popular parties, if nothing else because the Jewish population in the cities accounted for between 30% and 50%.

Throughout the existence of the USSR Soviet historical sciences claimed that the leading role in the February Revolution was played by the Bolsheviks. This assertion was far from the reality. At the beginning of the revolution the Bolsheviks were a small party; in Petrograd it had no more than 2,000 members. Vladimir Lenin, the leader of the party, and other members of the Central Committee were in exile in Switzerland. And only as more and more chaos started to set in in the country did the Bolshevik party grow in size as a result of its aggression and populism.

In the first few weeks after the February Revolution trade unions started to form in Belarus. By the end of March unions of shoemakers, printers and railway workers had formed in Minsk. They took the decision to adopt the 8-hour working day and implement a salary increase. However, in the current state of chaos, the implementation of these decisions was impossible.

Those parties with a national dimension made active progress, laying claim to the role of the political centre. The largest and most influential of these was the Belarusian Socialist Association, which had about 10,000 active members.

In July 1917 the Second Congress of revolutionary organisations was held in Minsk, which was dominated by the Belarusian Socialist Association. Under its influence the congress delegates called for the unification of all parties around their fundamental idea: the creation of a Belarusian national autonomous state within a democratic federal

Russia. But when, one month later, local government elections started in Belarus, the Belarusian Socialist Association did not receive any support.

In 1917, the broad masses of the Belarusian population and soldiers on the Western Front supported the SRs and Cadets. These parties agreed that the future fate of the country had to be determined by a Constituent Assembly, elected in a democratic manner, and its first issues would be ruling on the matter of an armistice, agrarian reform and the national question. The programme of the Bolshevik party completely dropped the general democratic stance from this, as its main objective was to establish a dictatorship of the proletariat. But the influence of the Bolshevik Party on the masses had grown exponentially. This can be explained by the fact that the Provisional Government in Petrograd led round-the-clock party debates, but did not take any action, failing even to put forward any concrete plans to stabilise the situation in the country and set about implementing the anticipated reforms. The propaganda of the Bolsheviks on ceasing the war with Germany at any cost was very effective, but at the same time the Provisional Government had decided to resume its offensive on the Western Front. In June, when the offensive began, under the influence of the Bolshevik propaganda tens of thousands of soldiers and workers went out in protest in Minsk, Vitebsk and Mogilev. The demonstrators demanded the immediate conclusion of a peace treaty without any annexations or indemnities. In July, there were mass demonstrations by soldiers on the Western Front who demanded the cessation of hostilities, the dissolution of the Provisional Government and the transfer of full powers to the Soviets of Workers' and Soldiers' Deputies. The Provisional Government issued an order to shoot discontented soldiers on the spot. With this, the diarchy effectively ended as the Provisional Government decided to abolish the Soviets. In Belarus, on the Western Front, mass arrests took place of all Soviet members, Bolsheviks and active soldiers. "Unreliable" military detachments were disbanded. All of this only contributed to the rapid "shift to the left" of the masses, bringing about far greater understanding of the Bolsheviks' radical appeals. The outcome of the struggle was fast approaching.

CHAPTER 10
The October Bolshevik Revolution
(1917)

I N THE NIGHT OF THE 25 TO 26 OCTOBER THE BOLSHEVIKS ORGANISED an armed assault by rebelling sailors and soldiers on the Winter Palace in Petrograd, the seat of the Provisional Government. All of its members were arrested and power was transferred to the All-Russian Congress of Soviets of Workers' and Soldiers' Deputies. The SRs did not agree with the arrest of the government and therefore left the Congress. In the first few days the Congress adopted the Decree on Peace and the Decree on Land and formed a government headed by Vladimir Lenin (1870-1924).

News of the fall of the Provisional Government immediately spread across Russia. The Minsk Soviet of Workers' and Soldiers' Deputies, the majority of which were already Bolshevik, issued its Decree No. 1, which declared: "All power to the Soviets!" As a result of this decision, Minsk prisons released 2,000 prisoners and deserters from which the First Revolutionary Regiment was formed. Two reserve infantry regiments went over to the Bolsheviks, taking with them a total of 5,000 people. The Soviet issued arms to hundreds of workers. In order to consolidate its power the Soviet sent its commissars to the railway station, post office and all other strategically important institutions and in the first few days established censorship over the print media. But by 27 October supporters of the Provisional Government, members of the Cadets, Bund and SR parties, set up a Committee in Minsk to save the revolution, as they believed that the Bolsheviks had usurped power. Having a significant advantage in terms of military strength (the committee to save the revolution had retained regiments of the Caucasian division numbering 20,000 people), the Committee demanded transfer of the power in the city, and the Bolshevik Soviet was forced to comply. But the Bolsheviks did not intend to yield power forever: they sent hundreds of propagandists to the army, and from there on 1 November an armoured train arrived in Minsk with 2 regiments of revolutionary soldiers. The Committee to save the revolution was disbanded and power was once again handed over to the Minsk Soviet of Bolsheviks. Throughout November, the Soviet regime, based on the one-party system of the Bolsheviks, was implemented across all Belarusian territory which was not occupied by the Germans.

The relatively easy victory of the Bolshevik revolution in Belarus can be explained by the fact that all layers of society were hoping for their most pressing and urgent issues to be resolved, primarily the issues of peace and land. The Bolshevik government immediately declared: "Peace for the people, land for the peasants!" and with this populist slogan millions of supporters were immediately won over. And it is easy to understand why: half of the country had donned military uniforms for World War I, and all of these people wanted peace. Almost two thirds of the Belarusian population were peasants, and they all dreamt of owning land. One of the most successful slogans of the Bolsheviks knocked the ground from under the feet of the other political parties. The Bolshevik leader Lenin swore in every speech that the Bolsheviks would do everything they could for the free national determination of Finland, Belarus and Ukraine, and this was a truly burning issue for these peoples (91).

On 19-21 November the Congress of Workers' and Soldiers' Deputies convened in Minsk. Out of its 560 delegates 480 supported the Bolsheviks. The Congress demanded that all civil servants and officials of government bodies submit to the Soviet regime and that all officers in the army who did not support the Bolsheviks be removed from their posts. The decrees of the Congress eliminated the old court system and announced the creation of revolutionary tribunals made up of three people who could, without any trial or investigation, hand down any sentences, including execution.

The policy of a range of Belarusian national organisations, including the Belarusian Socialist Association, was quite distinctive, as their stance was based on the need to create a sovereign Belarusian state. They supported the victorious Bolshevik Soviet regime in Russia and Belarus, but refused to recognise the central Russian government.

In the first few weeks of Soviet power the government managed to conclude an armistice with the Germans and cease hostilities on the Western Front. But the Bolshevik government did not have enough experienced officials to implement such revolutionary changes as exiting the war, transferring land from landowners to peasants, and implementing an 8-hour working day. The seizure of political power was not supported by a readiness for constructive action, or most importantly, the necessary experience and knowledge. For decades to come all of this predetermined the hardships in the socio-economic development of Russia and Belarus and demanded intensive efforts from the people, and even many victims. The first misfortune was the famine of 1918 when the whole country started to establish Poverty Committees which had the right to steal from the more prosperous peasants and to take away their corn, and if they failed to comply to shoot them. Corn supplies in the country did not increase as a result of such measures.

The October Bolshevik Revolution took place in the form of an armed coup, after which they immediately established a dictatorial form of government referred to as the "dictatorship of the proletariat", which was in reality the dictatorship of the Bolsheviks. This could not help but lead to confrontation in society, to military confrontation between the most diverse forces of society and the Bolsheviks. The SRs and Mensheviks (former associates of the Bolsheviks in the fight against the autocratic powers) immediately clashed with the new regime as they could not see any realisation of the principles of freedom and democracy in society for which many of them had been forced into penal servitude or put in prison during the tsarist era. The radical laws of the new government on the nationalisation of all businesses – even small ones – trade bans, the forcible seizure of corn from the peasants, labour service, etc. All of this dealt a painful blow on different sectors of society and led to civil war. But it should be noted that in Belarus the civil war was not especially widespread. This was due to the fact that the Belarusian upper bourgeoisie did not have any significant political unions of their own, and therefore could not organise any resistance against the new regime. Only the Belarusian Socialist Association occupied a staunch anti-Bolshevik position, uniting officials, clergy, intellectuals and youths.

After the October Revolution the question of Belarusian statehood was once again posed for the Belarusian people. On 5 December 1917 the All-Belarusian Congress took place, which was attended by 2,000 delegates. It was the first so highly representative and well-attended popular forum in the history of the Belarusian people. The Congress delegates expressed their disagreement with the policies of the Bolsheviks, believing that the revolution in St. Petersburg had led to anarchy, the loss of freedoms won through the February Revolution, and political terror. The Congress elected an executive committee which, after some time, in March 1918 adopted a declaration on the creation of a Belarusian National Republic (BNR). The declaration stipulated freedom of speech and of the press, of assembly and to strike, freedom of conscience and the equality of all languages of all the nationalities of Belarus. Only those who did not support the October Revolution and who were active opponents of Bolshevik ideas were elected to the BNR government. Primarily this included members of the SRs and the Belarusian Socialist Association. On 25 March the government adopted a decision to withdraw the BNR from Russia as a free and independent state (92). The national leaders adopted a white-red-white flag as the national flag (also adopted later after independence in 1991, but later banned under Lukashenko's dictatorial regime), and the *Pahonia* (the emblem of the Grand Principality of Lithuania) was chosen as the coat of arms of the new republic.

But the government of the independent Belarusian National Republic did not receive widespread support. The *Rada* (council) of the BNR tried to implement the idea of independence externally. This was a big mistake. The new government's policy of collaborationism with Germany, which at the time occupied almost half of Belarus, could not possibly bring success. The Bolshevik party published in their leaflets the wording of the letter from the cabinet of BNR ministers to the German Kaiser: "... we live in the hope that international forces will tear us away from Soviet Russia and unite us with Lithuania under the protectorate of Germany..." as well as the wording of a telegram in which the BNR government thanked the German Kaiser for liberating Belarus from the Bolsheviks and asking for assistance in the establishment of a new sovereign state in alliance with the German Empire (93). Once these documents had been made public, there was a political crisis in the BNR government which completely paralysed its activities. Members of the Jewish Bund left the government, and the Belarusian Socialist Association, which had until now been the main political force in Belarus, dissolved and ceased to exist. Members of the BNR government in most cases emigrated. Evidently, German did not in any way comment on the flirtation of the Belarusian government and the ideas of an independent Belarus as it had too many of its own problems to engage in a direct confrontation with the Bolsheviks in Soviet Russia. The new state received no formal legal recognition, and its creation remained on paper alone. The nations party to the Entente also did not recognise the Belarusian National Republic.

In this regard, the words spoken at a rally of Belarusian emigrants in St. Petersburg on 14 April 1818 were almost prophetic: "For three hundred and forty-seven years royal Poland has oppressed Belarus, and for the one hundred and twenty years which followed it was tyrannised by Russia. And now you Ukrainians aspire to expand your northern borders at the expense of Belarusian land into the Chernigov, Minsk and Grodno Provinces. You Lithuanians aspire to get our Kovno and Vilno Provinces... You Poles, profiting from the fact that Belarus was once on the eastern borderlands of your kingdom, want all of Belarus, from Białystok to the Dnieper, to be included in your newly created kingdom" (94). In this unusually tense and dramatic period of history all nations were concerned about solving their own problems.

There is no consensus among modern historians about the legitimacy of the Belarusian National Republic. In Soviet scientific and educational literature there is not a word about its creation, and in the period after the collapse of the USSR many historians greatly exaggerated the significance of this. But, of course, the declaration of the BNR was the first attempt at creating an independent state on ethnic Belarusian territory.

As a result of the collapse of the European empires on the political map of Europe many new states appeared: Hungary, Austria, Czechoslovakia, Poland, Finland, Estonia, Latvia and Lithuania. The last five of this list came from the former Russian Empire (95). Belarus was not so successful.

In November 1918, in connection with the outbreak of the revolution in Germany, the Red Army launched an offensive on the Western Front and quickly began to take back German-occupied Belarus. On 10 December 1918 the German troops left Minsk, and by March 1919 the whole of Belarus had been liberated. But at the same time, in February 1919, Polish legionaries began to advance on the Belarusian territory that had formerly been occupied by the German forces.

After Germany's defeat in World War I, Poland was restored as an independent state, and immediately the question was raised about its borders. Although the Polish politicians disagreed on exactly what status the eastern territories of the former Polish-Lithuanian Commonwealth should have, i.e. Belarus, Lithuania and part of Ukraine, they unanimously advocated their return to Polish control. The Soviet government, which had inherited all of the imperial ways of the tsarist regime, wanted control over the entire territory of the former Russian Empire and was not prepared to give Belarus to Poland. This could only result in military conflict. 10 Polish divisions launched an offensive towards Minsk and Vilno. In March 1919 they occupied Brest, Slonim and Pinsk. The Poles' rapid advance was aided by the rising protests within Belarus against the Soviet regime and Bolshevik Party. In many localities where Poles arrived they immediately started to revolt against the local Bolshevik Soviets. Anti-Bolshevik and anti-Russian landowners and petty bourgeoisie welcomed the Polish troops. In August-September 1919 the Poles reached the Berezina River; half of Belarus had been taken. The Poles eliminated the Soviet control in the occupied territories, abolishing the existing laws, and restored private ownership. The Red Army retreated to Russian territory, and then the Bolshevik agents started to organise a guerrilla movement in Belarus. The guerrilla groups were truly massive, numbering hundreds of people. This was not because they wanted Bolshevik rule, but because at the time the country had thousands of homeless and derelict armed people who had nowhere to go.

By the summer of 1920 the Red Army had won several decisive victories on the Eastern and Southern Fronts in the Civil War, and it now had free resources for the Western Front to authorise a counterattack on Belarus. In July, the Poles were ousted from the major cities of Minsk, Vilno, Grodno and Brest. The Red Army's successful offensive raised concerns to the west. On the 12 July the Foreign Secretary of Great Britain Lord Curzon sent a note to the Soviet Government urging them not to step beyond the line from Grodno to Brest. This ultimatum was rejected and the Red Army continued its offensive. In response Great Britain threatened that if the Soviet troops entered Warsaw then within three days the entire British naval fleet would start military operations in support of Poland. But the advance of the Red Army, which was launched with the aim of liberating Belarus from the Poles, had already taken on a different colouring. The Bolshevik Party had attempted to export its revolution to Western nations. The commander of the Red Army, M. Tukhachevskiy, an ardent Bolshevik, called not only for Poland to be taken, but to advance to Berlin too. But the anticipated support of the Polish proletariat and peasantry was not justified. Conversely, Poland had been overcome by a mass nationalistic and patriotic movement to defend their own recently proclaimed independence. Having halted his army just outside Warsaw, M. Tukhachevskiy started to retreat. The Entente Nations, especially France, offered tremendous support in the form of provisions and arms to the Polish army, and on 15 October 1920 the Poles once again successfully took Minsk. Battles continued all Autumn and Winter on Belarusian soil, with brigades and guerrilla groups formed from Belarusian nationalists fighting on the side of the Poles. Gradually the Polish army was driven towards Warsaw, but the Soviet Government realised that it could not keep all of Belarus as part of Soviet Russia as the anti-Bolshevik and anti-Russian sentiment was too strong. On 18 March 1921 a peace treaty was signed in Riga between the Soviet Union and Poland. No representatives of Belarusian organisations were invited to attend the negotiations. Western Belarus, with Grodno, Brest, half of the Minsk and Vitebsk Provinces, were ceded to Poland under the Riga Treaty. This area was approximately 108,000 square kilometres and had a population of 4 million people. Thus, only one third of Belarusian territory (60,000 square kilometres with a population of 1.65 million people) remained part of Soviet Russia. This was the political outcome of the October Bolshevik Revolution and Civil War. A new era had started for Soviet Belarus: the establishment of communism under Moscow.

PART 7

THE ESTABLISHMENT
OF COMMUNISM

(1920-1991)

CHAPTER I
Socio-political life in the 1920-30s

AFTER THE END OF THE CIVIL WAR THE NEW COMMUNIST government of Soviet Russia was faced with the question of organising domestic life and setting up a structure for the new state. It was clear that a return to a unitary state, as the Russian Empire was, was impossible and so it had to seek out new forms of political coexistence for the various peoples of the vast country. The Bolshevik government was dominated by two main ideas for the union: the principle of autonomy (advocated by Stalin) and the principle of a union of independent states (advocated by Lenin). Stalin proposed including all of the young Soviet republics in Russia as autonomous states, whereas Lenin's plan called for the creation of a union of independent Soviet republics, which would even give them the right to secede from the union. Lenin's plan received greater support in the republics and was therefore adopted for implementation.

On 30 December 1922 Moscow saw the opening of the 1st All-Union Congress of Soviets, which adopted a declaration on the creation of the Union of Soviet Socialist Republics (USSR). Belarus became part of the USSR as an independent republic, although this right was only in principle and not in reality. In 1924, Belarus was assigned the territory which had become part of Russia following the chaos of the first few post-revolutionary years: this included districts in the Vitebsk, Smolensk and Gomel provinces. As a result of this voluntary gesture on the part of the Soviet Government, the territory of Belarus increased by more than twofold compared with the outcome of the

Riga Treaty of 1921, and its population was 4.5 million, more than 70% of whom were Belarusians. The administrative unification of territories which were both historically and ethnographically homogeneous was of course beneficial to economic relations and facilitated the creation of well-connected economic systems, now based on new ownership principles.

The main feature of the political life of the 1920s was the formation of the one-party system. The national democratic movement split in this period, with members of other parties moving over to side with the communist Bolsheviks.

The Bolshevik Communist Party of Belarus (BCPB) was established in 1918 and immediately started to take action to eliminate other parties. In March 1921 the party liquidated the Jewish Workers' Bund, but a large proportion of its members voluntarily moved over to the BCPB. The terrorist methods of the Central Committee of the BCPB left dissidents no choice, or at least their choice was somewhat limited: emigration (if lucky), execution (a certainty), or adherence to the Communist Party. In early 1921 mass arrests and executions of members of the SR party were carried out, whose numbers were five times more than the Communist Party and also controlled a 8,000 strong youth organisation. The lifeless SRs were disbanded in 1924. The decisive and harsh imposition of the totalitarian regime across all republics of the USSR quickly stripped all remaining political forces of any illusions that they held on to. The Government in exile of the Belarusian National Republic (BNR), which still existed in Berlin, announced its dissolution and the termination of its struggle against the Soviet Powers at a meeting in October 1925. Perhaps an announcement in 1923 by the Government of the USSR offering full amnesty to all members of anti-Soviet organisations operating in 1917-1920 played a role in this. Many of them, believing in the amnesty, returned to Belarus and worked extensively in the cultural and scientific fields, greatly enriching these disciplines. But in the 1930s, a common destiny awaited all of the returned political émigrés, irrespective of their position and rank: execution as "enemies of the people" or many years spent in Gulags.

With the rapid departure of all opposition from the political arena, the ruling Communist Party devoted all its efforts to consolidating its position. In 1922 there were 4,834 members of the BCPB, and by 1929 this had increased to 33,380 members. The majority were conscientious people from working or peasant backgrounds with low levels of education, supporting the idea of creating a fair socialist society and inspired by the slogan of "he who was once nothing will become everything". Statistics indicate that the intelligentsia in the first few years of the Soviet rule did not join the party. According to the party census of 1927 30% of the party's members did not even have a primary education, and those with a higher education only made up 0.6% (96).

By the end of the 1920s the Communist Party had retained control over all aspects of social, political and cultural life. Sometimes its measures seemed entirely absurd: for example, even Belarusian grammar spelling rules, which had been adjusted in 1926, had to be coordinated with a specially-created committee under the Central Committee of the BCPB.

On 11 April 1927 the Constitution of the Belarusian Soviet Socialist Republic was adopted. It proclaimed the BSSR a socialist state led by a dictatorship of the proletariat. It was established that the power in the republic lay with the Soviets of Workers' and Peasants' Deputies. Basic rights were established, the most important of which were implemented in practice, including the right to free education for all and the right to medical care.

By the end of the 1920s the process of knitting together the party and state apparatus had come to an end and a centralised hierarchy was established made up of secretaries of the party's organs. After a short period of certain liberal and economic freedoms aimed at improving the economy devastated by the Civil War, the Communist authorities once again established an administrative command structure which had proven its effectiveness during the Civil War. The slightest deviations from official views on the methods and forms of social development led to immediate political reprisals. In the 1920s this was simply a case of removing people from positions and isolating them from everyday life in society. The leadership in Moscow closely monitored the Communist Parties in the republics, regularly sending commissars to them from the central authorities. Out of all the senior members of the Communist Party of Belarus from 1924 right up to 1953 (the year of Stalin's death), there was not a single Belarusian.

But the ruling party could not entirely reckon with the national sentiments of the population it had subjugated, and moreover, was forced to adapt its state apparatus to the language of the majority. In the early 1920s in Belarus there were 4 officially recognised languages: Belarusian, Russian, Polish and Yiddish. For some time the slogan "Workers of the world, unite!" was even written on the coat of arms of the Belarusian Soviet Socialist Republic in the four languages, which did not occur in any other republic. To more rigorously pursue its policies and propaganda, the Bolsheviks decided to impose restrictions on languages. To this end, in Belarus (and in the other republics) a programme of "Belarusisation" was announced in 1924. But the communist powers could only allow the Belarusian language and culture to be consolidated and disseminated under its guidance and supervision. In June 1924, a government committee was set up to oversee this Belarusisation in the BCPB. The political amnesty of 1923 and the return to Belarus of hundreds of émigrés (who were mainly leading scientists or cultural figures) greatly aided this process. Thanks to the return of the émigrés, the University of Minsk, which opened in 1921, finally managed to take on enough qualified teachers.

The programme of Belarusisation involved the translation of all paperwork and teaching in educational establishments into the Belarusian language, the teaching of "Belarusian Studies" in schools, and the appointment of locals to local government positions, rather than newly arrived residents. But given that the urban population was multinational, and there were 4 official languages under the Constitution (Russian, Belarusian, Polish and Yiddish), the policy of Belarusisation was relatively mild and short-lived. In the late 1920s, with the end of the period of liberalism and small-scale economic freedoms, Belarusisation came to an end. In 1927, at the Congress of the Bolshevik Communist Party of Belarus it was declared that national democracy was a progressive phenomenon during the struggle against capitalism and autocracy, and that now, under the dictatorship of the proletariat, national democracy was counter-revolutionary ideology which put national interests above class interests. The Bolsheviks, who had always been able to find simple solutions to complex issues, announced that social support for the national sentiments came from the kulak class (according to the Communists, all peasants who lived under somewhat more prosperous conditions than the poverty-stricken fell under this class). This created the ideological foundations for mass repression against the peasants in future. The over-enthusiasm for national culture was recognised not only as harmful, but dangerous too. In 1929 the Central Committee of the Communist Party adopted an official stance whereby national democracy was seen as "the main danger at this stage in the construction of communism". Linked to this was the NKVD (the People's Commissariat for Internal Affairs, the forerunner of the KGB). In 1930, the Cheka "exposed" the counter-revolutionary organisation "The Union for the Liberation of Belarus". In this case 108 people were arrested, all members of the higher circles of the Belarusian intelligentsia: the academics V. Lastovskiy, I. Lesik and S. Nekrashevich, professors A. Smolich and D. Petrovskiy, the minister for agriculture D. Prishchepov, the minister for education A. Balitskiy, writers M. Goretskiy and Y. Pushcha, secretary of the Central Committee of the BCPB I. Vasilevich and many more. All of those involved in the case received long prison sentences; death sentences had not yet become widespread – this would occur in the next 5 to 6 years. At the beginning of perestroika in 1988 the Belarusian KGB, at the request of the Institute of History, gave an official response in relation to this case: "After careful examination of archival materials no documentary evidence has been found on the existence of the organisation "The Union for the Liberation of Belarus". In other words, 108 people, the cream of Belarusian sciences and culture, were convicted and sent to Gulags on the basis of a falsified trial.

Political life and social consciousness in Belarus in the 1930s were full of controversy. On the one hand, there were significant advances in the economy and improvements in living standards. But on the other hand, there was a constant struggle against the slightest manifestations of political dissent, eliminating some of the best members of the intelligentsia and high ranking military personnel. The country was under the rule of a dictatorship led not just by one party, but by one person, its leader Stalin. The emotional and ideological basis for his dictatorship came from his cult of personality, the cult of an infallible leader. The roots of this lay in the administrative command system formed in the 1930s to govern all aspects of social life. The bureaucratic apparatus merged with the party and virtually transformed into a special social class. As a result of the knitting together of the state and party apparatus, the role of elected council deputies reduced significantly. Methods of governance were dominated by total centralisation and state terror against any dissenting and potentially dissenting citizens. But when the new Constitution was adopted in Belarus in 1937, it was almost the most democratic in the world at the time. It stated that the supreme ruling body was the Supreme Soviet, which at the time was a complete sham, and proclaimed numerous democratic freedoms, which, in reality, had not even been mentioned.

The end of the 1930s saw the repression against "enemies of the people" rise to a totally different scale. By this time, amid Stalin's cult of personality, the country had fully established a brutal totalitarian regime. The party leadership turned into a punitive body. "Enemies of the people" were needed as scapegoats for failures in the economy, to sow fear in society, and therefore to prevent any resistance from dissidents. In addition, out of the accused "enemies of the people", the government was able to create a labour army one million strong which would not be protected by any social guarantees or labour laws.

Once the state security agencies had dealt with the Belarusian intellectuals in 1930-32, accusing them of nationalism, the repression was directed against figureheads of Jewish and Polish culture and the clergy, especially Catholics. A wave of repression against Catholics began after the Pope wrote an open letter in defence of the religion which had been toppled by the Soviet regime. He called on the entire Christian world to pray for the victims of the Communist regime. On 19 April 1930, all Catholic churches in Western Europe held services in support of the Christians in the USSR. Soviet propaganda immediately referred to this action as a "crusade" for global capital against nations of workers and peasants (97).

Using the terminology of the time, "Belarusian national fascists", "Trotskyists", "Polish spies" and "Zionists" all faced arrest for their involvement in various counter-revolutionary, espionage and subversive organisations, which in reality never existed.

Senior members of the Communist Party did not trust their own party committees and held regular "party purges". During such a purge in 1933 numbers in the Communist Party of Belarus reduced from 65,000 to 38,000 members. During the period of exchange of party documents from 1935 to 1936 party numbers once again reduced, and on 1 January 1937 there were only 31,937 members. Thus, as a result of brutal political terror, the Communist Party lost more than 40% of its members, but was quickly replenished with new faces (98). By the start of the Great Patriotic War in 1941, there were 72,000 communists among its ranks. The new members were significantly different to the eliminated party elite, as they were well aware of the rules of the game, did not have any new communist ideas and ideals, and joined the party to make a career according to the established rules of complete subordination of juniors to seniors.

In 1937, during the greatest repression, dozens of Communist Party secretaries and trade union and Komsomol leaders were arrested, resulting in significant losses among the scientific and creative intelligentsia: 26 academics, a considerable number of rank-and-file scientists and university teachers, and more than one hundred writers and journalists were sent to the Gulag. Having purged the party of intelligentsia, the state security organs began to purge within themselves in a vicious dog eat dog environment. In 1939 more than half of the NKVD (People's Commissariat for Internal Affairs) were shot, including five chairmen of this punitive organisation which quickly replaced one another in this position: B. Berman, L. Zakovskiy, I. Leplevskiy, A. Nasedkin, R. Rapoport and all of their deputies.

It should be noted that ordinary workers knew nothing about the illegalities taking place due to false propaganda; they continued to support the Communist Party with enthusiasm as it tried to convince them that they lived in the most fair and happy society and that it was simply "enemies of the people", who had to be ruthlessly eliminated, who were interfering with them achieving complete happiness.

By the mid-1930s the international situation in Europe worsened. It was obvious that war was brewing. The Soviet Government attempted to negotiated with Great Britain and France regarding mutual assistance in the event of aggression by Germany, but they refused the offer. On 23 August 1939 in Moscow, after lengthy preparation, a non-aggression pact was signed between the USSR and Germany for 10 years. The Treaty had secret protocols which defined the scope of Germany's and the Soviet Union's respective influences in Europe. Western Belarus, which was at the time part of Poland, was under the Soviet sphere of influence.

On 1 September 1939 Germany invaded Poland, starting World War II. The Polish army was not in a position to put up any opposition to the invasion, the Polish government fled the country and by mid-September, the German troops reached Western Belarus. With this, on 17 September the Red Army crossed the Soviet-Polish border, with the attack order stating that the Soviet troops "must defend the lives and property of the inhabitants of Western Belarus and Western Ukraine". The advance of the Red Army was not met with any resistance, with Polish military detachments surrendering on the whole without a fight, and by 25 September they controlled the entire territory of Western

Belarus. The Soviet newspapers wrote that the fraternal Belarusian and Ukrainian peoples had finally been liberated from Polish occupation and were reunited with the fraternal Russian people. On 28 September a second treaty was signed with Germany in Moscow regarding friendship and non-aggression, in accordance with which Lithuania was also handed over to the Soviet Union. After Lithuania's occupation by the Red Army, the Soviet Government, without approval from the Belarusian SSR Government, gave Lithuania the city of Vilno and the Vilno Province. Thus, Belarus lost one of its most important cultural and historical centres. In all of the territories of Western Belarus and Lithuania occupied by Moscow they immediately started to implement measures to establish Soviet power.

On the question of the new territories' accession to the Soviet Union Moscow showed the foresight of preserving at least a semblance of purity and legality. On 1 October the CPSU Central Committee adopted a resolution "On the question of Western Belarus and Western Ukraine". It ordered the convocation of an elected National Assembly in these republics, but also elaborated the wording of the decisions which should be adopted by these National Assemblies. The Belarusian National Assembly convened in Białystok on 28-30 October. It adopted a Declaration on the inclusion of Western Belarus into the Belarusian SSR and on the nationalisation of land, the banks and industry. A response from Moscow did not take long: on 2 November the corresponding decision was made by the Supreme Soviet of the USSR. The Belarusian people, who after World War I had lived in two separate states, in the USSR and in Poland, were now reunited. The Belarusian SSR increased its territory to 101,000 square kilometres (a twofold increase) and the population grew from 5.6 million to 10.3 million. Immediately, new administrative divisions were set up on the annexed territories and party and Komsomol organisations sprung up everywhere.

CHAPTER 2
The Great Patriotic War
(1941-1945)

T HE FIRST MONTHS OF THE WAR. ON 22 JUNE 1941, WITHOUT warning, Nazi Germany attacked the USSR along its entire border from the Baltic to the Black Sea. The war which had started went down in Soviet and Belarusian history under the name of the Great Patriotic War.

Preparations for an attack on the Soviet Union were started by Germany immediately after it had captured the European nations. A key document was a plan named "Operation Barbarossa", signed by Hitler in December 1940. This plan consisted of a set of military, political and economic actions. In the military part of the operation he planned a "Blitzkrieg" in the first few days to crush the Red Army. There were plans to capture Moscow by 15 August at the latest. The German rulers were convinced of the Red Army's weaknesses and the fragility of the Soviet political system and assumed that with the first few military defeats of the USSR as a multinational state, it would fall apart and collapse. The General Staff of the Wehrmacht promised the Führer victory within a maximum of 16 weeks.

By the start of the war with the USSR, Germany relied on the economic potential of almost the entirety of Western Europe. At the time of the attack on the USSR its army numbered 8.5 million soldiers and officers. 5.5 million were sent to fight on the Eastern Front together with four German air fleets each with 5,000 combat aircraft, as well as the air forces of Finland and Romania. Nazi Germany set itself the goal of eliminating the USSR, seizing new territory, destroying or forcing millions of people out of Belarus, Ukraine and the European part of Russia beyond the Urals.

The Germans commenced their attack on Belarus with a powerful military bombardment of the border regions, before going on the offensive with ground forces. At the same time, German aircraft bombed cities, airports, railway junctions and Red Army positions. On the first day alone of the war, 538 military aircraft which had not managed to take off were destroyed at Belarusian airfields, and the entire Air Force of the USSR lost 1,200 aircraft within the first week, accounting for 40% of the entire fleet.

The attack on the USSR was launched by three army groups: "North", "Centre" and "South". The "North" army group was to seize the Baltic states and all ports on the Baltic Sea, including St. Petersburg (then Leningrad). The "South" army was sent to Ukraine and the North Caucasus to seize corn and oil. The "Centre" group was faced with the most important task: the rapid defeat of the Soviet troops in Belarus before advancing on Smolensk and Moscow.

The first powerful blow was dealt by the "Centre" army in the region of the cities of Brest and Grodno, where the sheer number of German troops and equipment exceeded the Red Army's numbers fivefold. Fighters at the Brest Military Fortress heroically defended their land. Border troops in the Brest Garrison numbered only 9,000, whereas the assault on the fortress by the Germans was backed by an infantry division of 17,000. According to the plan, the fortress was to be taken by midday on the first day of the war. But the garrison, entirely surrounded, and without food or water, and with an acute shortage of ammunition and medication, fought for almost a month. The Soviet soldiers hoped for and expected an attack by the Red Army to lift the blockade, but in the first month of the war the Red Army suffered stunning losses and retreated far to the east, continuing its retreat in complete chaos. About 4,000 of those defending the fortress from the Brest garrison were captured; the rest were killed.

The main strategic goal of the "Centre" army group was to take Minsk, Smolensk and then Moscow. On 28 June, near Minsk, troops from several Soviet armies were killed, more than 330,000 Soviet soldiers and officers were taken prisoner and 3,500 tanks were destroyed. During its defence Minsk was destroyed, the city burned, through the constant bombardment of the German air force. The evacuation of the city was not organised due to a lack of time and the total chaos that reigned, but the high-ranking leaders of the Party and Government had already left the city on 24 June. Official archives and documents were not removed, and from these the occupiers quickly learnt the names and addresses of government workers and party organisations, as well as members of their families. Using these documents, in the first few days the occupiers carried out mass arrests and executions in Minsk.

The surrounded 153rd Soviet Division defended Vitebsk for almost a month. It was impossible to keep the city, but the Soviet soldiers withstood two German armies before they eventually broke through the encirclement, battling through the front line and joining up with the Red Army. On 9 July Vitebsk was surrendered. On 14 July, in battles near Vitebsk in the town of Orsha, the Germans first experienced the mighty blow from a battery of new Russian weapons: rockets, which later came to be named "Katyusha".

The defence of Mogilev lasted 23 days. On 12 July the battle lasted for 14 hours with the Soviet army destroying 39 enemy tanks that day. On 16 July the city was completely surrounded, but still for 10 days the Red Army soldiers continued to fight bravely. Together with them the city's militia, comprising 1,000 men, and a police battalion of 250 continued to defend the city. 230 soldiers from this battalion, led by their commander Captain V. Vladimirov, were killed in the defence of Mogilev.

The courage that the Soviet soldiers showed in hopeless situations held back huge enemy forces and was of considerable moral and motivational value. Faced with an unexpected, but powerful resistance in Belarus, the German forces had to stop the offensive at the end of July and switch to the defensive to strengthen the flanks of the armies.

On 4 August Hitler arrived in the Belarusian town of Borisov and heard of the losses of the German army. It became clear to him that the hopes of victory within two months had not been fulfilled and that the war was looking to be far more drawn out (99).

In late August, the German army went on the offensive again, encountering no resistance from the Red Army which had retreated to Moscow and united with other forces for future battles. By early September, the entire territory of Belarus was occupied. Battles in Belarus over the first two months of the war thwarted Hitler's "blitzkrieg" plans and allowed them to strengthen their defences on the road to Moscow, which played a significant role in the further course of the war.

THE OCCUPATION REGIME. Having captured Belarus, the German occupiers began to establish a "new order", the aim of which was to eliminate the Soviet power and to loot national resources and national treasures. The ideological basis of the fascist methods was the theory of the "racial superiority" of the Aryan race over other peoples, which gave Germany the right to world domination, requiring new "living space" ('lebensraum') for the master race. The targets of Nazi Germany among the peoples of the USSR were identified in 1940 in the "Ost" plan and the "Directives for the governance of the economy in the occupied Eastern provinces" (the so-called "Green Folder"). These documents stressed that the war in the East would be different from the war in the West as it would seek to fully destroy the country, army and people. Hitler declared: "We must destroy the Slavic population; it is our mission to protect the German population. I have the right to destroy the millions of people of inferior races which breed like worms". Under the "Ost" plan, on USSR and Polish soil there were plans to eliminate 120-140 million people. A separate document of the "Ost" plan was dedicated to Belarus, in which it stated that only 25% of the population be left as a labour force, and 75% were to be eliminated or expelled to concentration camps. According to the maps drawn up for the "Ost" plan, from Belarus' western border on the Grodno to Brest line, the regions of Pinsk, Mozyr and all of the woodlands were to be entirely cleared of the local population to be settled by German colonists.

To implement its policies the occupiers created ancillary administrative and police bodies in the localities from opponents of the Soviet regime and a variety of collaborators. These governing bodies were under the constant supervision of the German military commanders. To maintain the "new order" in Belarus, 5 Wehrmacht security divisions were placed in Belarus, consisting of 160,000 people in total (100). In addition, the German authorities sent several pro-fascist groups from Ukraine and a Lithuanian battalion from Vilnius which was used to fight guerrilla and underground movements were sent to Belarus. The Lithuanian battalion, in particular, immediately engaged in punitive operations against the Jews and Communists: within just one month from 5 October to 7 November 1941, the Lithuanian battalion killed 43,000 civilians in mass executions.

The occupiers set up a system of camps. Prisoners were held in separate SD and SS camps, civilians were placed in labour camps, and Jews were put in ghettos. In total 260 concentration camps were in operation in Belarus. In the death camp at Trostinets near Minsk, over the three years of the occupation, 206,500 people were killed (101). The number of victims at this camp places it fourth behind Auschwitz, Majdanek and Treblinka.

One of the largest death camps was the Minsk ghetto which the Germans created on 19 July 1941. The ghetto was surrounded by a high wall topped with barbed wire. Jews could only work outside the ghetto with special permits. Any person found in violation of the rules was shot. During the occupation of Minsk, more than 100,000 Jews were killed at the ghetto (102).

After a guerrilla movement had spread across Belarus, the occupiers engaged in particularly brutal widespread reprisals. In February and March 1943 punitive counter-insurgency operations were carried out under the rather romantic name "Winter Magic" ('*Winterzauber*'). During these operations, 158 villages and their inhabitants were robbed and burned to the ground. One of these villages was Khatyn, whose inhabitants were suspected to have links to the guerrillas. On 22 March 1943 a punitive detachment was sent to the village, and all of the inhabitants, including women, the elderly and children, were herded into a large barn which was loaded with straw, doused with petrol and set alight. Those who tried to escape were shot on the spot. Among the peasants were families with many children, including, for example, the Baranovskiy family, which had 9 children, and the Novitskiy family with 7. The fire burned 149 villagers to death, 70 of which were children under 15 years of age. The village itself was completely destroyed. This method of mass destruction was applied by the Nazis to 628 Belarusian villages during the occupation. 186 of them were never restored as they were burned to the ground along with all their inhabitants (103).

To implement their genocidal policies the Nazi soldiers of the Wehrmacht and SS subjected the Belarusian people to ideological indoctrination. In the publication for Wehrmacht personnel heading to the Eastern Front *Memo to German Soldiers* it said: "You have no heart and no nerves; they are not needed for the war. Do away with your pity and your sympathy, kill every Russian, do not stop if there is an old man or a woman, a boy or a girl standing there in front of you, kill them – by doing this you will save yourself from death and secure the future of your family and be forever celebrated".

In 1969 in Belarus, not far from Minsk, a "Khatyn" memorial complex was opened which served as a monument to all of the destroyed villages. The complex is the only village cemetery in the world, with 185 graves, symbolising each of the perished villagers. The tomb of each villager has in it symbolic ashes, in the centre of which is a pedestal in the form of a flame and an urn with soil from the destroyed village.

THE GUERILLA MOVEMENT. The resistance movement started in Belarus immediately after its occupation. Guerrilla detachments were formed from the local population and the huge number of Red Army soldiers which were surrounded in the first two months of the war and ended up at the enemy's rear. Within the first few weeks of the war, the "Centre" army command group received regular reports that the army's supplies were being affected by the guerrillas destroying railways. By Winter 1941, 430 guerrilla detachments numbering 8,300 people were on Belarusian soil (104). The defeat of the German army near Moscow in December 1941 not only fostered courage in the patriots who had already fought, but also contributed to a rapid growth in guerrilla numbers. The battle near Moscow showed that the war would be long and that the Germans, despite their might, could be vanquished. This caused a sudden uptake of local residents joining guerrilla detachments. In May 1942 a central guerrilla command headquarters was formed, and from this time forward their actions were organised and strategically planned. In Spring and Summer 1942 a guerrilla detachment succeeded in freeing vast swathes of territory from the occupiers, thereafter creating guerrilla-led free zones. In the woodlands an October Free Zone was created which was controlled by the guerrilla detachment of Fedor Pavlovskiy (1908-1989), numbering 3,000 men. In the Mogilev Province the guerrillas liberated the Klichev District and the city of Klichev from the Germans. In the Vitebsk Province, not far from the city of Surazh, in Summer 1942, a guerrilla detachment led by Minay Shmyrev (1891-1964) managed to break through the front line along a 40 kilometre stretch and create the so-called Surazh Gates. As a result of this success, the guerrillas, sitting at the rear of the Germans, were able to receive an uninterrupted supply of food, weapons and military equipment, and they started to send well armed and trained Soviet diversionary groups into occupied zones. After several unsuccessful attempts to eliminate the Surazh Gates, the Nazi occupiers resorted to their usual methods of repression: capturing and shooting Minay Shmyrev's four young children: Liza (14 years old), Sergey (10), Zina (7) and Misha (4).

Fedor Pavlovskiy and Minay Shmyrev were named Heros of the Soviet Union (the highest level of military honour in the USSR) for their courage and heroism in the guerrilla struggle. The title of Hero of the Soviet Union was awarded to a total of 448 Belarusian soldiers and officers, 240 of which were guerrilla fighters.

Guerrilla detachments destroyed German garrisons, carried out attacks against government officials and collaborators, freed arrested hostages, and damaged communications lines. In 1943, when the front had drawn nearer to Belarus, and the time of liberation was near, the number of guerrillas rose to 155,000 people. This was a huge force. In 1943 the guerrillas received 20,000 rifles, 11,000 sub-machine guns, 1,235 machine guns, and 100,000 mines through the Surazh Gates from the Red Army in unoccupied Russia. In the period 1943-1944 all of the guerrilla detachments started the large-scale Rail War. This operation was set to paralyse the communications of the German army at a time where in Russia, near Kursk, for several months there had been a raging tank battle which proved decisive in the war between Germany and the USSR. The victory at Kursk was the final turning point in the war, after which the Red Army went on the offensive on all fronts, arriving in Berlin in April 1945.

The guerrilla struggle in Belarus, in spite of the unimaginable brutality of the occupation regime and its punitive operations, were truly mass and popular in nature. Such a phenomenon was not witnessed in any other occupied region of the Soviet Union. The following figures really reflect the scale of the guerrilla war in Belarus and its importance for the war in Belarus and its significance in terms of the final victory over Germany: over the three years of fighting at the enemy's rear 500,000 German soldiers and officers were killed, including 47 generals, 11,000 German trains were derailed, hundreds of kilometres of railway were blown up, and 1,355 tanks, 18,000 vehicles and 305 aircraft were all destroyed (106).

OPERATION BAGRATION. By Summer 1944 the situation on the Soviet-German front was entirely in favour of the Red Army which held the strategic initiative. The plan to deal the decisive blow to the German "Centre" army was discussed at the General Command Headquarters in May 1944 and was named Operation Bagration. It was named in honour of the Russian General Petr Bagration who became famous during the war between Russia and Napoleon in 1812. In this plan, they sought to break through the defences of the German army in the centre of the Eastern Front, crush the "Centre" army group and eliminate them one by one.

Operation Bagration took place from 23 June to 29 August 1944. On 23 June 1944 the Red Army broke through the front and began its mighty offensive. Now, just like it was for the Soviet armies in the first two months of the war, all of the German divisions were surrounded in "pockets". On 25 June near Vitebsk the Red Army encircled and destroyed 5 divisions of the German army, and on 26 June Vitebsk was liberated. In the Vitebsk "pocket" the Nazis lost 50,000 soldiers and officers. The city, which was on the front line, had been completely destroyed. When the Red Army entered Vitebsk, the commanders immediately ordered measures to assist the civilian population. Orders were given to draw up lists of survivors to offer them food. The list was compiled in the first few days of the city's liberation. Only 118 people were left of the population which had once been 180,000 before the war.

At the same time as the events in Vitebsk, the First Belarusian Front army surrounded 6 divisions of the German army near Bobruisk, encircling 40,000 people.

The occupation of Minsk lasted for 1,100 days. On the morning of 3 July, after a long bombardment of the city, tank divisions of the First Belarusian Front broke into the city, supplanted the main enemy forces and took the capital. To the east of the city, within the Minsk "pocket" the 105,000 thousand strong German army was surrounded. The city lay in ruins and after the war it was almost entirely rebuilt, except for a few small areas in the centre. During the occupation, more than 70,000 inhabitants were arrested.

The Red Army moved swiftly and triumphantly to the west. On 14 July Pinsk was liberated, on 16 July Grodno, and on 28 July Brest, a historical milestone between Belarus and Poland.

During the operations to liberate Belarus, the German "Centre" army group was entirely destroyed and huge losses were suffered by the reserve troops which were sent to Belarus from Germany, Norway, Italy and Holland. Thus, as a result of Operation Bagration the strategic situation on the Eastern Front changed entirely. The Red Army entered Polish territory and approached the borders of Germany. According to the assessment of the outcome of Operation Bagration by the German command, it was seen as an even greater catastrophe for the Wehrmacht than the defeat at Stalingrad. The offensive in Belarus, in terms of its scope, the number of military forces involved, and the speed of the military operations, was one of the largest battles of World War II, and the battle completely overwhelmed the German generals. The concentration of a huge number of German forces on the Eastern Front and the quick advances of the Red Army in Summer 1944 created conditions for the opening of a second front, on the subject of which several years of unsuccessful negotiations were held with the anti-German coalition government. On 6 June, British, American and Canadian troops supported by the French Resistance commenced its operations for an Allied invasion of Normandy, before advancing on Paris, liberating the city, and then attacking the Franco-German border. Thus, the West finally started to take action, which Russians refer to as the Second Front.

◆

The Belarusian people made irreparable sacrifices on the altar of victory in World War II. By 1942, Moscow had set up an Extraordinary State Commission (ESC) to establish and investigate the crimes of the German army on occupied territory. Two years later, a similar commission was set up in Belarus. The commission's staff gathered data on casualties and damage, interviewed witnesses and investigated sites of mass graves. It was found that on Belarus SSR territory the German occupiers had killed 2.2 million citizens and prisoners of war (107). ESC acts and documents have been recognised as evidence at the Nuremburg Trials against German war criminals. In the post-war period, especially during perestroika, this figure has been questioned by some academics, citing both higher figures (3.5 million) and lower (700,000). Demographic calculations of the losses using modern computer methods reconcile the most popular views on the subject and have again led academics to the figure put forward by the ESC in 1945 – more than 2 million. Thus, if we consider only the direct losses during the war years, then every fourth citizen in Belarus was killed, and taking into account the demographic consequences, not even every third citizen was counted in the country.

———◆———

During the period after World War II, thousands of scientific papers were written in the field of global historiography describing and analysing the events of the war. The most extensive and general works were written by American academics, who published a 99 volume history of the war, and by British academics, who published a 66 volume version. Japan even released a 100 volume history. A lot of papers have been written in France, Belgium and especially in Germany. Unfortunately, it cannot be ignored that American, French and British historians are often over-zealous in upholding the national and official stances in their research and strive to highlight the importance of the contributions of their governments to the defeat of Nazi Germany. As a rule, their works exaggerate the significance of the Second Front which only opened in 1944, and underestimate the contributions of the Red Army, with which the burden of the most global operations of World War II lay. The main front in World War II was the Soviet-German front, which involved between 190 and 270 divisions from Nazi nations. (Anglo-American armies came up against 8-20 divisions in North Africa, 9-26 division in Italy, and 56-75 divisions in Western Europe). The main German forces were lost on the Soviet-German front, with the losses of the Nazi army amounting to 10 million people, which was 73% of the total number of deaths over the entire period of the war.

CHAPTER 3
The period 1945-1991

THE VICTORY IN THE GREAT PATRIOTIC WAR CAME NOT ONLY FROM a sense of pride and patriotism among the Belarusian people, but also hopes of a better life. Demobilised soldiers and officers returned from the front, many of whom had seen life in European nations and started to relate differently, more critically, to the surrounding Soviet reality. Therefore, in the first few post-war years there were several attempts to create an underground anti-Communist organisation, especially in the western provinces of Belarus. The underground organisation "Chaika" ('gull') was made up of students in Brest and Baranovichy and "The Union of Belarusian Patriots" were active in Postavy and Glubokoye. These organisations did not set out to commit terrorist acts or to overthrow the existing government, but simply offered damning critiques of the ruling powers, promoted the values of democracy, and held political discussions which, under the totalitarian regime, required great courage.

Immediately after the victory over German, Stalin restored the strict totalitarian policies, started mass arrests and executions, and sent people away to concentration camps. Stalin used the war victory exclusively as an important bargaining chip to consolidate the authority of the Communist Party and himself, the all-powerful and ingenious leader. The hopes of the broad masses for a democratisation of social life did not materialise. All soldiers who had been taken prisoner by the Germans and who had returned home after the war were immediately sent to the Gulag, and all those who lived in occupied territory were under suspicion. In 1947, in a similar way to the 1930s, new fabricated trials against "enemies of the people" were held. Belarusian student underground organisations were uncovered in 1946-1947 and those involved were greeted with the fate which befell all dissidents in the Soviet Union: they were sent to the Gulag.

But it was not just small-scale student organisations which were set against the Soviet regime. For several years after the war armed terrorist groups operated in the Belarusian SSR, formed from the remnants of the Polish army, Ukrainian nationalists which had fled to Belarus, and all those who openly served the Germans during the occupation and now feared reprisals. These gangs were especially numerous and active in the western districts of Belarus which before the war had belonged to Poland. The nationalisation of the land and the creation of kolkhozes (collective farms) gave rise to protests among the local population, and the disgruntled joined the guerrilla groups which now fought not only against the German occupiers, but against the Soviet regime. The "Forest Brothers" group raided village Soviets, killed the leaders of the kolkhozes, and burned grain stores. The authorities were forced to place three times as many police in the western regions of Belarus as any other areas, and they were authorised to shoot anyone suspected of ties to the "Forest Brothers" without trial or investigation. But gradually these gangs lost their social foundations among the local population, as they in reality transformed into entirely criminal organisations. By 1952, all of these gangs in Belarus had been completely eliminated.

Over the entire period from 1946 to 1953 (the year of Stalin's death) there was a new wave of crackdowns in the USSR. In Belarus, the pre-war and post-war repression was associated with L. Tsanavy, the People's Commissar for Internal Affairs. He instigated the arrests of thousands of people and falsified trials against senior officials in the republic, academics and intellectuals. In 1947, a resolution was adopted by the Central Committee of the Communist Party in Moscow "On the work of the Central Committee of the Bolshevik Communist Party of Belarus" in which it stated that "the lack of Bolshevik criticism of works by Belarusian writers by the party has led to the emergence of many unprincipled and erroneous works incorrectly depicting Soviet reality". L. Tsinava immediately launched mass arrests of writers. Over 2-3 years more than 100 writers and journalists were arrested, and only about 20 of them returned from the camps after rehabilitation. In 1951, on a charge of spying for Yugoslavia, the Belarusian SSR Minister for Education and Enlightenment P. Saevich was shot. The President of the Belarusian SSR Academy of Sciences A. Zhabrak was stripped of all duties and titles for publishing academic papers on genetics in the American journal "Science". These are just some examples of the lawless killings of members of the Belarusian sciences and culture. Meanwhile, large quantities of Stalin's works and his biographies were translated into Belarusian and published to be studied in all educational institutions.

The crackdown on the ideological front masked the poor condition of the economy well. During the war years more than 10,000 industrial enterprises were destroyed in Belarus (85% of pre-war numbers), power stations and railways were destroyed, and 209 out of 270 cities were destroyed, including major cities such as Minsk, Vitebsk, Gomel, Orsha and Polotsk where 80-90% of the housing stock was destroyed. 380,000 Belarusian residents were deported to work in Germany (108). The inefficient agriculture, forced into kolkhozes, could not provide the country with food. The harvest in 1946 was half less than the pre-war harvest: there was not enough equipment and manual labour and it was just women and the elderly working in agriculture. In 1946-1947 there was a famine in Belarus with food being distributed according to a strict quota and ration cards. Farmers did not receive any salary, they worked for the sate for "work-day units", and depending on the number of days they had worked they received a miserly amount of food. No measures were adopted to provide material incentives for work, and on the contrary, heightened labour discipline was introduced through commanding and repressive methods. In June 1948 a decree "On the eviction to remote regions of persons refusing to work in agriculture" was adopted. From the western districts of Belarus alone more than

8,000 peasant families were sent to Kazakhstan and Siberia and their land was taken from them to transform them into kolkhozes. And as a rule, due to class considerations, the most prosperous and productive private farms of those who opposed the kolkhozes were destroyed. All of this led to the living conditions of peasants being not much better than they were during serfdom. Only in the second half of the 1960s did the agricultural situation improve somewhat.

◆

The international political status of Belarus grew considerably after World War II. In April 1945, an international conference in San Francisco, convened to found the United Nations, adopted a decision to include the Belarusian SSR among the founding members of the organisation. This was the international community's recognition of the huge contribution of the Belarusian people to the victory over Nazi Germany. Stalin persistently sought to include Belarus and Ukraine in this international body, citing the huge losses of the two republics during their occupation. At the Yalta Allied Conference, Prime Minister Churchill agreed with Stalin. "I sympathise with Belarus," he said in his speech at the conference, "which fought a tyrant and was victorious, shedding its blood". The Belarusian SSR delegation and representatives from Ukraine and the USSR participated in all of the sessions of the General Assembly from the very first days of the UN. Under a decision by the Relief and Rehabilitation Administration, set up by the UN to support those nations which suffered most in the war, in 1947 Belarus received goods and technology valued at 63 million dollars and monetary support in the order of 23.5 million dollars. In 1946, on the initiative of the Belarusian SSR, the UN General Assembly adopted a resolution on the extradition and punishment of war criminals. Later, with the active involvement of the Belarusian SSR, the *Convention on the Non-Applicability of Statutory Limitations to War Criminals* was adopted and the principles of international cooperation to seek out, arrest, extradite and punish war criminals were agreed. But the wider development of Belarus' international relations was hindered by a number of circumstances: the cold war between opposing political systems, the policy of "closedness" in Soviet society, and the practice of suspicion towards those who had been in contact with representatives of other nations.

Stalin's death on 5 March 1953 was a turning point for all aspects of life in the Soviet state. In September 1953, the position of first secretary of the Communist Party of the Soviet Union, the head of state, was awarded to Nikita Khrushchev. He realised that the totalitarian regime established in the USSR in the early 1930s was obsolete and required, if not total abolition, then at least some modernisation. A period of some democratisation then ensued, as the party tried to return to collective, and not individual decisions on political and state affairs. The Ministry of Interior Affairs was immediately stripped of all departments dealing with political repression. A key role in this democratisation of society and the improvement of living conditions was played by the 20th Communist Party Congress in February 1956. Khrushchev's speech at the congress was devoted to condemning Stalin's cult of personality and stressing the need to overcome its effects. Investigations began on the rehabilitation of victims of repression. In Belarus alone from 1956 to 1962, 29,000 people were rehabilitated and returned from camps and prisons. Across the country monuments to Stalin started to be dismantled. In Minsk, for example, in just one night a huge monument to Stalin was dismantled and destroyed on October Square. With this wave of democratisation there came a range of measures to enhance the rights of all of the union republics which were part of the USSR. The party's Central Committee finally granted the republics greater autonomy over political and economic issues. In 1956, the Central Committee of the Belarusian Communist Party, for the first time since the 1920s, was able to choose its own first secretary, as opposed to being sent a protégé from Moscow. The first secretary was the first ethnic Belarusian to occupy the position in the entirety of Soviet history: K. Mazurov.

Over the few years of Khrushchev's "thaw", as historians have dubbed this period, there were significant positive changes in the spheres of culture and literature. Many works which were banned under Stalin were published and cultural relations were expanded with Western European nations. But this period was not without its twists peculiar to the Communists. According to a statement made by Khrushchev in 1961 at the 22nd CPSU Congress and a newly adopted party programme the people were promised that communism would be established in the USSR within the lifetime of one generation, by 1980. This promise was not fulfilled.

In October 1964, Khrushchev was removed from office as the first secretary "for numerous errors in the governance of the country and for voluntarism". He was replaced by Leonid Brezhnev, whose governing term came to be known in Soviet history as a "period of stagnation". In the 1970s there were again trials of dissidents and strict censorship on literature and art. The attempts to reform the economy and to democratise society adopted in the 1950-60s gave way to conservative views and methods which led to the stagnation of the economy and economic crisis. Having put a man in a position with the only means to achieve his party's ideological aims, and having completely deprived him of interest as a result of his work, the Soviet state lagged behind the more advanced nations in all economic respects. At the same time citizens were alienated from the government authorities due to the monopoly of the single party system suppressing any dissidents. The ideological pressure evoked political apathy in the people and cynical attitudes towards social values; society was contained by lifeless dogmas which nobody have believed in for a long time. The economic difficulties of the 1970-80s led to low living standards among Soviet citizens, incomes did not increase in the population, and many foods were governed by quotas and rationed. The pace of development in all economic industries steadily declined. All of this led to the discrediting of the Soviet system as a whole. A radical reform of the economy, and inevitably the political system with that, became an objective necessity.

In April 1985, the post of first secretary of the CPSU came to be occupied by Mikhail Gorbachev. He strongly reiterated the need for reform, which later came to be known as "perestroika" ('restructuring'). Perestroika was aimed at all aspects of Soviet society, and special significance was attached to the democratisation of Soviet society. A paradoxical situation existed where the initiator of the reforms advocated not opposition to the government regime, but support for the very communist party which had led the country to a standstill. The party recognised the need for openness and the political revival of private entrepreneurial initiatives. The principle of "glasnost" ('openness'), which Gorbachev so extensively spoke about, called for the phasing out of CPSU control over ideology and actual implementation of rights to free speech and a free press. Censorship of the media was almost entirely removed, and this led to the publication of large numbers of historical and journalistic works which mercilessly criticised the Soviet society built by the communist powers over the last 70 years and the very methods by which it was created. By 1990, authoritarian control over social life and thought finally ceased to operate, and in the Soviet republics national processes started to grow. For the most part the Belarusian leadership sided with the national opposition, and the Supreme Soviet increasingly raised the question of full independence from the Soviet Union. Since 1990, the destruction of the single economic space which was the USSR started to take place, accompanied by a drop in production and uncontrolled inflation. This angered the general public and opposition against the central authorities in the Kremlin started to become widespread.

The foundations for the independence of the Belarusian SSR were laid on 27 July 1990. On this day the Supreme Soviet of the Belarusian SSR adopted the Declaration on the Sovereignty of the Belarusian SSR and set in motion a programme to transition to a market economy, which was the only alternative to the collapsed administrative command system. The basic principles of the state programme were guarantees of freedom of enterprise and freedom of economic choice.

From 19 to 21 August 1991, a group of high-ranking party leaders attempted a coup in Moscow to take revenge and restore the control of the Communist Party over the country. However, their actions were quickly neutralised by supporters of the new policy and democracy. After the elimination of the attempted coup all activities of the Communist Party were stopped in all of the Union's republics with party committees of all levels dissolving themselves. The attempted coup contributed to the rapid acceleration of political processes, and created conditions for the consolidation of the republic's sovereignty. The central authorities were paralysed and union laws and presidential decrees were not carried out. The actual power was already in the hands of the Union republics. On 25 August 1991, the Supreme Soviet of the Belarusian SSR adopted the resolution "On ensuring the political and economic independence of the Belarusian SSR". All enterprises and organisations under union control were transferred into Belarusian ownership. On 19 September the Belarusian Soviet Socialist Republic was renamed the Republic of Belarus and its national symbols were defined: a new state coat of arms and flag.

On 8 December 1991, Russian President Boris Yeltsin, Chairman of the Supreme Soviet of Belarus S. Shushkevich and Chairman of the Supreme Council of Ukraine Leonid Kravchuck signed an agreement in the Belarusian village of Viskuli on withdrawal from the USSR and the formation of a new Commonwealth of Independent States. The treaty stated that the USSR as a subject of international law had ceased to exist. With this ended the history of the "evil empire" and the era of the construction of communism. For the first time in its history, Belarus was faced with the task of building a new independent democratic state.

PART 8

RECENT HISTORY

(1991-2012)

CHAPTER I
The Outgoing Century

THE DESTRUCTION OF THE COMMON ECONOMIC SPACE OF THE USSR, which had already begun in 1989-1990, was accompanied by a steady decline in production across all of the republics. By 1991 Belarus witnessed a fall in both industrial and agricultural output by 30-35%. Shop counters were empty and stable foods were rationed. Such a sharp fall in living standards coincided with the first years of Belarus' independence and lodged a negative view of independence in the public mind set. For many, especially the older generations, the collapse of the USSR was perceived not as the end of a dramatic period of totalitarianism, but as a historical tragedy which brought about the ruin of all the familiar structures, poverty and lawlessness. At many businesses in the larger cities there were workers' strikes. Those involved were demanding an increase in their salary which was dwindling before their very eyes due to the constant inflation. The inexperienced young government of the newly formed state pursued a policy of artificial price regulation to prevent growing discontent among the people, but there was no way that it could be successful and prevent landslide inflation. By 1993, the average wage was one quarter of the amount in 1991. The state switched its printing press onto full capacity, throwing increasing amounts of money not secured against commodities into circulation.

After gaining its independence Belarus started to form a new government. All of the former ministries of the Soviet Union were placed under the control of the Belarusian government. One structure underwent practically no changes at all and did not even change its name: the KGB. This body managed to keep its own property, including some of the best buildings in each city, and its own staff. Society, which was occupied with solving painful economic problems, and in reality struggling for its very survival, paid no attention to the structure which very soon started once again to persecute dissenters.

The Belarusian military district of the Soviet Army was declared the Belarusian Army, and from Autumn 1991 Belarusian citizens started to undergo their military service exclusively on Belarusian territory. Since its inception, independent Belarus proclaimed peaceful policies. In Autumn 1991 all nuclear missiles were removed from its territory and returned to Russia. On 23 May 1992, Belarus signed the Lisbon Protocol, in accordance with which it pledged to sign the Strategic Arms Reduction Treaty and declared itself a nuclear-free country.

An important event in the foundation of the independent state was the development and adoption of a new Constitution. The Supreme Soviet of the Republic adopted a Constitution on 15 March 1994. Under this Constitution, the position of president was introduced, but the main state power still remained with the parliament, the Supreme Soviet. In July that year, the first presidential elections were held in Belarus. In the second round of voting, the winning candidate was Supreme Soviet Deputy Aleksandr Lukashenko, who at the time was the head of the "Communists for Democracy" faction in the Supreme Soviet and was famous for his scandalous and vulgar populist speeches.

Lukashenko's career is remarkable for its diversity, changing his workplace and role numerous times, and actually not working anywhere for more than 2 to 3 years. His last positions before being elected Supreme Soviet Deputy were: Deputy Director of the "Udarnik" Kolkhoz in the Shklow District; Deputy Director of the Construction Materials Complex in the city of Shklow; and then Secretary of the Lenin Kolkhoz Party Committee. In 1990, on the wave of social upheaval caused by perestroika, he was elected to the Supreme Soviet of the Belarusian SSR.

At the time, when the glasnost proclaimed by Mikhail Gorbachev actually removed all forms of censorship, it was common to show on television live broadcasts of Supreme Soviet sessions and all of the debates held there, which would have been entirely unthinkable in the former totalitarian communist society. Thousands of people for hours watched the political coverage thereby becoming, albeit passively, part of the political process. Lukashenko quickly came to be a prominent figure, thanks to his strong and critical speeches, in particular on corruption, and extremely populist oratory style. For example, when the Supreme Soviet ratified the Belavezha Accords, which marked the end of the USSR, Aleksandr Lukashenko, according to some sources, was the only deputy who voted against the agreement, and according to other sources, abstained. Later Lukashenko declared that the disintegration of the Soviet Union was "the greatest geopolitical catastrophe of the 20th century".

From the very first few days of his rule, Aleksandr Lukashenko conducted a clear policy of rapprochement with Russia and was categorically opposed to any nationalist slogans. He immediately clashed with the Belarusian Popular Front party who championed the ideals of national cultural development. The so-called "language problem" which had been aggravated in the wake of perestroika in the late 1980s had become a battlefield for political games. The problem was that the active Russification of Belarus carried out by the Communist Party during the Soviet era led to a sharp decrease in the use of the Belarusian language. Now the Popular Front party was linking this problem to the desire for true independence, democracy and the country's own national policies. Back in 1990, thanks to the efforts of the Popular Front, the Supreme Soviet adopted a law "On languages in the Belarusian SSR" in which Belarusian was declared the official language. Russian was simply guaranteed "equality with all other languages used by citizens in Belarus". This law caused considerable controversy in society, as approximately 80% of the population spoke in Russian and were against Russian losing its status as an official language. Even many members of the Popular Front saw the law as premature and overly extreme. President Aleksandr Lukashenko took advantage of these sentiments and initiated a referendum on the official language and state symbols. He wanted to pit the masses against the his sworn enemy and main political rival, the Popular Front. But at the same time, Aleksandr Lukashenko sought to resolve another even more important issue: consolidating his own personal power.

The referendum addressed four questions:

- making Russian an official language

- amending the state flag and emblem

- supporting the president's actions aimed at economic integration with Russia

- amending the Constitution to give the president the right to dissolve the Supreme Soviet should the Constitution be violated.

Clearly, the fourth question was the most pressing for Lukashenko. A favourable decision on this matter would significantly expand the president's personal power. At the same time, the ambitious Lukashenko actively sought widespread popularity in Russia, as he expected that under favourable circumstances he could even become president of Russia, or at least lead the Russian union state.

Lukashenko's proposal to hold a referendum evoked strong protests from the Belarusian Popular Front deputies on the Supreme Soviet, as Belarus' Constitution clearly granted only the Supreme Soviet the right to decide on a national referendum. But the president said that he would take full responsibility for the referendum and that it would not require any decision by the Supreme Soviet. Out of protest, all of the Popular Front deputies, led by Z. Poznyak, and members of the Belarusian Social Democratic Party, led by O. Trusov, held a hunger strike in the Supreme Soviet hall and refused to leave the government building. In the night from 11 to 12 April, under the pretext that word had been received that the building was rigged with mines, OMON special riot police burst into the hall together with members of the president's security service. They forcibly expelled the deputies, many of whom were beaten. The next day, President Aleksandr Lukashenko did not try to make any excuses for himself, declaring simply that he personally ordered the removal of the deputies from the Supreme Soviet building for their own safety.

On 12 May, the Belarusian Popular Front issued a statement in which they called on the Belarusian people to vote no to all four questions in the referendum. Thus, the party went against the wishes of the president, who was very popular at the time, and lost.

The referendum went ahead of 14 May 1995. All of the motions were passed. In the various regions, 75-83% of the population voted yes to all four questions. The Soviet flag and Soviet coat of arms once again returned to independent Belarus (with minor changes to small details). In the evening after the polls had closed and the first preliminary results had been declared, the Head of Presidential Affairs I. Titenkov personally climbed on to the roof of the Government Building, ripped down the white-red-white flag and tore it to shreds. From then on, the abolished white-red-white flag and coat of arms of the Grand Principality of Lithuania, the "Pahonia", came to be symbols of opposition in the fight against Lukashenko.

The results of the referendum laid the foundations for the consolidation of presidential power at the expense of the legislature. The nationalist ideas of the Belarusian Popular Front showed their unpopularity. It should be noted that the referendum vote was not subjected to any criticism or doubts on either side. It was the first and last national referendum in Belarus recognised by law.

By 1996, the conflict between the president and parliament intensified on all aspects of public life, and the country entered into a period of political crisis. The parliament insisted on carrying out market reforms, extensive privatisation, preserving sovereignty and consolidating society on the national idea. One of the most pressing political issues was the question of integration with Russia. In April 1996, an agreement was signed between Russia and Belarus on the establishment of the Union of Sovereign Republics. Russia opened up all of its markets to Belarus and started to supply raw materials and energy at discounted prices. As a goodwill gesture, Belarus had its debts written off at $1 billion dollars for previous energy supplies. In protest against this agreement, the opposition organised a demonstration in Minsk on 26 April, the 10th anniversary of the Chernobyl nuclear power plant disaster, which was attended by 50,000 people. The demonstrators came bearing white-red-white flags and slogans such as "We don't want to go back to Russia", "Lukashenko is a Russian agent", and "For independent Belarus". This was the first mass anti-government protest.

To shift the situation in his favour Lukashenko decided to use the already well-proven method and again proposed to hold a national referendum. This time he put forward questions of changes and amendments to the Constitution. These changes were due to transform the parliamentary-presidential republic into a presidential republic. In response the Supreme Soviet proposed including in the referendum an opposing question, on abolishing the position of President. The conflict was so strong that the Constitutional Court of the Republic of Belarus was forced to intervene. The court sided with the Supreme Soviet deputies and recognised the eighteen Presidential Decrees adopted over the previous year as inconsistent with the Constitution. The court ruled that all of the referendum questions on changes to the Constitution could only be advisory in nature, and in no way binding, since according to the current Constitution any changes to its provisions could only be made by decisions handed down by the Supreme Soviet. One of the judges of the Constitutional Court, V. Pastukhov, declared: "adopting provisions of the Constitution through a referendum is the same as entrusting a surgical operation to a nurse".

But Lukashenko ignored the decision of the Constitutional Court. He knew that standing in his way to absolute power were only the laws of the Constitution and the Supreme Soviet. Despite the fact that the decision of the Constitutional Court were final and could not be appealed, President Lukashenko issued a decree on the binding nature of all referendum questions, while accusing the Constitutional Court of "attempting to limit the constitutional right of citizens to take part in a referendum". This populist rhetoric covered up the president's direct violation of the country's Constitution. Moreover, the decree made a direct threat against those government bodies "which might stand in the way of the referendum", warning of closure and dissolution.

In a speech on 9 October, Aleksandr Lukashenko made his views clear: "My attempts to establish constructive cooperation with the Supreme Soviet have failed. Only as a result of constitutional reform can we finally do away with the endless and pointless political battles and focus on the issues that most concern our people. It is through strong leadership today that we can save our state and economy. Under a weak president our home-grown liberals and DUMBOcrats, with their talk of the good of the people, will leave us exposed in our own country".

Lukashenko did not hide his admiration for "strong" leadership in the past. It is worth nothing an interview he held with the German newspaper Handelsblat on 23 November 1995. Quote: "German order developed over the centuries. Under Hitler this development reached its peak. This is in line with our understanding of a presidential republic and the role of the president in it. Hitler formed a mighty Germany thanks to his powerful presidency. It was the 30s, a time of great crisis in Europe, and Germany rose up thanks to its powerful government". This interview caused quite a stir in the media in Western Europe. The reference to Hitler, thanks to whose "strong" leadership the "mighty Germany" was formed, and this from the president of a country which calls itself "democratic" was a sign that the Republic of Belarus was in danger.

From 19 to 20 October the Belarusian People's Assembly sat in Minsk, attended by 5,000 representatives from industrial enterprises and organisations. The resolution adopted announced support for the president's political policies and condemned the actions of the opposition "aimed at dividing society and destabilising the country". On 18 and 19 October the opposition forces held a National Congress "In Defence of the Constitution against the Dictatorship", attended by approximately 1,500 people. Members of the Supreme Soviet started to collect signatures to begin the impeachment of the president. The country was witnessing an acute political crisis and schism in society. Faced with this situation, Lukashenko endeavoured to hold a referendum as quickly as possible to change the Constitution, after which nobody could oust him from office.

The acute crisis, involving two branches of the government, had an impact not only in Belarus, but around the globe. Public opinion in Western nations supported the opposition and condemned the usurpatory actions of Lukashenko. For example, on 17 October, the US State Department declared: "Not wishing to continue working alongside the parliament, President Aleksandr Lukashenko is going down a path to split the country".

On 14 November, a few days before the referendum, by order of President Lukashenko, the Chairman of the Central Electoral Committee for Elections and Republican Referendums, the active leader of the opposition and experienced lawyer V. Gonchar, was illegally removed from office. Speaker of the Supreme Soviet S. Sharetskiy referred to this event as "the beginning of a forced government revolution". Under the Constitution, the appointment and removal of the Chairman of the Central Electoral Committee did not fall under the president's remit, but rather that of the Supreme Soviet. The president's security services forcibly expelled Gonchar from his office. An immediate response was issued by the Chairman of the Constitutional Court V. Tihinya, who sent an appeal to President Lukashenko to overturn his decision to dismiss Gonchar, since the president had exceeded his constitutional mandate. The President ignored the request.

The demonstrative dismissal of the Chairman of the Central Electoral Committee practically paralysed the working of the committee on the eve of the referendum. The president personally appointed L. Ermoshina, an ardent supporter of Lukashenko (who remains in office to this date), to the role of Acting Chairman. The Speaker of the Supreme Soviet S. Sharetskiy said "The Republic has seen the beginnings of an unconstitutional seizure of power and the establishment of a dictatorship".

Mass propaganda was published in the state media in support of the president and his draft amendments to the Constitution. According to a group of international observers from the European Media Institute, virtually all television and radio airtime (more than 90%) was handed over to supporters of the president. People were exposed to mass indoctrination with citizens being called upon dozens of times every day to show support for the initiatives of the president. All regions saw the establishment of referendum preparation headquarters and nearly all executive authorities acted as presidential canvassers.

In this challenging environment, on 24 November 1996 the referendum was held, largely shaping the future course of Belarus' development. The main question, the very reason for the organisation of the referendum, was worded as follows: "For the adoption of the Constitution of the Republic of Belarus with the amendments and addenda proposed by President Aleksandr Lukashenko", with 70.4% voting in favour and 9.3% voting against the motion. The same referendum provided responses to other key questions: 82% voted against private ownership of land and 80% voted against the abolition of the death penalty. (Belarus is still the only country in Europe where the death penalty has not been abolished.)

The rhetoric of Lukashenko and his populist promises of a wonderful life if the people granted him unlimited power found sufficient support among the broad masses. The idea of a union with Russia amid the reigning economic devastation turned out to be salutary, as many believed that their stronger "big brother" would not leave them in the lurch. Sympathies for Russia were entirely natural in a country where 80% of the population spoke Russia and the centuries of common history between the two culturally close peoples naturally played a huge role in the public consciousness. Lukashenko was particularly popular among the elderly who shared nostalgia for the former USSR. He skilfully took advantage of these features in the Belarusian people to combat the nationalist opposition, and as a result was victorious in the struggle. The young, inexperienced and not yet existent democracy in Belarus had lost out to the fierce thirst for power of the new leader. As soon as the new Constitution had been adopted on 27 November, Lukashenko declared that his five-year presidential mandate would start afresh, namely not from his election date in 1994, but from the date on which the new Constitution was adopted in November 1996, thereby extending his rule by two years.

On 29 November Lukashenko issued a decree dissolving the Supreme Soviet, and out of those deputies who supported the constitutional reform he set up a new "pocket parliament", the National Assembly House of Representatives. There are no other examples in history when parliamentary deputies were not elected, but rather appointed by the president. The European Union and the US have not recognised the legitimacy of the new parliament where the deputies were appointed rather than elected. Those members of the Supreme Soviet who were not appointed to the new "parliament", led by Speaker S. Sharetskiy, continued to view themselves as the only legitimate parliament and represented Belarus on the international stage. Until 2001, their delegations were welcomed into the Parliamentary Assembly of the OSCE.

In actual fact, the events and results of the referendum were a constitutional coup. Out of protest against the usurpation of power by President Lukashenko, eight judges resigned from the Constitutional Court in Belarus, led by its Chairman V. Tihinya, Prime Minister M. Chigir, Employment Minister A. Sosnov, and Deputy Foreign Minister A. Sannikov. The OSCE (Organisation for Security and Co-operation in Europe) and the European Parliament declared the referendum and its results illegal. "The new Constitution of Belarus is illegal and does not meet the minimum democratic standards and violates principles of the rule of law and the division of powers". This was the assessment of the European and international institutes expressed by the President of the Parliamentary Assembly of the Council of Europe, L. Fisher.

Political and public life started to be saturated with developments in 1999.

The Belarusian Popular Front and the United Citizens' Party did not recognise the new Constitution created by Lukashenko or the extension of his mandate. They sought to organise and hold presidential elections in the Summer of 1999, as set out as a fundamental law of the country prior to Lukashenko's modifications. All of Lukashenko's opponents rallied around these parties and deputies of the defunct Supreme Soviet, led by V. Gonchar. To Lukashenko, the danger of these opposition actions, going down a course to hold "alternative elections", lay in the fact that the regime that he had set up could fall apart like a house of cards. If the opposition succeeded in organising and holding elections on the basis of the 1994 Constitution, it would mean that the opposition had publicly proven the first great crime of the government, the constitutional revolution of 1996, resulting in the illegitimacy of the incumbent President Lukashenko.

Political crisis again brewed in the country. Amid this backdrop, in 1999 the disappearance of key opposition leaders was particularly striking: former Interior Minister Y. Zakharenko, former Speaker of the Supreme Soviet and Chairman of the Central Electoral Committee V. Gonchar and A. Krasovskiy, a businessman funding the opposition, all disappeared. Law enforcement agencies launched an investigation into their disappearance, but the inquiries have never given any results. To many it was clear that these individuals were abducted to kill them for political reasons. In Belarus, and in many other European countries where Belarusians live, 16 September, the day of Gonchar's and Krasovskiy's disappearance, sticks in the memory. In 2010, a documentary film called *The Godfather* was filmed in Russia which directly expressed suspicions of President Lukashenko's and his security service's involvement in the abduction and murder of the opposition leaders.

The opposition's attempt to organise alternative presidential elections came to nothing. Western societies officially recognised the end of President Lukashenko's powers in 1999 and his further tenure has been declared illegitimate.

In December 1999, in St. George's Hall in the Kremlin, Presidents Aleksandr Lukashenko and Boris Yeltsin signed a treaty establishing a Union State. Integration under this agreement went quite a long way. For example, it called for the creation of a common parliament based on elections held in both countries. Lukashenko nurtured the idea of a possible running in the Russian presidential elections in 2000, and for that he needed a union treaty according equal political rights to the citizens of both countries. He hoped that he could overpower the old and weakening Yeltsin at the elections. After signing the treaty, in the early 2000s there were active attempts to implement the articles and provisions of the treaty, but as a result they were unsuccessful. Both parties had differing views on the various issues of building the new Union State, which, however, did not stop more and more new demagogic and populist resolutions from being adopted. For example, a decision was adopted to introduce a common currency from 2008, which was never implemented. It was obvious that Belarus could not integrate into the economy and political situation of Russia without losing its sovereignty. Vladimir Putin's declaration in 2002 on the possible incorporation of Belarus into Russia as a federal subject was also not conducive to integration. This statement was met with great public indignation in Belarus. But, nevertheless, the rhetoric of the "friendship between the two fraternal Slavic peoples" continued, as it was a sure means to divert the public consciousness from real problems. Belarus' economy could not do without two very important things: Russian energy resources and the Russian market. The people started to refer to the constant rhetoric of a rapprochement with Russia as "oil and gas in exchange for kisses".

Belarus' foreign policy in 1999 was significantly affected by events in Yugoslavia. The NATO military operation from March to June 1999 provoked a strong reaction in the governments of Russia and Belarus. Lukashenko, speaking before the National Assembly, declared that a new global divide had begun, and that the bombing by NATO revealed the true goals of Western democrats to appropriate the criminal right to punish other nations. In the same speech, the President called on the West to stop pressuring Belarus, noting that Europe and the US were financing opposition media in Belarus and "revanchist" forces. The Belarusian President declared: "All of these gestures... will receive an adequate response. We are not Yugoslavia; we are able to protect ourselves, whatever the cost". In April 1999 Lukashenko visited Belgrade where he held talks with Yugoslav President Slobodan Milošević regarding the accession of Yugoslavia to the Union of Russia and Belarus. Such talks were held both in the Russian State Duma and in Yeltsin's government. A quote from the Chairman of the Russian State Duma G. Seleznev stated: "This Union is possible, and the argument that we have no common borders is irrelevant; the same applies to the US state of Alaska". Obviously, the war in the Balkans ended with the collapse of Yugoslavia, and so the issue was dropped.

Alongside these powerful political events, 1999 went down in history as the year of hyperinflation in Belarus. The National Bank introduced more and more new notes into circulation, and in 1999 there was even a 1 million rouble and 5 million rouble denomination (for comparison, in 1991 the highest denomination note was 100 roubles). The value of one US dollar reached 320,000 roubles, and the minimum guaranteed wage was 1 million, i.e. three US dollars. From 1 January 2000, the government was forced to announce denominations having removed three zeros from the values. Now, the dollar was worth 320 roubles (on 1 January 2012 the value of the dollar was 8,100 roubles).

In 1999, the country held a census. According to data from the census, there were 10,045,000 people in Belarus, representing 130 nationalities. 81.2% of the population considered themselves Belarusian.

By the year 2000, positive economic development had started to set in. The pre-crisis levels of 1990 had finally been surpassed in terms of industrial production and household income. The government increasingly spoke about "five-year plans", just like during the Soviet era and the construction of communism. A highly telling event in this regard was the Second All-Belarusian Assembly, attended by 2,500 delegates in Minsk. The assembly (not the government) adopted a programme of socio-economic development for the next five years. According to this programme, there were provisions for wage increases by 2005 to 250 US dollars, and old-age pensions to 120 US dollars. All of this still did not resemble the Soviet Union, in which all national assemblies spoke *ad infinitum* about "improvements", "increases", "advances", "introduction", "development", etc.

CHAPTER 2
The Incoming Century

BEFORE THE 2001 PRESIDENTIAL ELECTIONS LUKASHENKO FULLY protected himself from any competition by removing all of his most powerful opponents. The foremost opposition leader V. Gonchar disappeared without a trace, the chairman of the most radical party the National Front, Z. Poznyak, and the former Speaker of the Supreme Soviet S. Sharetskiy were forced to emigrate, the former prime minister M. Chigir was imprisoned on charges of "negligent performance of his duties", and the former deputy chairman of the Supreme Soviet G. Karpenko died under mysterious circumstances at the age of 49.

By this time, President Lukashenko had concentrated all of the main economic and information resources of the country in his own hands and had enlisted the support of the new Russian President Vladimir Putin. The Central Electoral Committee was permanently taken over from 1996 by Lukashenko's supporter L. Ermoshina, and all of her employees were subjected to a strict selection process based on their allegiance to the president. All of this ensured his victory in the elections in September 2001, at which he received 75% of the votes. His main rival, Chairman of the Belarusian Federation of Trade Unions V. Goncharik, took 15% of the votes.

The Belarusian opposition, the US and the European Union did not recognise the results of the elections, stating that there were numerous violations in the way in which they were conducted and that they did not meet democratic standards.

The term of the new presidency of Aleksandr Lukashenko was due to expire in 2006. Under the current Constitution he could not stand for president for a third time. So he decided again to use the method of a referendum and again to change the Constitution. Unlike the Supreme Soviet, which in 1996 upheld the law and fought against the despotism, for which it was ultimately broken up, in 2004 his "pocket parliament" had absolutely no objections to the referendum. Opinion polls conducted by Russian and international companies, in particular The Gallup Organization / Baltic Surveys, showed that the majority of the population did not support Lukashenko's initiative to extend his presidency. But on the eve of the referendum there was a fifty per cent increase in wages in the public sector and in the state old-age pension. Television news broadcasts each day opened with announcements that on the day of the referendum goods would be sold without trade margins at polling stations, and visuals showed rows of appetising sausages. And through such simple methods the president bought the loyalty of his citizens.

On 7 September 2004 President Lukashenko issued a decree on a referendum. The question for the referendum was solely: "Do you authorise the first president of the Republic of Belarus Aleksandr Lukashenko to stand as a candidate for the presidency of the Republic of Belarus in the presidential elections and do you accept the following wording of part one of Article 81 of the Constitution: 'The President shall be elected for 5 years directly by the people on the basis of universal, free, equal and direct suffrage by secret ballot'?" This wording did not seem to evoke any misgivings, but the guise was this: when this wording from the Constitution was adopted, the second half of article 81, which dealt with the restrictions on electing the same president more than twice, disappeared. Thus, any limitation of the presidential mandate was eliminated from the Constitution.

The decree on the referendum to change the Constitution seriously worsened relations between Minsk and the West. Thus, the US Congress passed an act expressing concern for the democratic and human rights situation in Belarus. In response, the Belarusian Foreign

Ministry declared that the US State Department was putting pressure on international observers, directing them towards a "premature negative assessment of the voting process in Belarus".

The referendum took place on 17 October 2004. The people voted "yes" to the question and the second half of Article 81 of the Constitution disappeared: "the same person can be president for no more than two terms". Thus, the vast majority (79%) of the Belarusian people agreed to Lukashenko standing as a presidential candidate not only for a third time, but for an unlimited number of times. If you do not believe that the results of the referendum were falsified then it has to be recognised that the Belarusian people voluntarily placed themselves in the hands of a dictator. The European Union and the US declared the referendum illegitimate.

The presidential elections approached, and a new article was introduced in the Criminal Code "On criminal liability for defamation of the state". Under this article, any citizen providing a foreign state or foreign organisation with "deliberately false" information about the political, economic, military or international position of Belarus could be imprisoned for 2 years. The main speaker in parliament during the discussion of this new law was the Chairman of the KGB, S. Sukhorenko. He stressed that the adoption of the law was a "preventative measure to prevent forcible seizure of power". Sukhorenko called on parliament to be vigilant and said that a number of Western nations, primarily the US, have repeatedly stated their interest in Belarus undergoing a similar change in government to the "Orange Revolution" in Ukraine. The KGB chief declared that the US was using the resources of international organisations to prepare special groups to take part in organising mass riots and protests during the presidential elections. All of this talk is clearly reminiscent of the Cold War, and many arguments even sounded more deceitful and aggressive than the period which had seemingly long been consigned to the past.

The opposition strongly opposed the new repressive law. The Belarusian Social Democratic Party issued a statement in which it called on parliamentary deputies to "do at least one decent deed and vote against the adoption of the law, thereby preserving their own dignity towards their children and grandchildren". But 93 deputies voted in favour of the law, with only 3 voting against. The European Union appealed to the Belarusian parliament to reconsider the matter and to reject the new law citing "the commitments of Belarus within the framework of the OSCE". Likewise, a statement was made by the US State Department spokesman Sean McCormack who accused the Belarusian authorities of violating international law and intimidating Belarusians on the eve of the presidential elections.

On 1 March, KGB Chairman S. Sukhorenko held a press conference during which he reported on uncovering a conspiracy by the radical opposition to seize power immediately after the presidential elections. In his words, KGB officers managed to get hold of the opposition's plans. These plans allegedly involved the organisation of a mass rally in the centre of Minsk during which bombs would be detonated in the crowd. After this, government buildings were due to be seized to completely stop the functioning of the government. To implement these plans the opposition, according to the assurances of the KGB chief, intended to involve "militants from Georgia, Ukraine and former Yugoslavia". On 16 March KGB Chief S. Sukhorenko informed the press that they had uncovered plans for four terrorist acts on the day of the elections. According to the information allegedly received by the KGB Chairman, explosions were going to be set off in the schools where the election candidates and polls were due to take place. Videos showing the arrested "terrorist" suggest that he underwent training for the acts at a camp in Georgia and sat exams with American instructors.

On 2 and 3 March 2006 Minsk held its third Belarusian Popular Assembly featuring an extensive paper lasting many hours on "A State for the People" by President Aleksandr Lukashenko. The assembly adopted another programme for socio-economic development over the next five years from 2006 to 2010. The motto of the new period was "A State for the People" and the main strategic objective was to build a strong and prosperous Belarus.

Under these circumstances, on 19 March 2006 presidential elections were held with Lukashenko receiving 82% of the vote. His opponents A. Kozulin, S. Gaydukevich and A. Milinkevich brought in votes ranging from 3% to 6%. At a press conference held for foreign journalists on the results of the elections, in response to questions about possible falsification of the results Lukashenko said that if the results were indeed rigged then they were only rigged in favour of the opposition candidates, as they, according to Lukashenko, were "assigned votes to get around the European indicators" upon his orders. It is safe to say that such brutality and political irresponsibility in the "confessions" of the country's president was never expected by anyone.

In the evening, after the announcement of the election results, roughly 30,000 people went out onto the central streets in Minsk to protest against fraud during the elections. Special OMON riot police violently dispersed the demonstrators. On 25 March A. Kozulin – one of the presidential candidates, leader of the Social Democratic Party and one of Lukashenko's most active opponents – was arrested, due to be released after five and a half years in prison. He was charged with "malicious hooliganism and organising mass riots". In prison Kozulin announced a hunger strike demanding that the situation in Belarus be discussed in the UN Security Council. After a closed meeting of the Security Council on the issue of human rights in Belarus, the US Senate passed a bill to impose economic sanctions against Belarus. Amnesty International has recognised Kozulin as a political prisoner. Under pressure from international forces, in August 2008 President Lukashenko was forced to issue a decree pardoning Kozulin. The renowned scientist, academic, professor emeritus of many universities and former rector of the Belarusian State University A. Kozulin left prison after two and a half years (of which 8 months was spent on hunger strike) a physically broken man and abandoned his political activity.

The European community and the US declared the elections illegitimate and inconsistent with international standards. The European Council Secretary General Terry Davis called the elections a farce. The newly elected President Aleksandr Lukashenko and 42 officials from the higher echelons of power were declared *persona non grata*, with the European Union and later the US banning them from entering their territory. The grounds for this were Lukashenko and his entourage being charge with systemic attacks on the rights and freedoms of citizens, repression against the opposition and restrictions on freedom of the press.

Recent years in the history of Belarus can be compared with the years of stagnation in the Soviet Union under Brezhnev. From an economic perspective, these years were characterised by:

- the preservation of Kolkhozes (collective farms) which devour subsidies from the state budget while remaining unprofitable;

- the predominance of state ownership;

- the command system of the government;

- the constant expansion of the bureaucratic apparatus to strictly control private business;

- the regular receipt of many billions in loans, primarily from Russia.

And from a political perspective:

- the complete centralisation of power in the hands of the president and his vertical channels;

- the rapid growth of punitive bodies (there are 1,500 policemen on all levels for every 100,000 inhabitants – the highest figure among former Soviet states);

- the decisive dispersal of all non-state media;

- the ban on the activities of the Belarusian Helsinki Committee and numerous other social organisations;

- the incorporation in the Criminal Code of a number of laws aimed at combatting dissent.

Society is constantly being pumped with the psychology expected of inhabitants of a nation surrounded by enemies or inhabitants of a besieged camp through all possible forms of propaganda, primarily state television (no other television is available in Belarus). It is therefore with good reason that many politicians in the European Union have repeatedly dubbed the regime in Belarus "the last dictatorship in Europe".

———————◆———————

The presidential elections on 19 December 2010 went according to the already well developed plan. When the results of the vote were announced, again showing Lukashenko's victory, roughly 50,000 people went out onto the streets in protest against electoral fraud. The authorities predicted this turn of events and the central square in Minsk was surrounded by armed OMON special forces and specialised vehicles to carry away those arrested. The demonstration was brutally subdued: people were beaten with batons and dozens were taken away to prisons. Over the course of the evening and night roughly 800 people were arrested. 725 of them were sentenced to various forms of imprisonment. At hearings no relatives or journalists were allowed under any circumstances. All seven opposition presidential candidates, the brightest and most successful of which were Andrey Sannikov (ordered by a court to spent 5 years in a maximum security prison), Vladimir Neklyaev (2 years' imprisonment) and Nikolay Statkevich (6 years' imprisonment), ended up behind bars.

In the morning on 20 December, police officers broke into the offices of the human rights centre "Vesna" and the editorial office of the website "Charter - 97"; employees were arrested and their documents and computers were seized. The New York Times wrote: "the political repression has surpassed everything that has happened over the 16 years of rule by the 'father of the Belarusian people'".

The President of the European Parliament, Jerzy Buzek, said that Lukashenko was holding power illegally in Belarus. But at a press conference held in Minsk on 23 December, Russian Ambassador A. Surikov announced his full support for the actions of the Belarusian authorities against demonstrators, as the opposition, in his words, were hoping for an orange revolution on the square.

The OSCE did not recognise the election results and accused the government of rigging. In response, the Belarusian government refused to renew the mandate of the OSCE Minsk office and effectively shut off access to the country for the organisation.

The Belarusian government has described the events of 19 December as an attempt by the opposition to overthrow the government. Lukashenko said in parliament: "We can all be certain of the fact that the opposition was preparing a coup. That's all, nothing more and nothing less. Everything was planned and carried out under the supervision of certain foreign special services".

After the presidential elections in 2010 160 officials, including Lukashenko's two sons, were declared *persona non grata* and were banned from entering the European Union. This time, the list not only included high-ranking government officials, but also members of the KGB, police officers and judges who had imposed sentences against demonstrators protesting on 19 December. In 2012, this list was expanded again, alongside the range of economic sanctions. In response, the Belarusian Foreign Ministry withdrew its diplomats from the EU and Poland, and recommended that the Warsaw embassy and diplomats from Brussels return to their countries to report Belarus' extreme discontent at the extension of the sanctions. In reality, the diplomats were being expelled from the country. In response to this riposte, the outraged ambassadors of all 27 countries of the European Union left Minsk and returned to their home countries. Until this time, the European diplomatic community had never witnessed such a situation. The conflict was resolved in just a few months.

In 2012, during Lukashenko's visit to Venezuela, the country's president Hugo Chavez declared a public holiday in Venezuela to mark the arrival of President Lukashenko and his son Nikolay. Lukashenko's response to this was: "As you rightly said, my little boy is here with us. This reflects the serious and permanent foundations of our cooperation, and there is now somebody to take over this cooperation in 20-25 years' time". These words by Lukashenko give us reason to believe that he fully intents to hand over power to his son. Clearly, there is no need to pass any judgements here about how far these views depart from the notion of "democracy".

Over the past decade Belarus has been sinking deeper into insolation from the civilised world. It is on friendly terms with some of the world's most odious regimes in Venezuela, Syria and Iran. And with its neighbours Lithuania, Latvia and Poland in particular it is in a state of on-going political conflict. The country's only steadfast ally is Russia.

Why does Russia support Lukashenko's leadership? Firstly, to Russia Belarus is a buffer zone, a so-called "strategic depth of territory". Russia's leaders, most of which, including Putin, are remnants of the old power structures and still see maps of Europe divided along Cold War lines in terms of East and West. Although global life has long since changed, they continue to see the European Union and NATO as outposts of a hostile civilisation. And should Belarus go over to the enemy camp, the boundary is moved 600 kilometres to the east. In addition, Belarus is Russia's most important ally in the former Soviet region. Without Belarus the Union State (which was not only difficult to create but took a long time), Customs Union, "collective defence system" and the "common economic space" lose all meaning. Thanks to Belarus the leaders in the Kremlin can maintain the illusion, both in their own minds and the minds of the people, that they have their own European Union, and their own NATO. And as for "Europe's last dictator", Aleksandr Lukashenko creates a backdrop against which Russia actually looks quite good in terms of compliance with European democratic standards and human rights. When Lukashenko speaks out from time to time about Washington's conspiracy against Belarus' sovereignty when all 27 EU deputies leave the country, and in one night alone 800 protesters are arrested, Vladimir Putin starts to seem quite civilised in the eyes of his western partners.

It is difficult to say precisely what the safety margin of the current political regime is in Belarus, and what will happen after its fall. In this book we have seen that from the very earliest days of this country's history, its geopolitical influence has been in Russia's shadow. And there can be no doubt that the same is happening now. Will Belarus succeed in retaining its statehood, or will it once again be part of an empire? Only the future will tell.

LIST OF REFERENCES

1. Novik E., Kachalov I., Novik N. Istoriya Belarusi s drevneyshikh vremen do 1210 goda. Minsk, 2012, p.11
2. Zagorulski E. M. Nachalo formirovaniya naseleniya Belorussii. Minsk, 1996, p.43
3. Shtykhau G. V. Kryvichy. Minsk, 1992, p.95
4. Sedov V. V. O proiskhozhdenii belorusov. Minsk, 1966.
5. Shtykhau G. V. Kryvichy. Minsk, 1992, p.102
6. Timoshchuk B. Vostochnoslavyanskaya obshchina v 6-10 vekakh. Minsk, 1978, p.100-103
7. Shirokorad A. B. Rus i Litva. Moscow, 2008, p.6
8. Starazhytnaya belaruskaya literatura. Minsk, 1990, p.22
9. Ermalovich M. Starazhytnaya Belarus: Polatski i Naugarotski peryyady. Minsk, 1990, p.29
10. Ignatouski U. M. Karotki narys gistoryi Belarusi. Minsk, 1991, p.35
11. Ivakin G. Yu. Kiev v 12-15 vekakh. Kiev, 1982, p.32
12. Dounar-Zapolski M. V. Gistoryya Belarusi. Minsk, 1994, p.38
13. Ermalovich M. Starazhytnaya Belarus: Polatski i Naugarotski peryyady. Minsk, 1990, p.124
14. Kozhedub A. Rus i Litva. Minsk, 2011, p.124
15. Novik E., Kachalov I., Novik N. Istoriya Belarusi s drevneyshikh vremen do 2010 goda. Minsk, 2012, p.25
16. Zhitie Efrosini Polotskoy. Polotsk, 2012, p.9
17. Zhitie Efrosini Polotskoy. Polotsk, 2012, p.12
18. Ignatouski U. M. Karotki narys gistoryi Belarusi. Minsk, 1991, p.72
19. Ermalovich M. Starazhytnaya Belarus: Vilenski peryyad. Minsk, 1994, p.24

20. Gayduk M. Paratunak. Minsk, 1993, p.153

21. Ermalovich M. Starazhytnaya Belarus: Vilenski peryyad. Minsk, 1994, p.13

22. Ermalovich M. Starazhytnaya Belarus: Vilenski peryyad. Minsk, 1994, p.74

23. Ignatouski U. M. Karotki narys gistoryi Belarusi. Minsk, 1991, p.87

24. Ignatouski U. M. Karotki narys gistoryi Belarusi. Minsk, 1991, p.89

25. Ignatouski U. M. Karotki narys gistoryi Belarusi. Minsk, 1991, p.89-90

26. Gayduk M. Paratunak. Minsk, 1993, p.268

27. Dounar-Zapolski M. V. Gistoryya Belarusi. Minsk, 1994, p.57

28. Ignatouski U. M. Karotki narys gistoryi Belarusi. Minsk, 1991, p.93

29. Statut Vyalikaga knyastva Litouskaga 1588. Teksty, davednik, kamentaryy. Minsk, 1989.

30. Ignatouski U. M. Karotki narys gistoryi Belarusi. Minsk, 1991, p.109

31. Shirokorad A. B. Rus i Litva. Moscow, 2008, p.247

32. Bednov V. A. Pravoslavnaya tserkov v Polshe i Litve. Minsk, 2002, p.79

33. Ignatouski U. M. Karotki narys gistoryi Belarusi. Minsk, 1991, p.116

34. Padokshin S. A. Reformatsiya i obshchestvennaya mysl Belorussii i Litvy (vtoraya polovina 16 - nachalo 17 veka). Minsk, 1970, p.95

35. Kozhedub A. Rus i Litva. Minsk, 201, p.223

36. Ignatouski U. M. Karotki narys gistoryi Belarusi. Minsk, 1991, p.117

37. Asvetniki zyamli belaruskay, 10-20 stagodze. Minsk, 2001, p.135

38. Asvetniki zyamli belaruskay, 10-20 stagodze. Minsk, 2001, p.458

39. Asvetniki zyamli belaruskay, 10-20 stagodze. Minsk, 2001, p.389

40. Asvetniki zyamli belaruskay, 10-20 stagodze. Minsk, 2001, p.29

41. Asvetniki zyamli belaruskay, 10-20 stagodze. Minsk, 2001, p.127

42. Asvetniki zyamli belaruskay, 10-20 stagodze. Minsk, 2001, p.69

43. Padokshin S. A. Reformatsiya i obshchestvennaya mysl Belorussii i Litvy (vtoraya polovina 16 - nachalo 17 veka). Minsk, 1970, p.146

44. Asvetniki zyamli belaruskay, 10-20 stagodze. Minsk, 2001, p.462

45. Picheta V. I. Belorussiya i Litva v 15-16 vekakh. Moscow, AN SSSR, 1961, p.547

46. Kozhedub A. Rus i Litva. Minsk, 201, p.222

47. Dounar-Zapolski M. V. Gistoryya Belarusi. Minsk, 1994, p.98

48. Dounar-Zapolski M. V. Gistoryya Belarusi. Minsk, 1994, p.100

49. Narysy gistoryi Belarusi. Chı-2. Minsk, 1995, p.135

50. Ignatouski U. M. Karotki narys gistoryi Belarusi. Minsk, 1991, p.123

51. Asvetniki zyamli belaruskay, 10-20 stagodze. Minsk, 2001, p.29

52. Ignatouski U. M. Karotki narys gistoryi Belarusi. Minsk, 1991, p.123

53. Novik E., Kachalov I., Novik N. Istoriya Belarusi s drevneyshikh vremen do 1210 goda. Minsk, 2012, p.133

54. Tarasau K. Pamyats pra lyagendy. Minsk, 1994, p.144

55. Chigrinov P. G. Ocherki istorii Belarusi. Minsk, 2007, p.149

56. Narysy gistoryi Belarusi. Chı-2. Minsk, 1995, p.233

57. Maldzis A. Belarus u lyusterku memuarnay litaratury 18 stagodzya. Minsk, 1982, p.98

58. Asvetniki zyamli belaruskay, 10-20 stagodze. Minsk, 2001, p.265

59. Gayduk, M. Paratunak. Minsk, 1993, p.185

60. Asvetniki zyamli belaruskay, 10-20 stagodze. Minsk, 2001, p.456

61. Asvetniki zyamli belaruskay, 10-20 stagodze. Minsk, 2001, p.323

62. Asvetniki zyamli belaruskay, 10-20 stagodze. Minsk, 2001, p.471

63. Maldzis A. Belarus u lyusterku memuarnay litaratury 18 stagodzya. Minsk, 1982, p.128

64. Maldzis A. Belarus u lyusterku memuarnay litaratury 18 stagodzya. Minsk, 1982, p.105

65. Maldzis A. Belarus u lyusterku memuarnay litaratury 18 stagodzya. Minsk, 1982, p.148

66. Ikanapis Belarusi 15-18 stagodzyau. Minsk, 1994, p.9

67. Kozhedub A. Rus i Litva. Minsk, 201, p.203

68. Asvetniki zyamli belaruskay, 10-20 stagodze. Minsk, 2001, p.202

69. Kazlou L., Tsitou A. Belarus na syami rubezhakh. Minsk, 1993, p.20

70. Dounar-Zapolski M. V. Gistoryya Belarusi. Minsk, 1994, p.249

71. Taras A.E. 1812, tragediya Belarusi. Minsk, 2012, p.143

72. Taras A.E. 1812, tragediya Belarusi. Minsk, 2012, p.176

73. Taras A.E. 1812, tragediya Belarusi. Minsk, 2012, p.181

74. Samusenko E. G. Belarus i Otechestvennaya voyna 1812. Istoricheskie ocherki i esse. Minsk, 2012, p.15

75. Taras A.E. 1812, tragediya Belarusi. Minsk, 2012, p.234

76. Belarus i voyna 1812 goda. Dokumenty. Minsk, 2011, p.238

77. Asvetniki zyamli belaruskay, 10-20 stagodze. Minsk, 2001, p.331

78. Dounar-Zapolski M. V. Gistoryya Belarusi. Minsk, 1994, p.272

79. Novik E., Kachalov I., Novik N. Istoriya Belarusi s drevneyshikh vremen do 1210 goda. Minsk, 2012, p.186

80. Istoriya Belorusskoy SSR. Minsk, 1977, p.126

81. Tarasau K. Pamyats pra lyagendy. Minsk, 1994, p.259

82. Dounar-Zapolski M. V. Gistoryya Belarusi. Minsk, 1994, p.279

83. Kanfesii na Belarusi. Minsk, 1998, p.103-104

84. Asvetniki zyamli belaruskay, 10-20 stagodze. Minsk, 2001, p.225

85. Spadchyna, vypusk 1. Minsk, 1989, p.41

86. Asvetniki zyamli belaruskay, 10-20 stagodze. Minsk, 2001, p.125

87. Dounar-Zapolski M. V. Gistoryya Belarusi. Minsk, 1994, p.450

88. Novik E., Kachalov I., Novik N. Istoriya Belarusi s drevneyshikh vremen do 1210 goda. Minsk, 2012, p.264

89. Novik E., Kachalov I., Novik N. Istoriya Belarusi s drevneyshikh vremen do 1210 goda. Minsk, 2012, p.264

90. Istoriya Belorusskoy SSR. Minsk, 1977, p.208

91. Kazlou L., Tsitou A. Belarus na syami rubezhakh. Minsk, 1993, p.24

92. Narysy gistoryi Belarusi. Chı-2. Minsk, 1995, p.56

93. Narysy gistoryi Belarusi. Chı-1. Minsk, 1995, p.60

94. Kazlou L., Tsitou A. Belarus na syami rubezhakh. Minsk, 1993, p.58

95. Kazlou L., Tsitou A. Belarus na syami rubezhakh. Minsk, 1993, p.59

96. Stanovlenie i krushenie odnopartiynoy sistemy v SSSR. 1917-1991. Gomel, 1995, p.90-91

97. Kanfesii na Belarusi. Minsk, 1998, p.187

98. Narysy gistoryi Belarusi. Chı-2. Minsk, 1995, p.206

99. Narysy gistoryi Belarusi. Chı-1. Minsk, 1995, p.275

100. Kavalenya A. A. Belarus naperedadni i u gady Vyalikay Aychynnay vayny. Minsk, 2004, p.53

101. Kavalenya A. A. Belarus naperedadni i u gady Vyalikay Aychynnay vayny. Minsk, 2004, p.53

102. Novik E., Kachalov I., Novik N. Istoriya Belarusi s drevneyshikh vremen do 1210 goda. Minsk, 2012, p.412

103. Novik E., Kachalov I., Novik N. Istoriya Belarusi s drevneyshikh vremen do 1210 goda. Minsk, 2012, p.412

104. Narysy gistoryi Belarusi. Ch1-2. Minsk, 1995, p.284

105. Narysy gistoryi Belarusi. Ch1-2. Minsk, 1995, p.289

106.Kavalenya A. A. Belarus naperedadni i u gady Vyalikay Aychynnay vayny. Minsk, 2004, p.106

107. Belarus u gady Vyalikay Aychynnay vayny. Minsk, 1999, p.167

108. Narysy gistoryi Belarusi. Ch1-2. Minsk, 1995, p.324

Glagoslav Publications Catalogue

- *METRO 2033* (Dutch Edition) by Dmitry Glukhovsky
- *METRO 2034* (Dutch Edition) by Dmitry Glukhovsky
- *A Poet and Bin Laden* by Hamid Ismailov
- *A Russian Story* by Eugenia Kononenko
- *Kobzar* by Taras Shevchenko
- *The Stone Bridge* by Alexander Terekhov
- *King Stakh's Wild Hunt* by Uladzimir Karatkevich
- *Depeche Mode* by Serhii Zhadan
- *Wolf Messing – The True Story of Russia's Greatest Psychic* by Tatiana Lungin
- *Herstories*, An Anthology of New Ukrainian Women Prose Writers
- *Watching The Russians* (Dutch Edition) by Maria Konyukova
- *A Book Without Photographs* by Sergei Shargunov
- *The Grand Slam and Other Stories* (Dutch Edition) by Leonid Andreev
- *The Battle of the Sexes Russian Style* by Nadezhda Ptushkina
- *Down Among The Fishes* by Natalka Babina
- *disUNITY* by Anatoly Kudryavitsky
- *Sankya* by Zakhar Prilepin
- *Andrei Tarkovsky – A Life on the Cross* by Lyudmila Boyadzhieva
- *Solar Plexus* by Rustam Ibragimbekov
- *Don't Call me a Victim!* by Dina Yafasova
- *Tsarina Alexandra's Diary* (Dutch)

More coming soon…